DOGS

Having A Ball!

Angela Hunt

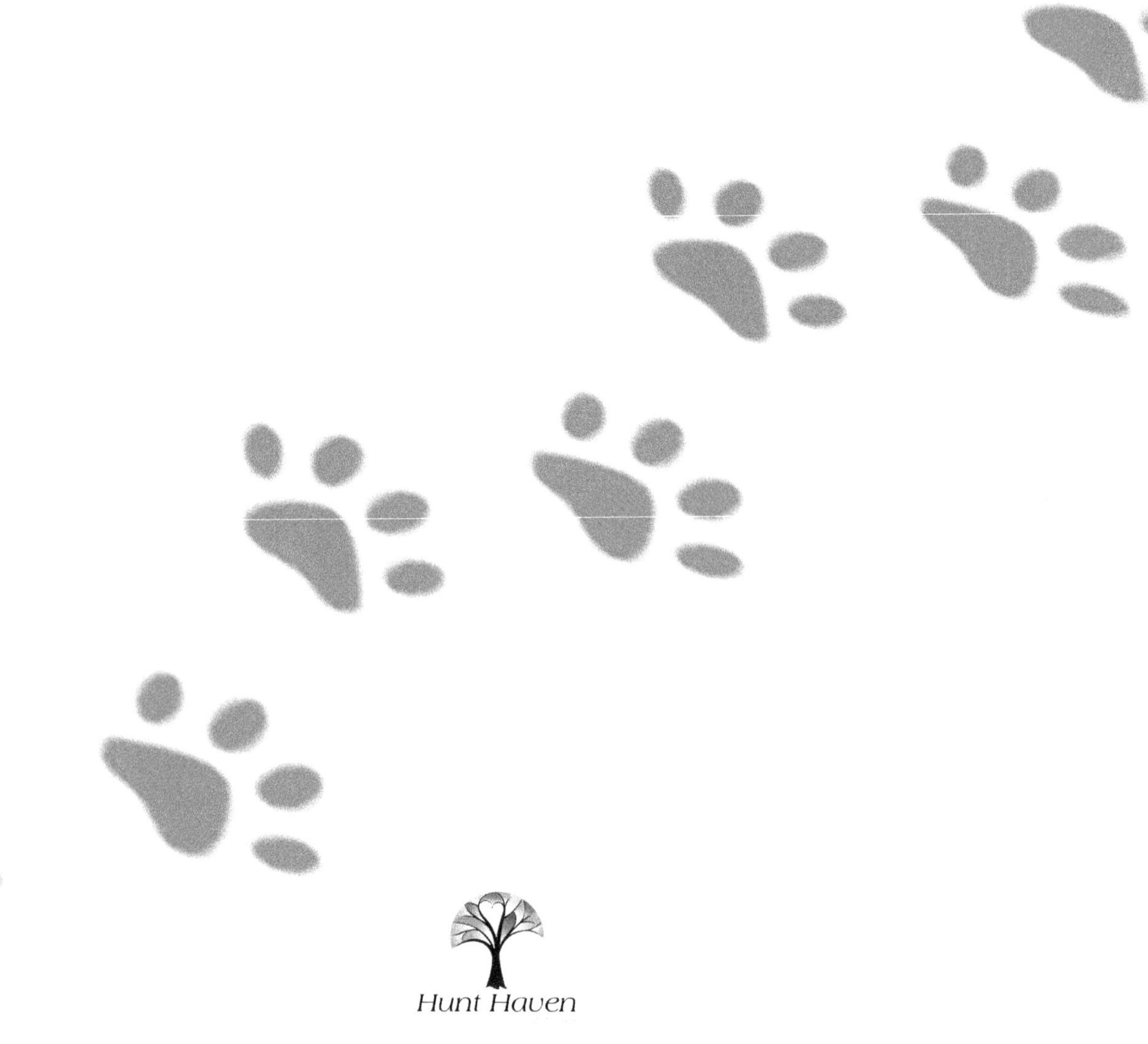

Published by Hunt Haven Press

First Edition.

ISBN print edition:: 978-1-7321990-5-7
ISBN ebook edition: 978-1-7321990-7-1

To all the wonderful people I have met who love and care for dogs, with huge appreciation for those who shared their furry family members with me. Wasn't it fun?

Specifically, *hugs* and *thanks* to:

Pam Smith, Tania FitzGerald, Deb Holland, Jesse Rappaport
Amy Ulrich, Lana DeBastos, Missy Lumbard, Cheryl Renner
Jan Whitlow, McLane Evans, Adrienne Busch, Cindy Crane
Tom Royal, Lisa Maker Bailey, Samantha Stepaniak, Julie Nikolov
Juli Rae Radloff, Inga Martinez, Rob Baerwalde, Eleanor Saleni
Cassy Combs, Douglas Perreault, Nicole Ledford, Marsha Laughter
Joe Testerman, Ginni Eichholz, Clint Meeks, Maureen Henderson
Rita Spillers, Claudia Claerhout-Saltz, Donna Bainter Naderhoff, Linda Russell
Valerie Brehm, Angie Panaro, Shannon Reed, Tiffani Oliver
Jane McKenzie, Katie Englebert, Michael Coleman, Barbara Hastings
Debie Scurr, Sherry Hardin, Cristina Jones, Diane Nally
Katie Bradford, Laura Spaulding, Merissa LaMacchia, Kimberly Valencia
Terasa Van Coppenolle, Irene Franklin, Sharon Fekete, Deborah Martohue
Emily Wohlrabe, Terry Meeks, Belinda Blease, Karen Altieri
Stephanie Percifield, Laura Kohler, Gisselle Padilla, Sharon Oliphant
Amanda Witt, Annie Boggs, Carissa Giblin, Rebecca Creveling
Judy Safer, Dawn McKinney, Sandra Combs

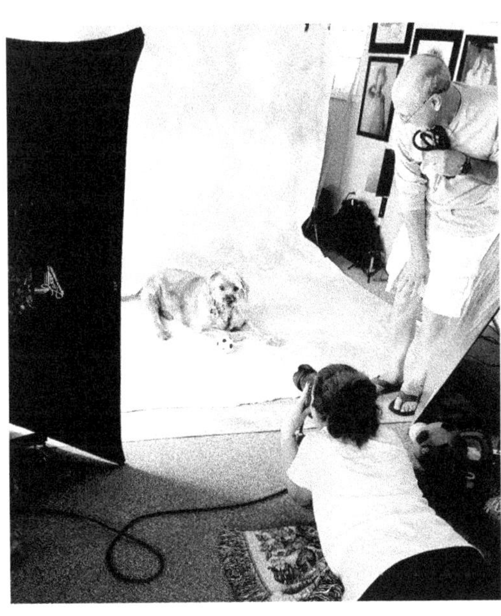

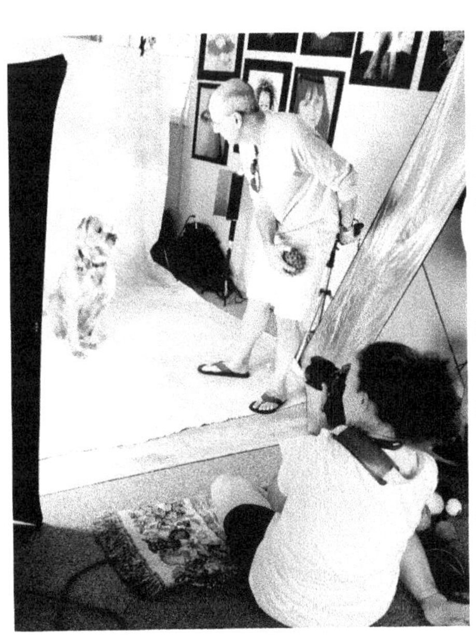

Photos © by Eleanor Saleni

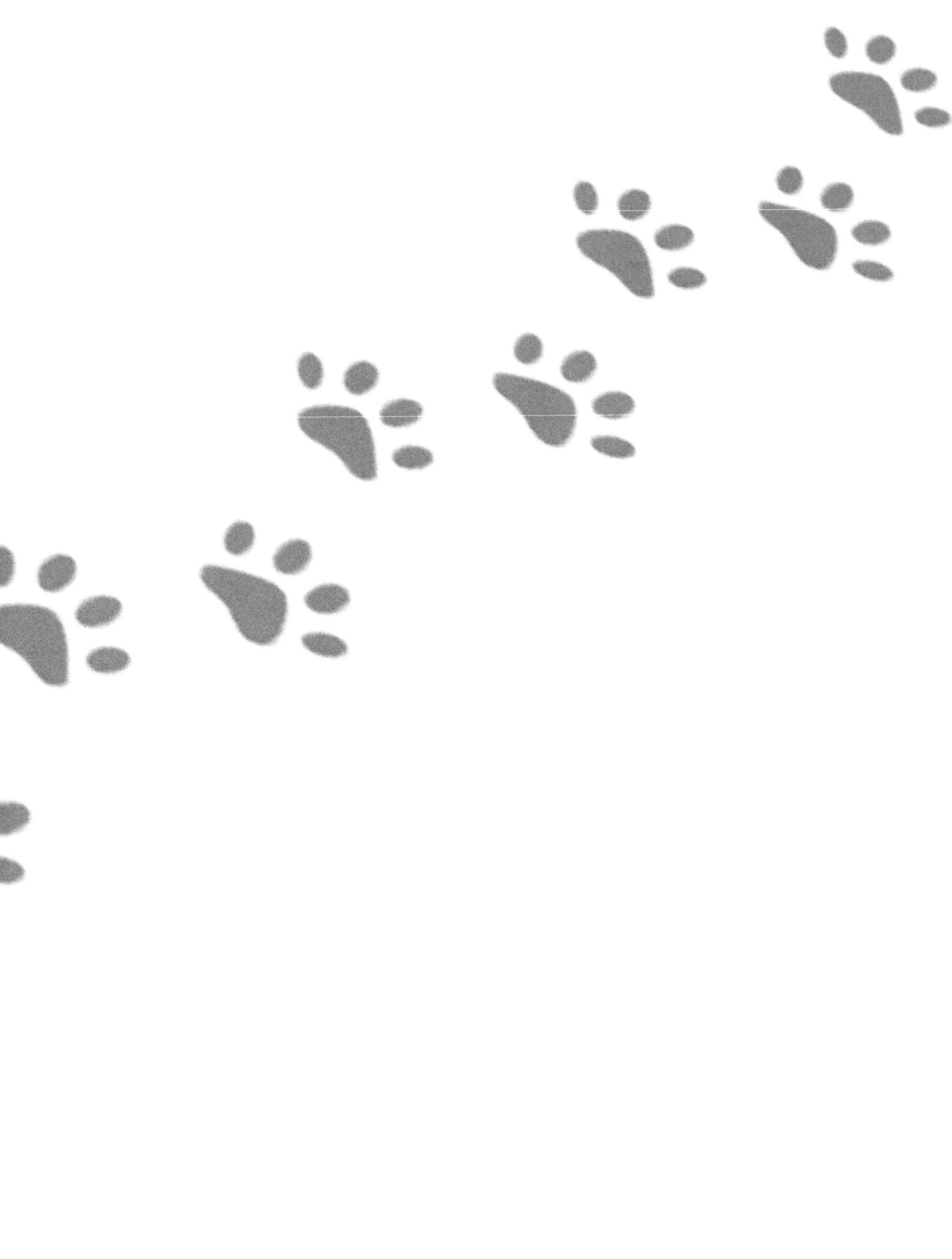

Author's Note

Thirty years into my first career, I decided to begin a second. Why? Because of the dogs.

I had begun to photograph adoptable dogs at my local SPCA, because dogs with good photos are adopted faster than those with shots taken behind a fence. So I started learning about photography, light and shadows, shutter speed and depth of field, and before I knew it, I was a part-time professional photographer. My second career is a labor of love, an investment of time, which is an investment of life. I love not only the dogs, but the big-hearted people who care for them, and I'm glad I can call so many "dog people" my friends.

My original vision for this book majored on photography and minored on story, but now that the book is nearly finished, I think each aspect carries equal weight. I began to hear amazing stories of dogs and their owners--funny stories, sad stories, poignant stories, and wonderful stories of second chances.

These stories have reinforced what I have always believed--that dogs are one of God's most precious creations, for they demonstrate unconditional love like no other creature.

I hope you'll settle back and enjoy this book of dogs and their stories . . . then go out and toss a ball to your favorite furry friend.

Angie Hunt
September 2018

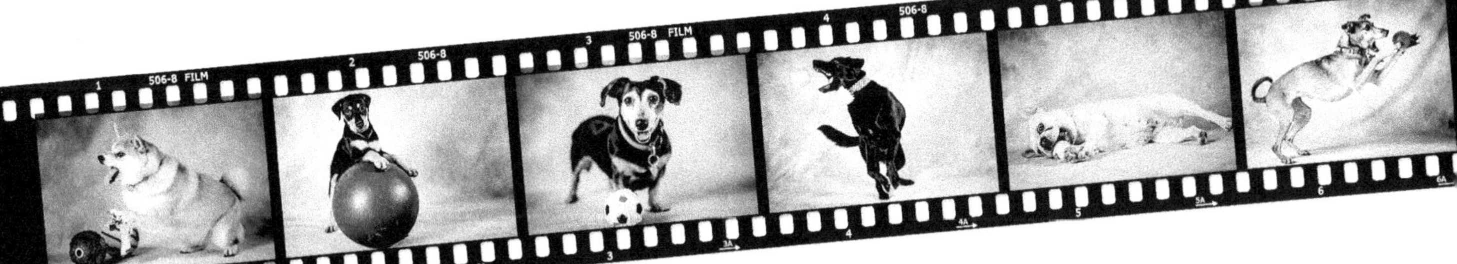

THE DOGS

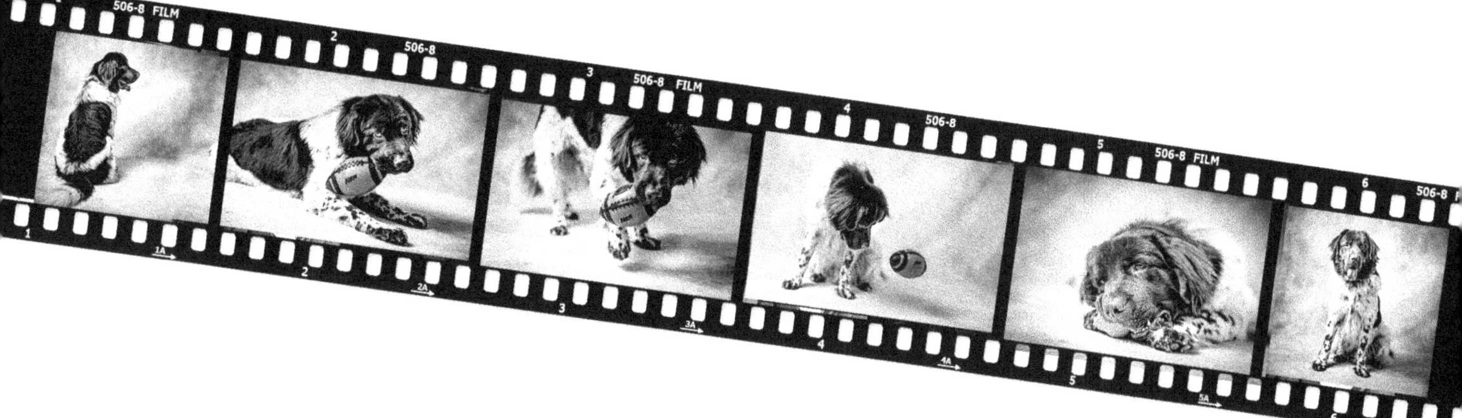

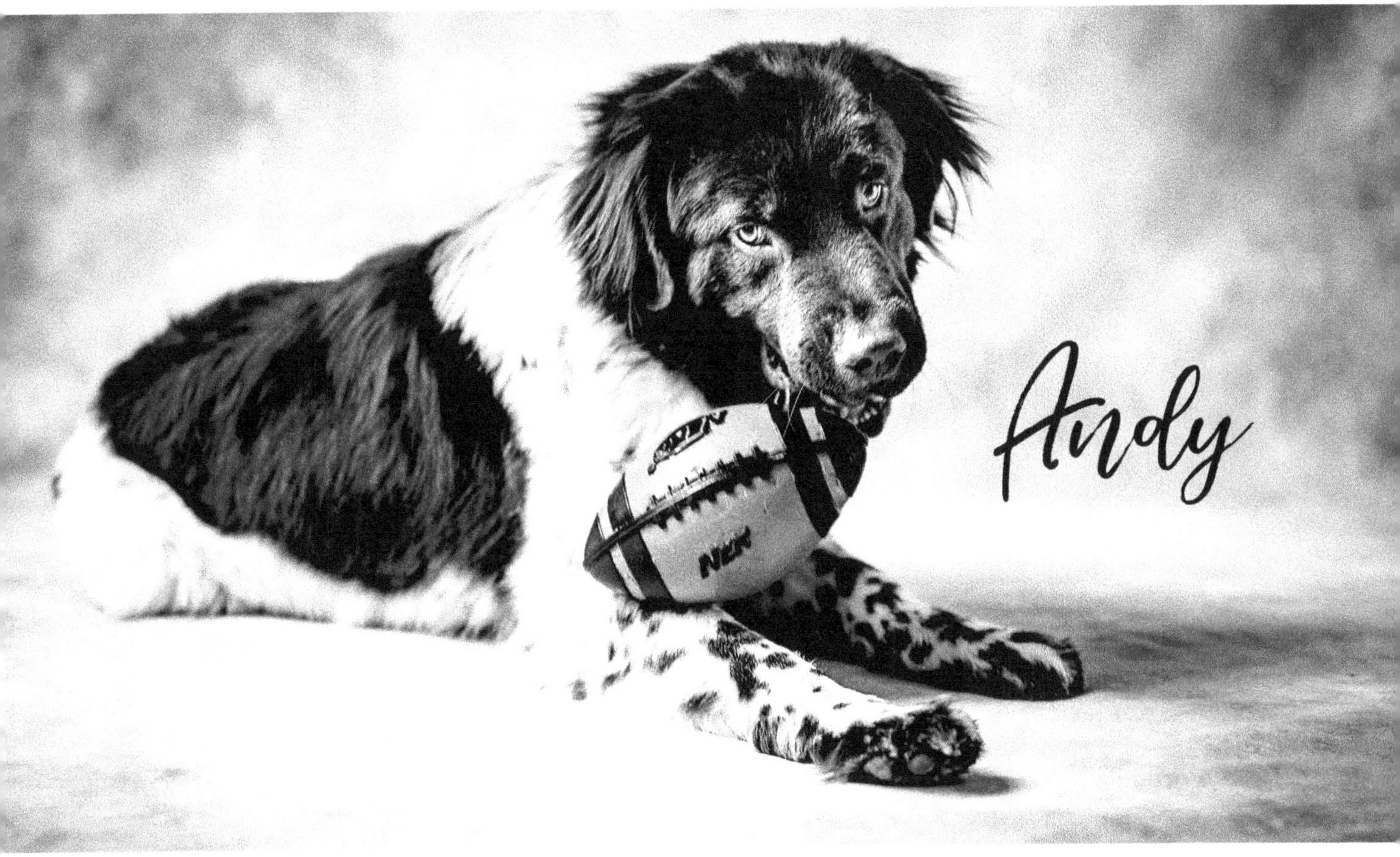

Andy

You might not believe that ANDY is practically a baby, but this Newfoundland is only one year old. He was rescued from a puppy mill, where for some reason he wasn't sold. He arrived at his forever home when he was six months old, and there he found doggie siblings to keep him entertained. His human mom says he's a clown and always into everything. His favorite toys are balls of all sorts--the bigger, the better--and he favors the kind that hold treats. He loves water wherever he can find it, and he hasn't met a human he didn't like. He loves to play with the family cats although, his mom reports, "the cats are not very happy about him living with us."

Asia

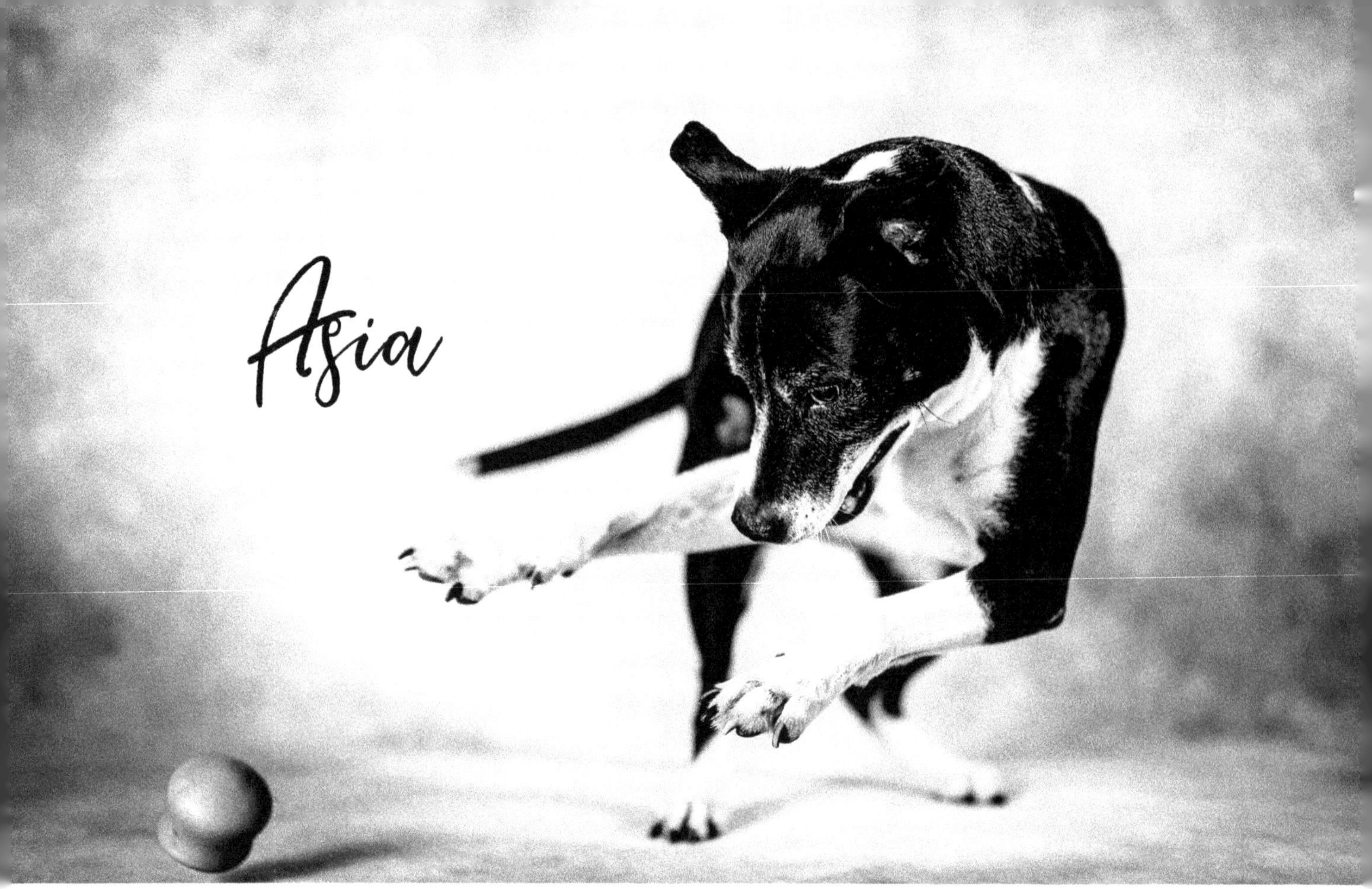

Nine-year-old ASIA, a pitbull terrier, behaves more like a puppy than a senior dog. She loves her knuckle bone and any toy that squeaks. Her human mom reports that Asia is her "emotional companion animal--she knows when I need to relax and cuddle." Asia's mom found her at the county animal shelter, and they've been together ever since. The worst thing Asia has ever done--and something her mom will never forget--is jump out of the car window at a stop light. Many dogs have done the same thing, but Asia jumped out of her mom's car and into the convertible waiting next to them.

No more open windows for Asia!

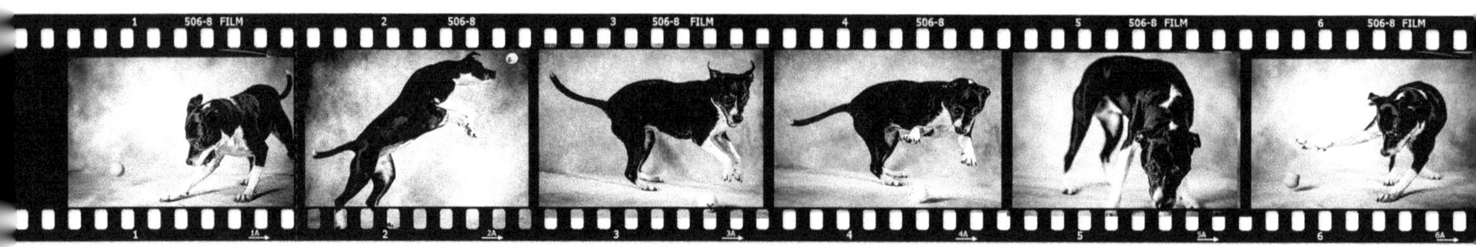

BABE loved basketball. Carrying them, that is. Babe, an English mastiff, came to her forever family via Mastiff Rescue. She was three years old when she arrived in her new home, and her previous owners had tried to make her into a guard dog, leaving her in a mechanic's garage all night and on a chain in daylight hours. But though Babe never shook her residual mistrust of men, she loved her new family and her new mastiff sibling. When he passed away at age nine, Babe followed him six weeks later because, the vet said, "her immune system failed." Why? Her owners believe she died of a broken heart.

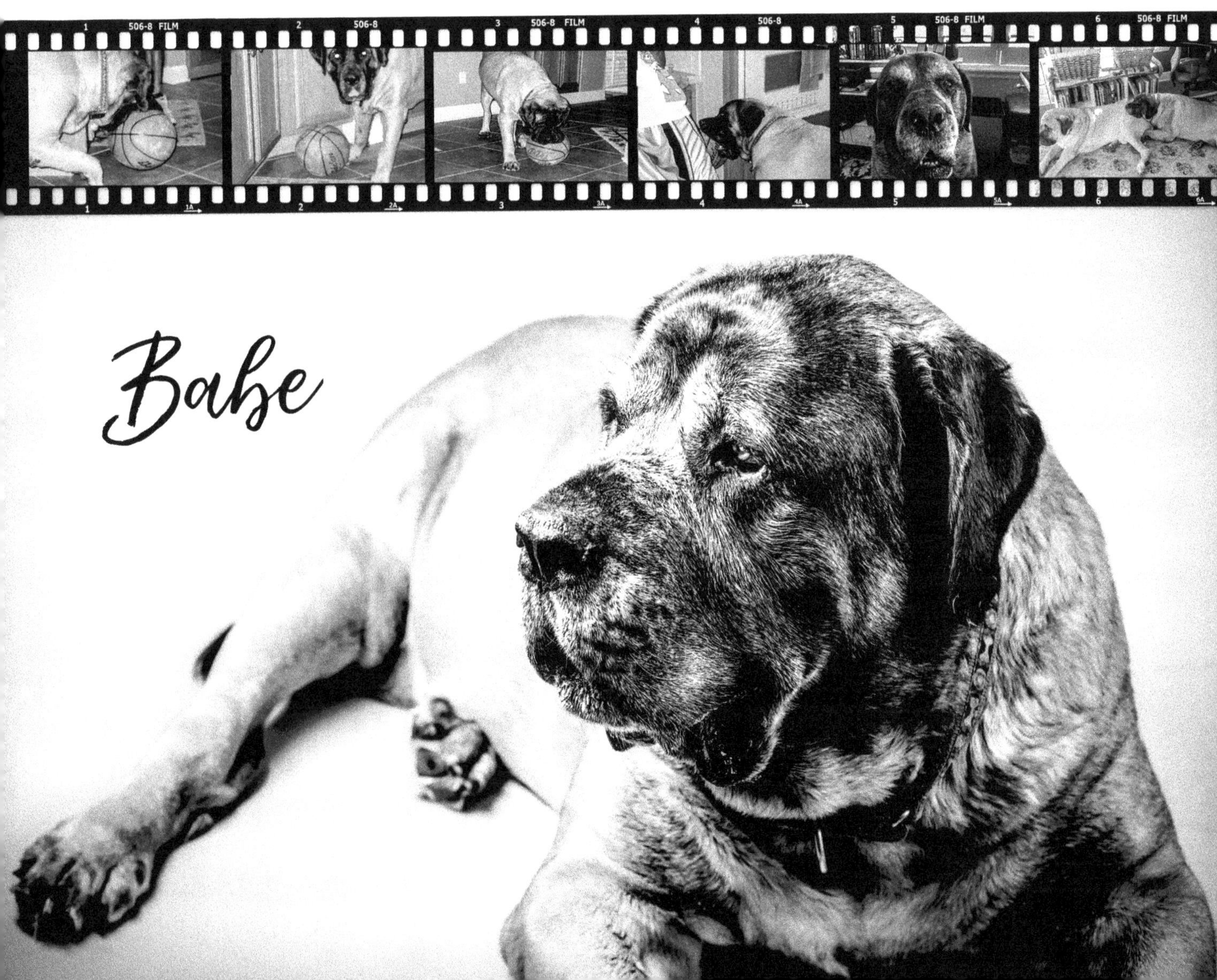

Bali

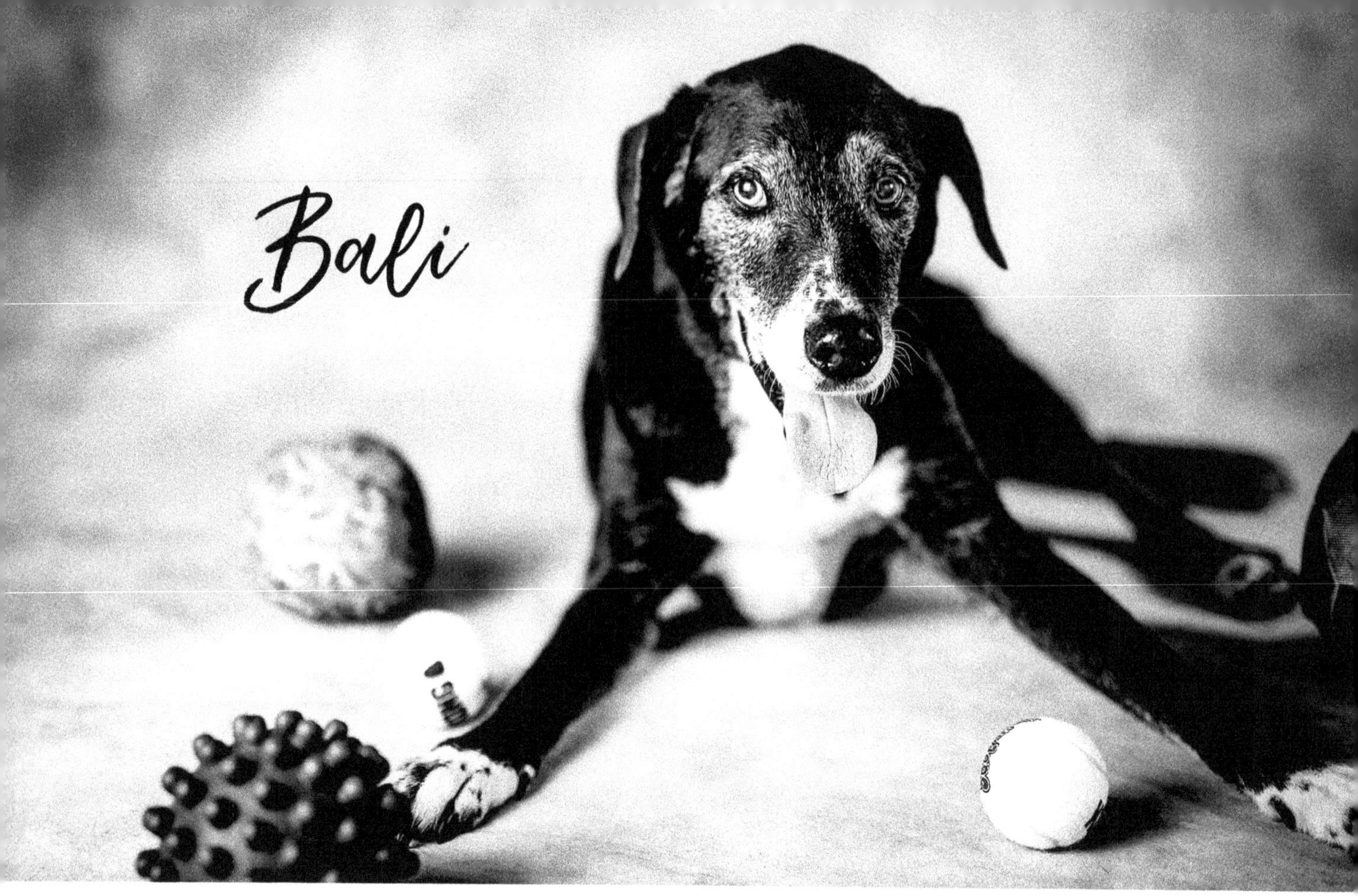

BALI is a New York girl--that's where she was found wandering the streets. Her present owner went from house to house, asking who might have lost the beautiful black dog with one blue eye and one brown, but no one claimed her. So Bali found herself adopted. The fourteen-year-old beauty's favorite toy is a Kong squeaker ball, but her favorite activity is snuggling with mom and talking in her own special language. This dignified girl is not without her faults--the worst thing she's ever done, says her mama, is roll around in dead things and carry the stink into the house. But stinky or not, she will always be welcomed back.
This girl will never wander again.

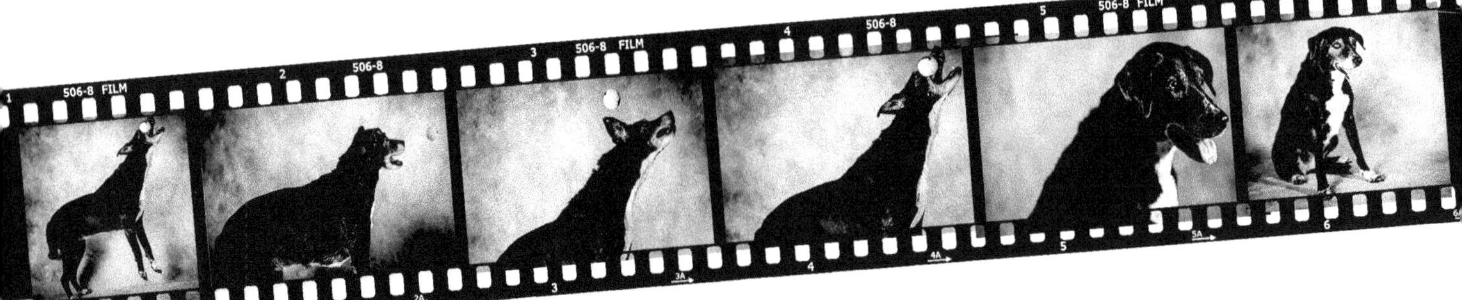

BEN is a large and handsome three-year-old Golden Retriever. His human mom reports that she and her husband found him on Craigslist--he was a "discount puppy" because he is half American, half English Golden.

But Ben doesn't know his pedigree is considered imperfect, and his owners don't care. He is much loved, and has lots of Kongs and tennis balls, his favorite things. His mom says the sweetest thing he does is sigh loudly and appropriately when the humans converse. The worst thing he's ever done? His dad is a teacher, and Ben once shredded all of Dad's students' tests--*after* they had been graded.

What did Ben have to say for himself? He sighed.

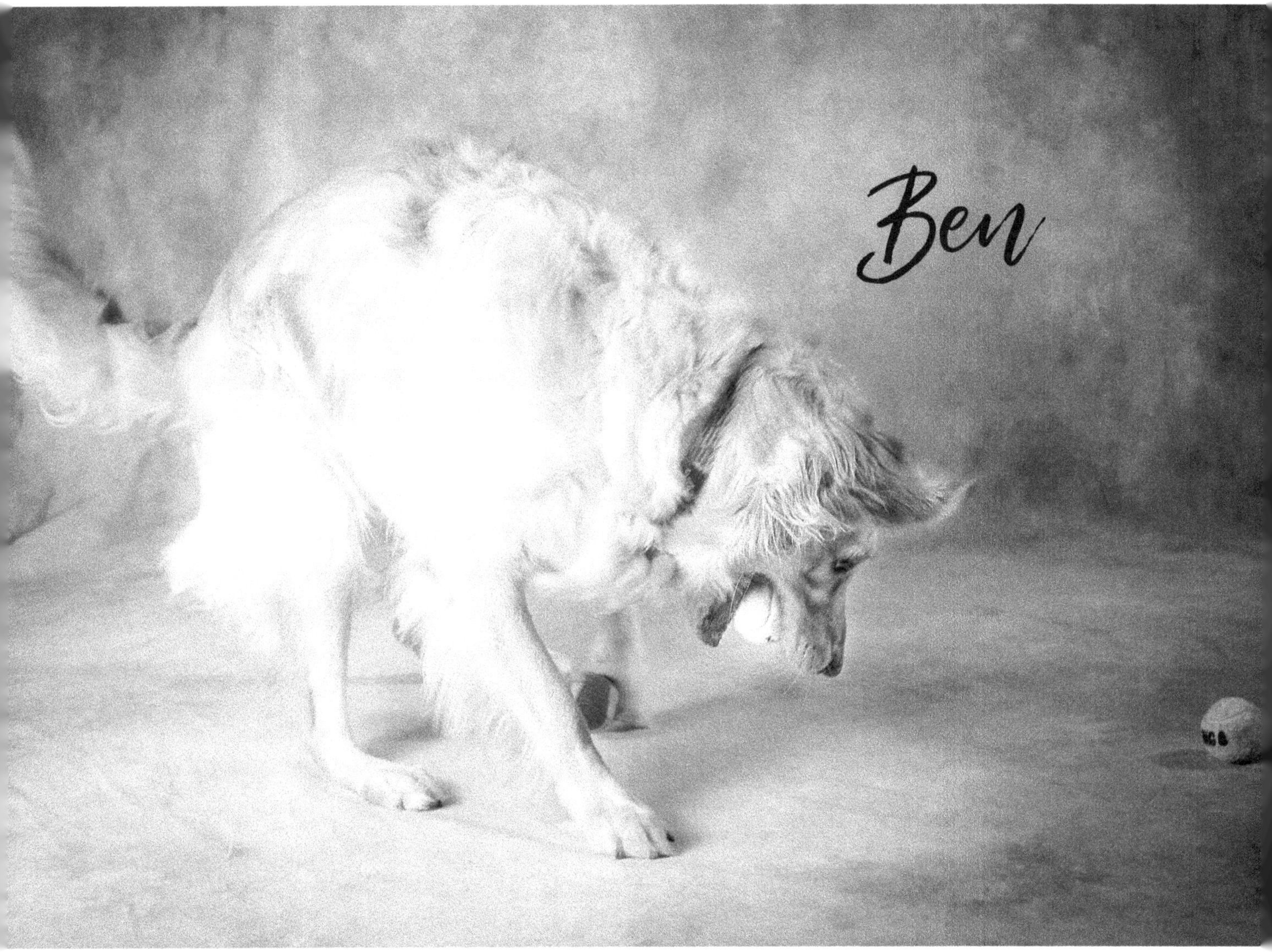

Ben

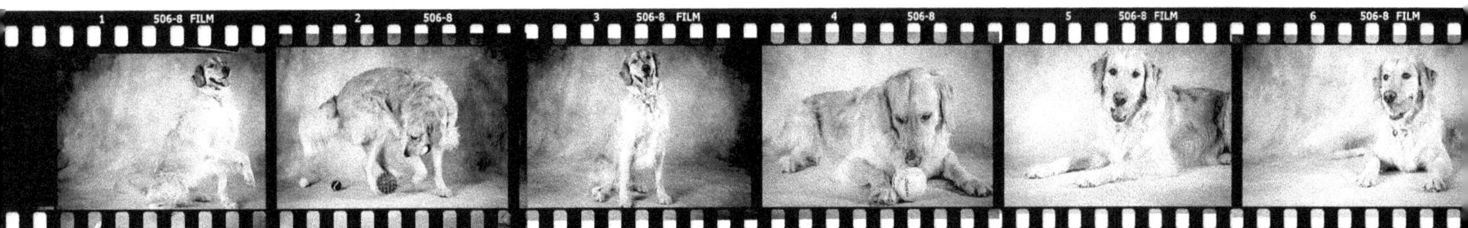

BINDI is much calmer than her brother, Skipper. An eight-year-old Havanese/Malti-poo mix, Bindi's favorite toy is her Nylabone. The sweetest thing she does? Her human mom reports that Bindi loves to lie on her back and be cuddled like a baby.

Only a trusting dog will do that.

Bindi isn't always calm, though. In her younger days she used to enjoy unrolling the toilet paper and grabbing things she shouldn't--like sharp objects.

She's more settled now, and that's a good thing.

Andshe's till adorable.

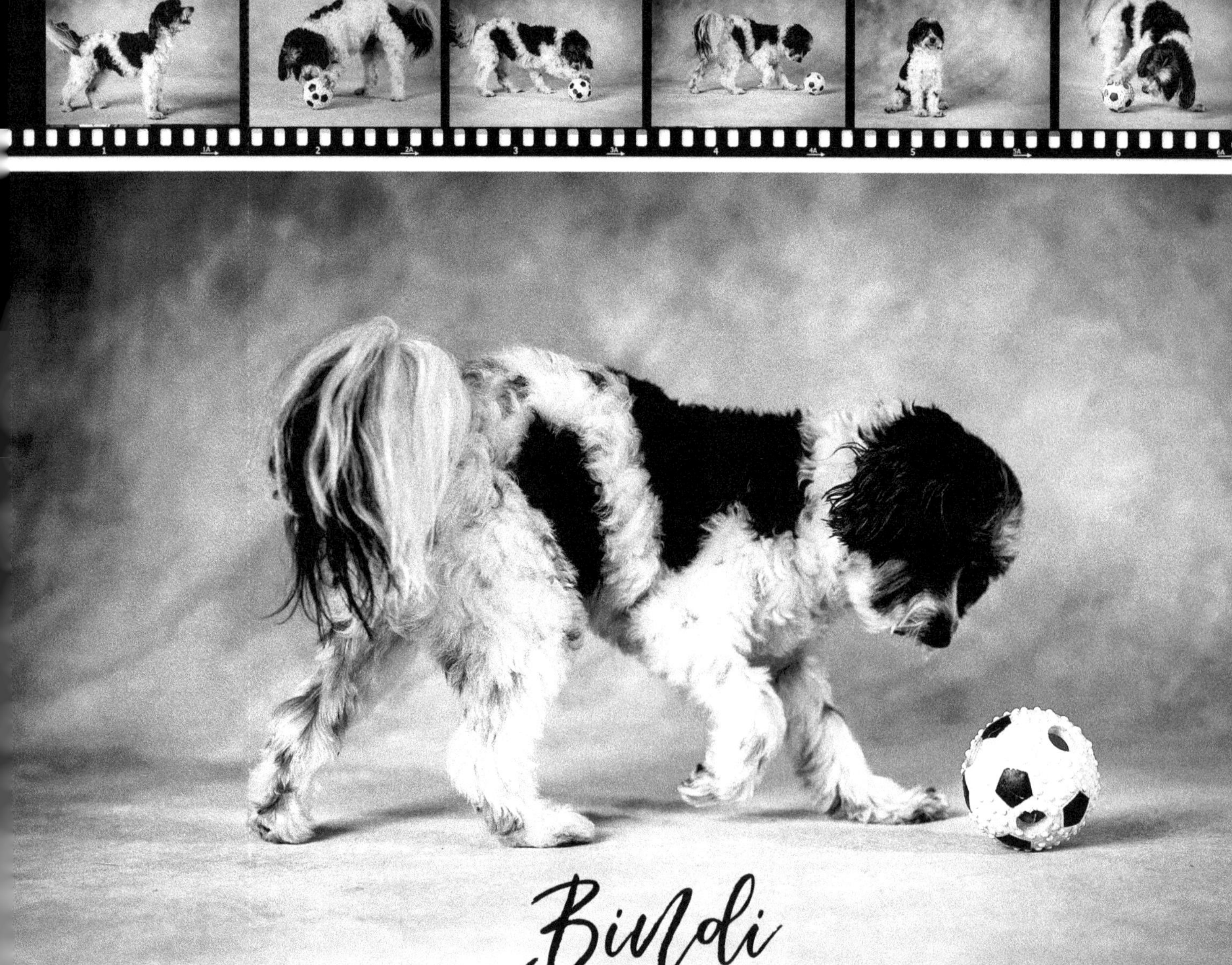

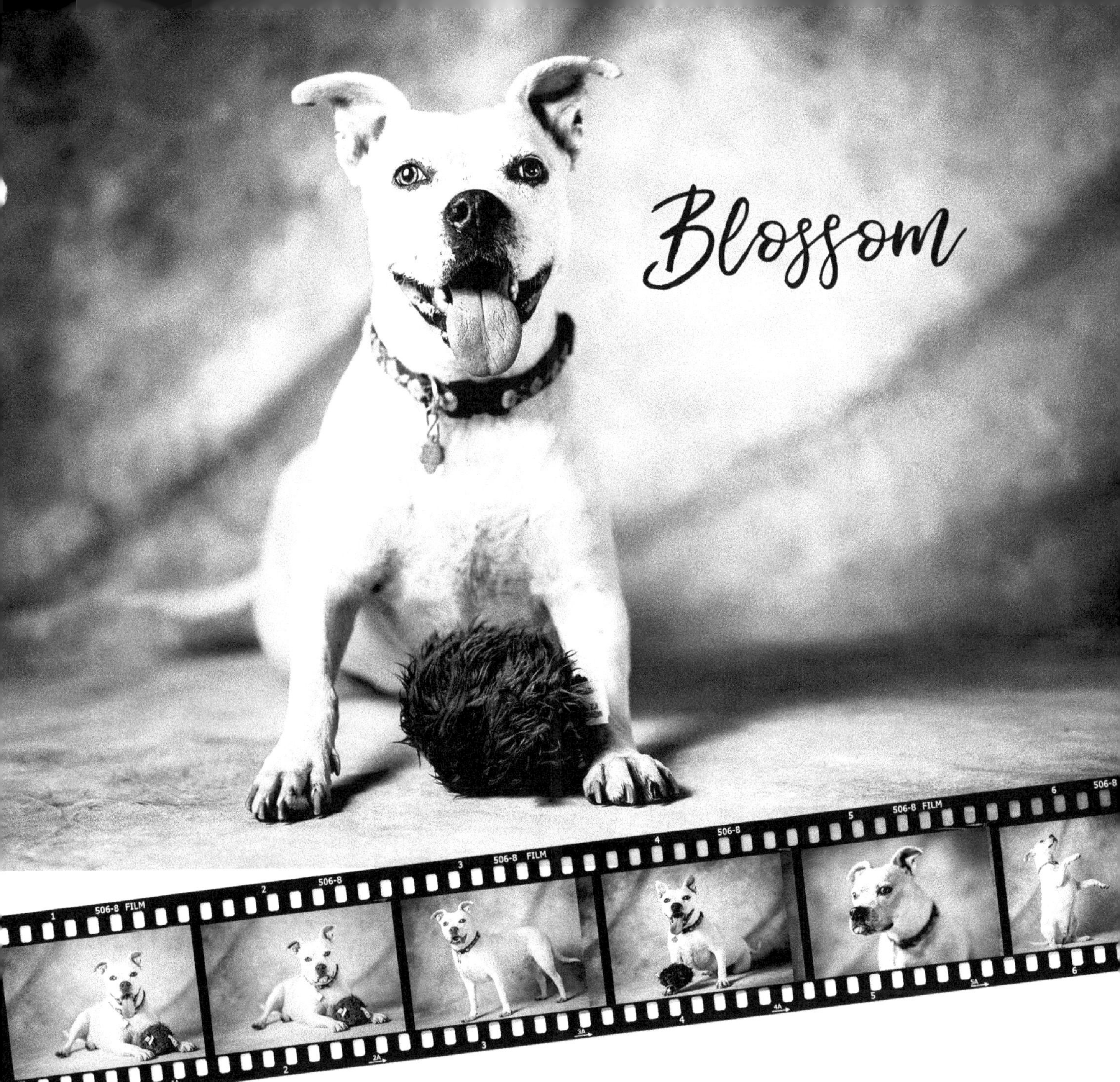

Blossom

Beautiful BLOSSOM loves her purple squeaky ball, often carrying it around the house and enjoying the noise. She is an American Bulldog/Pit mix, which explains her devoted and sweet nature. She has a German Shepherd sister who's a bit anxious, and Blossom calms her by giving her kisses. She was found in a Southern Florida orange grove, emaciated and suffering from severe mange. An animal rescue group sent her to the Suncoast Animal League to escape 2016's Hurricane Matthew, and Blossom was fostered by a family who just couldn't say goodbye. They realized she was meant to be forever home . . . with them.

Boogie

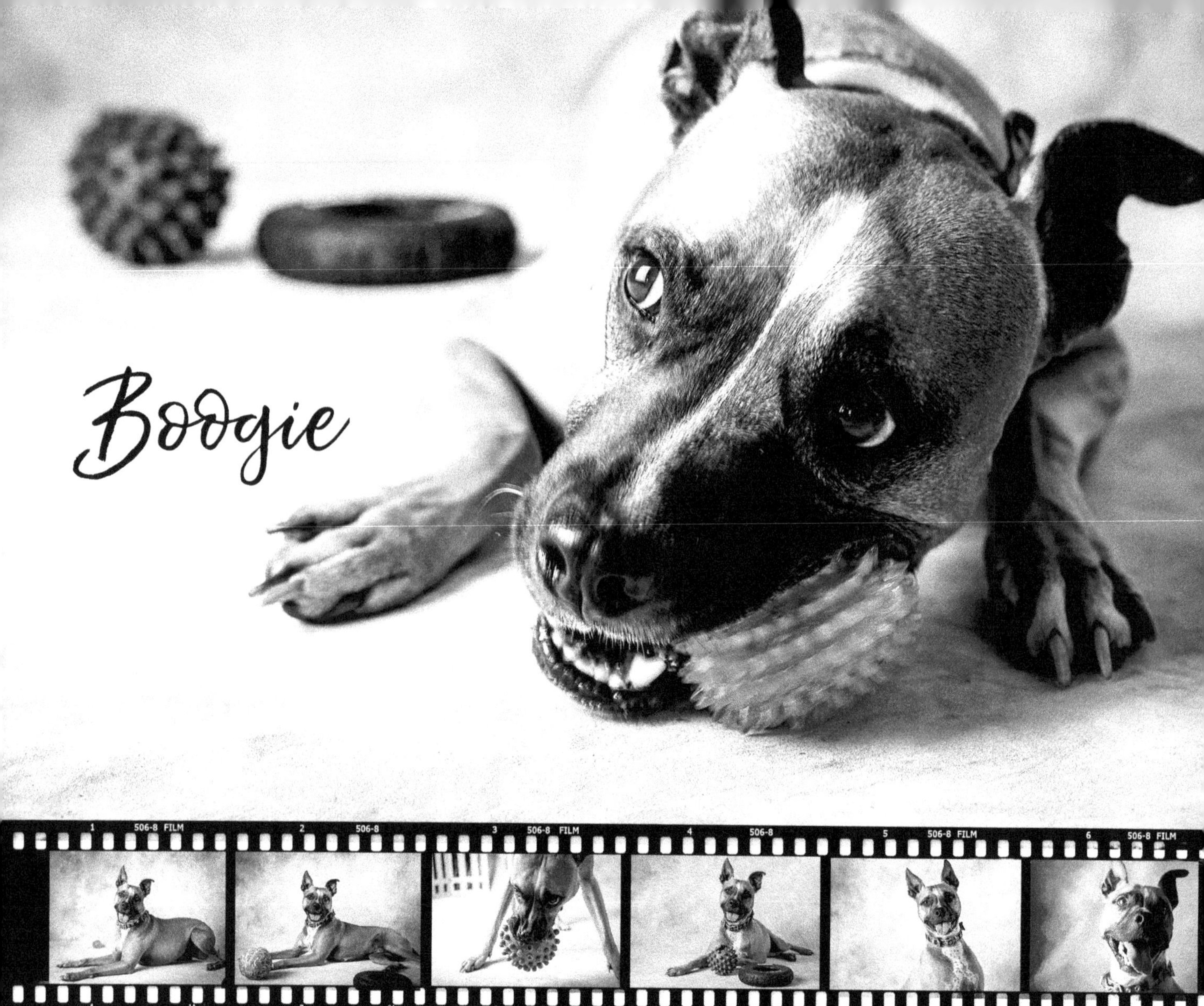

BOOGIE (a la *Boogie Woogie Bugle Boy*) loves his tire and any ball that squeaks. His life changed the day his human mom visited the Hillsborough County animal shelter looking for an older female dog . . . and then she saw that face. Those ears. That energy. And she fell in love. Boogie is a four-year-old Boxer mix who tested his new mom's love and patience in the first few months. Once while she was at work, his separation anxiety spurred him to eat the door frame off the door. But his mom has been patient and Boogie has grown more confident, learning tricks and relishing the time with his new mom and extended family.

Life is grand for this Boogie boy.

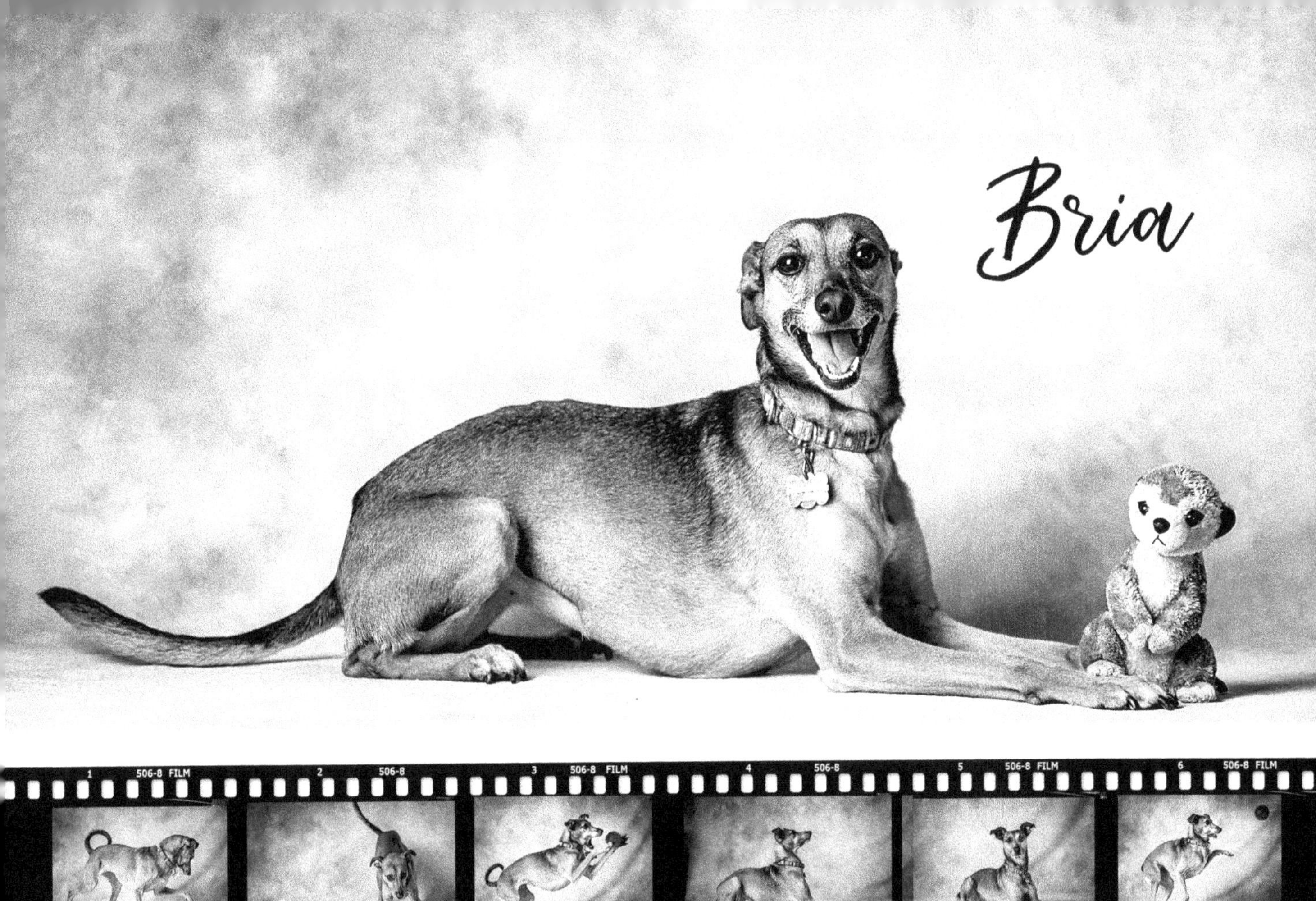

Bria

Lively BRIA is an eight-year-old, twenty-five pound Italian Greyhound/Whippet mix who really knows how to play with a ball. In fact, she has a pink ball she knows as "Pinkie," and it's her favorite thing. Her family was fostering her for the SPCA--she had come in as an emaciated stray--when the dad of the family adopted Bria as a Valentine present for his wife. "Best present ever," says Bria's mom. "She's our youngest and littlest dog, so she gets away with everything!" Bria has a tendency to tear up her bedding, but when she's in trouble she "flirts"--she gazes at her humans with those big brown eyes and melts their hearts. *Brio* is Italian for *vivacious*, so *Bria* suits this little girl to a T!

Buster

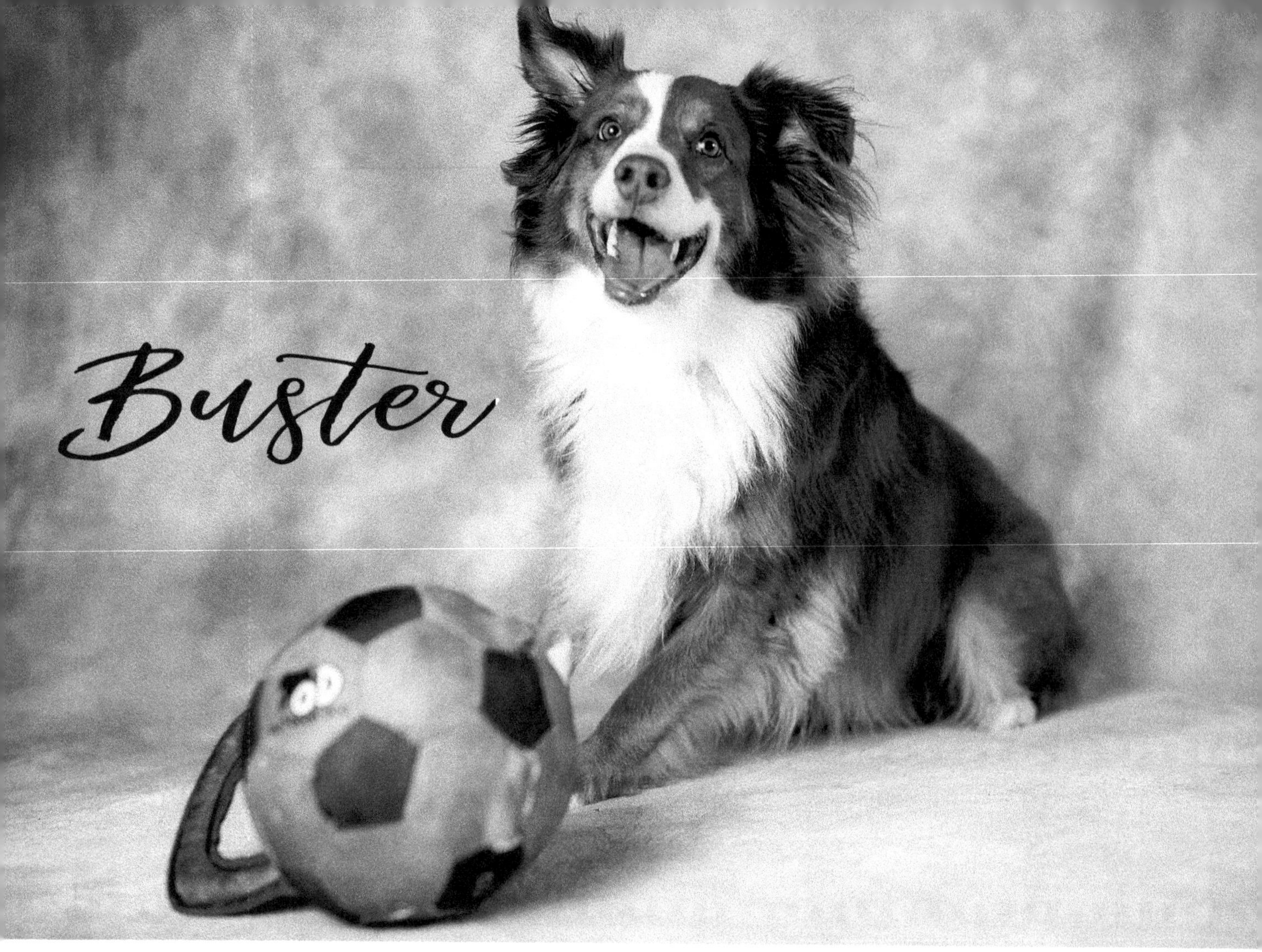

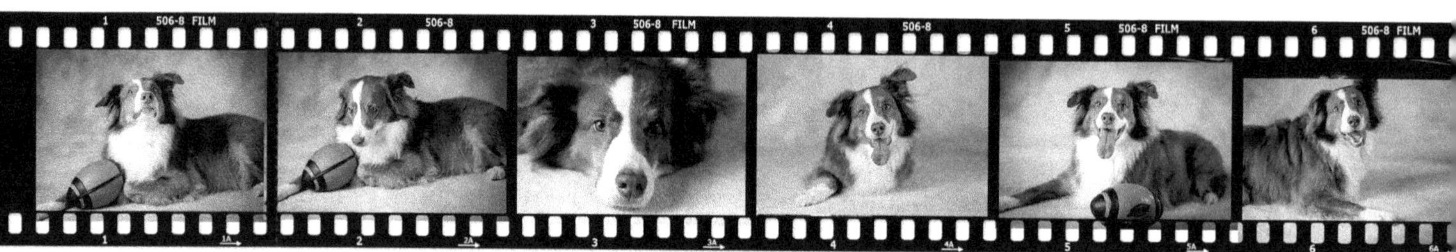

BUSTER is an active five-year-old Australian Shepherd who came from a reputable breeder. His favorite toy is a squeaky octopus and the funniest thing he does is hide his snacks upstairs under his humans' bed. When he was a puppy, he grabbed a rotisserie chicken off the kitchen counter, took it upstairs, and hid it under the bed. The gig was up, of course, when his family noticed he was extremely *greasy*. That Buster! Good thing he is loved.

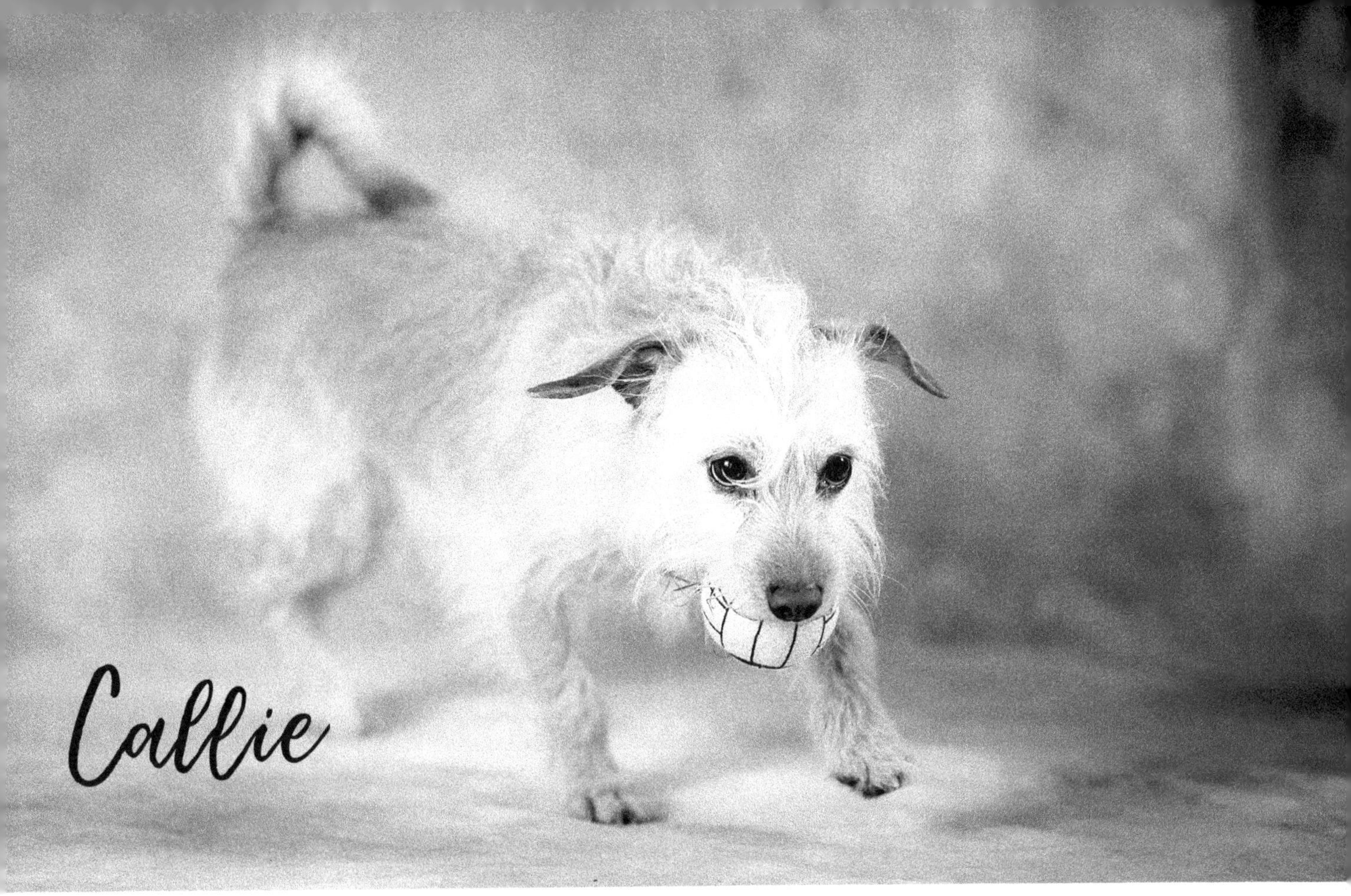

Callie

No one is exactly sure of CALLIE's genetic heritage--Jack Russell and something, perhaps? But one thing is certain--if not for a kind bystander, this little girl would not be brightening the days and nights of her forever family. In her former life, Callie was wandering the streets, flea-infested and pregnant, when she was hit by a car. A stranger stopped and took her to a vet, and after discovering that she had a broken pelvis, the vet called animal services but they could not come get her. After resting that weekend, she was taken to Florida Big Dog Rescue, where she was rehabbed and later adopted by her family. Callie's surviving puppy was adopted as well. Now Callie is quite attached to her family, and will search while making little throaty noises if she can't find at least one of them. This "cuddle dog" has responded to their love with unconditional love in return.

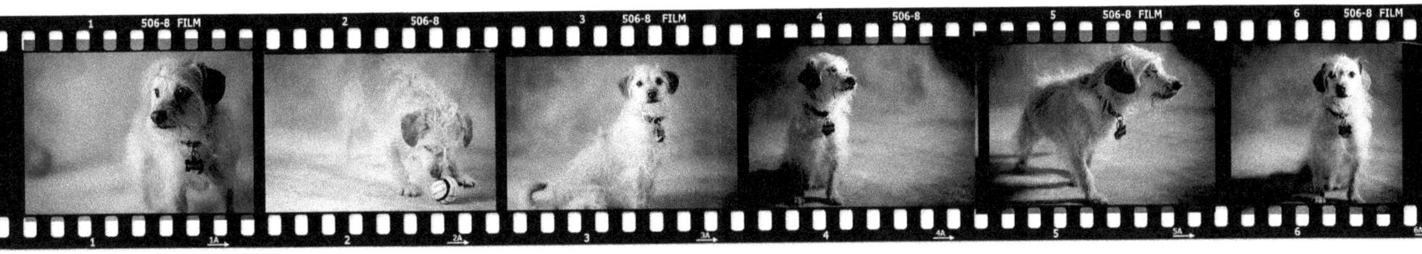

CARDI is an active, sweet, six-month-old Bully mix who loves to play with balls, ropes, anything you offer her. The most endearing thing she does, says her mama, is sit beautifully whenever she wants attention. (She's been to obedience school, so she knows sitting is a Good Thing.) Cardi loves to tease her older brother, Rigby. She snuggles any time she can and loves to play in water. Sometimes her mama finds her sitting in the shower, just waiting for the water to come on. What a treasure--and to think she was on petfinder.com, patiently waiting for her mama to find her.

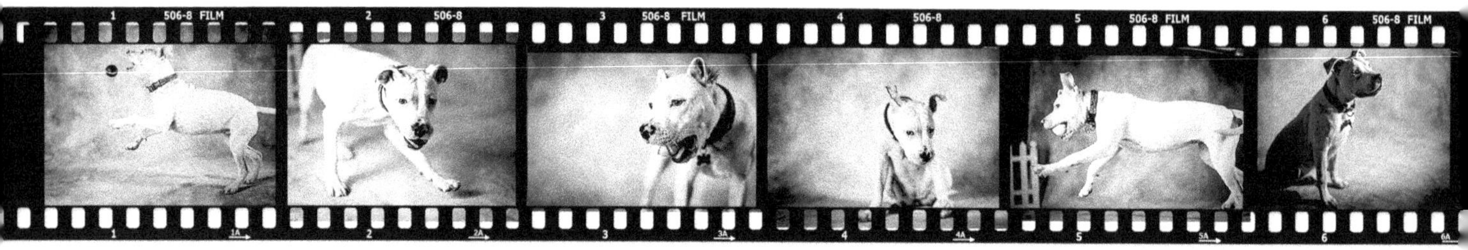

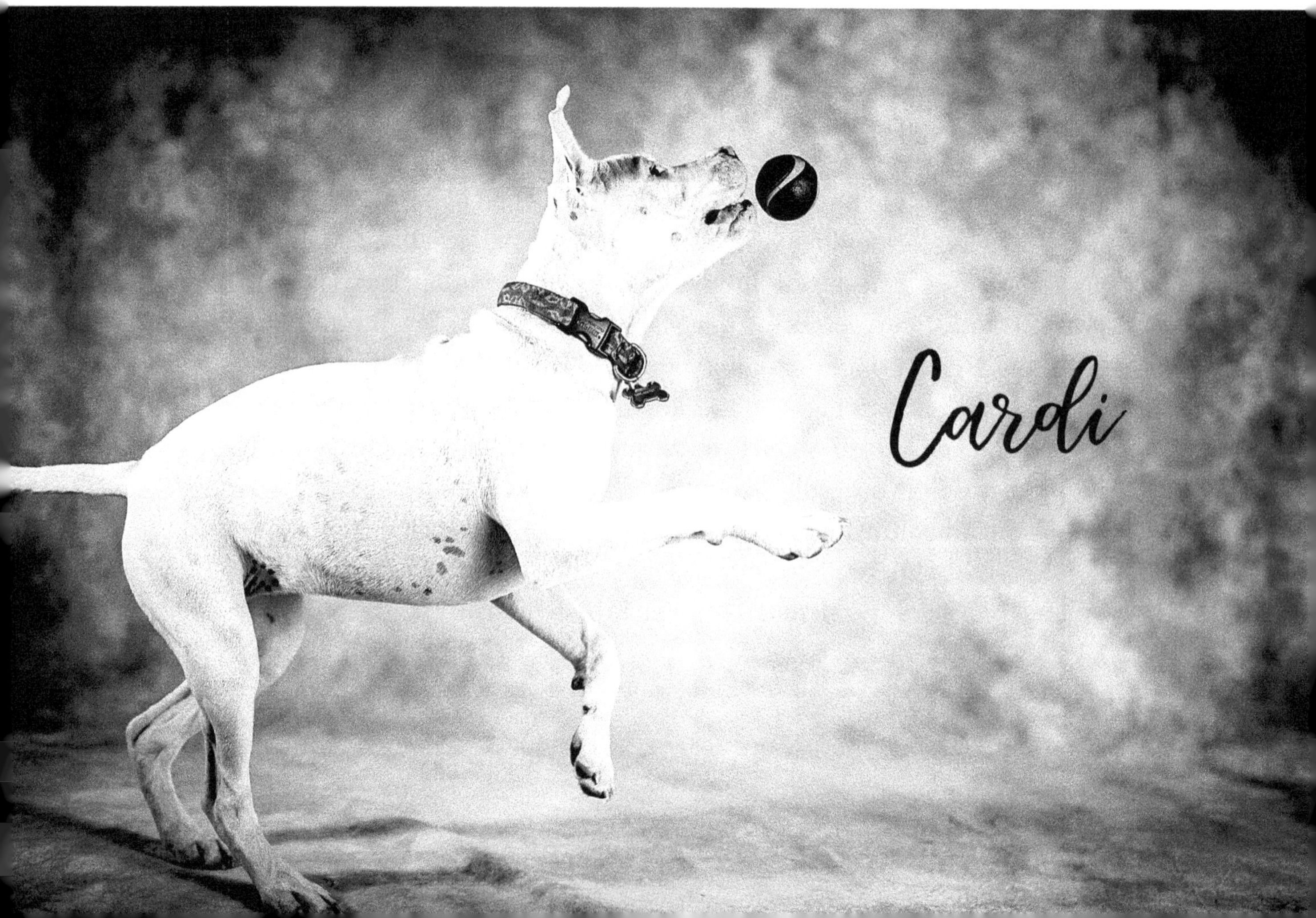

Cardi

CASSIE is a dignified 13-year-old German Shepherd/Collie mix. Her mom found her listed on Craigslist, and they've been together ever since What Cassie loves most, says her mama, is sqeaker toys, but even more than that, Cassie loves to cuddle. She's a verfied snuggle dog. Like her younger sibling Mushu, Cassie also loves to get into the trash, but Mom has learned to keep the really stinky stuff out of reach. Look into those eyes . . . there. You can see the gentle soul within.

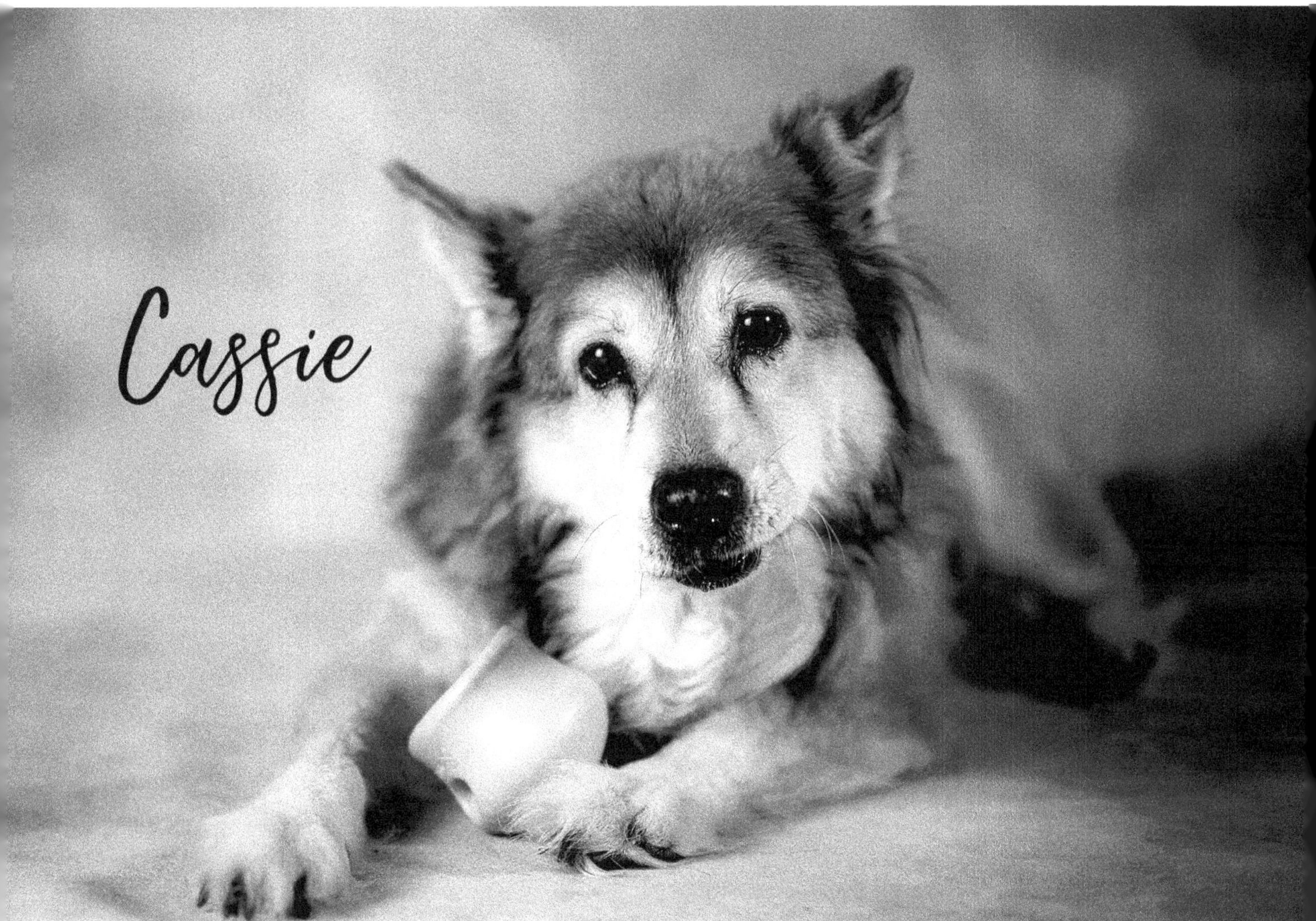

Cassie

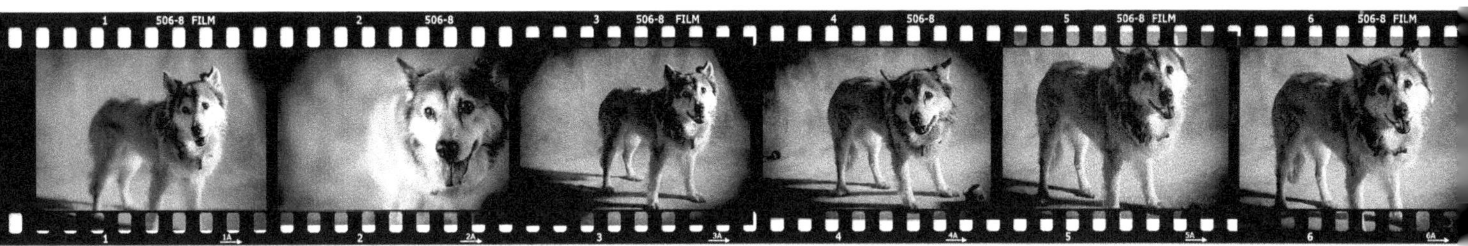

Four-year-old CHARLIE BROWN loves socks more than anything--even more than balls. The chocolate Labrador Retriever has quirks--for one, he loves to "lick" the vapor of hot coffee coming off the cup. To taste it? Who knows?

Second, whenever the family has company, Charlie Brown pulls all the toys out of his toy box, as if inviting the guest to play.

And third, at the dog park, Charlie B says hello to all the other dogs by back-kicking dirt all over them. Guess he has his own way of greeting the guys. .

This energetic boy loves the water, like most Labs, and doesn't bark--unless the doorbell rings. Maybe he's wirelessly connected.

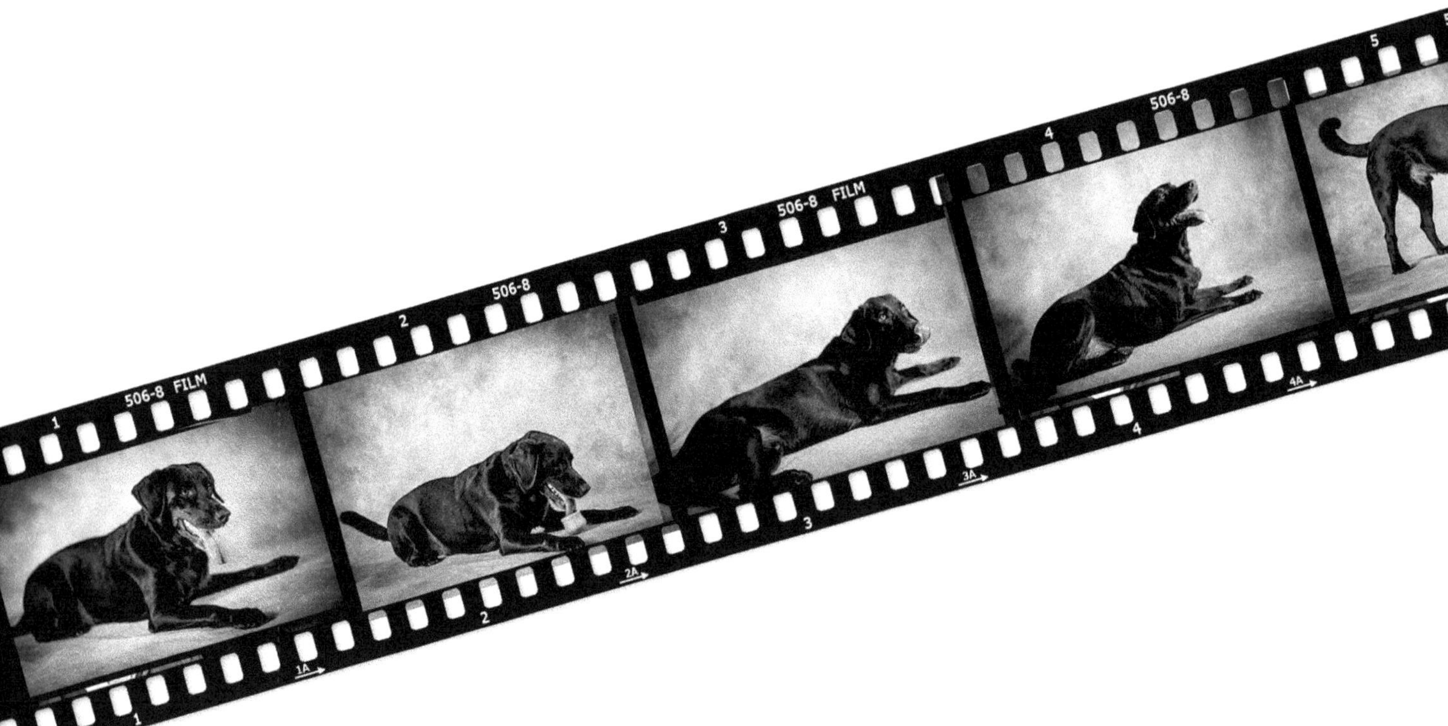

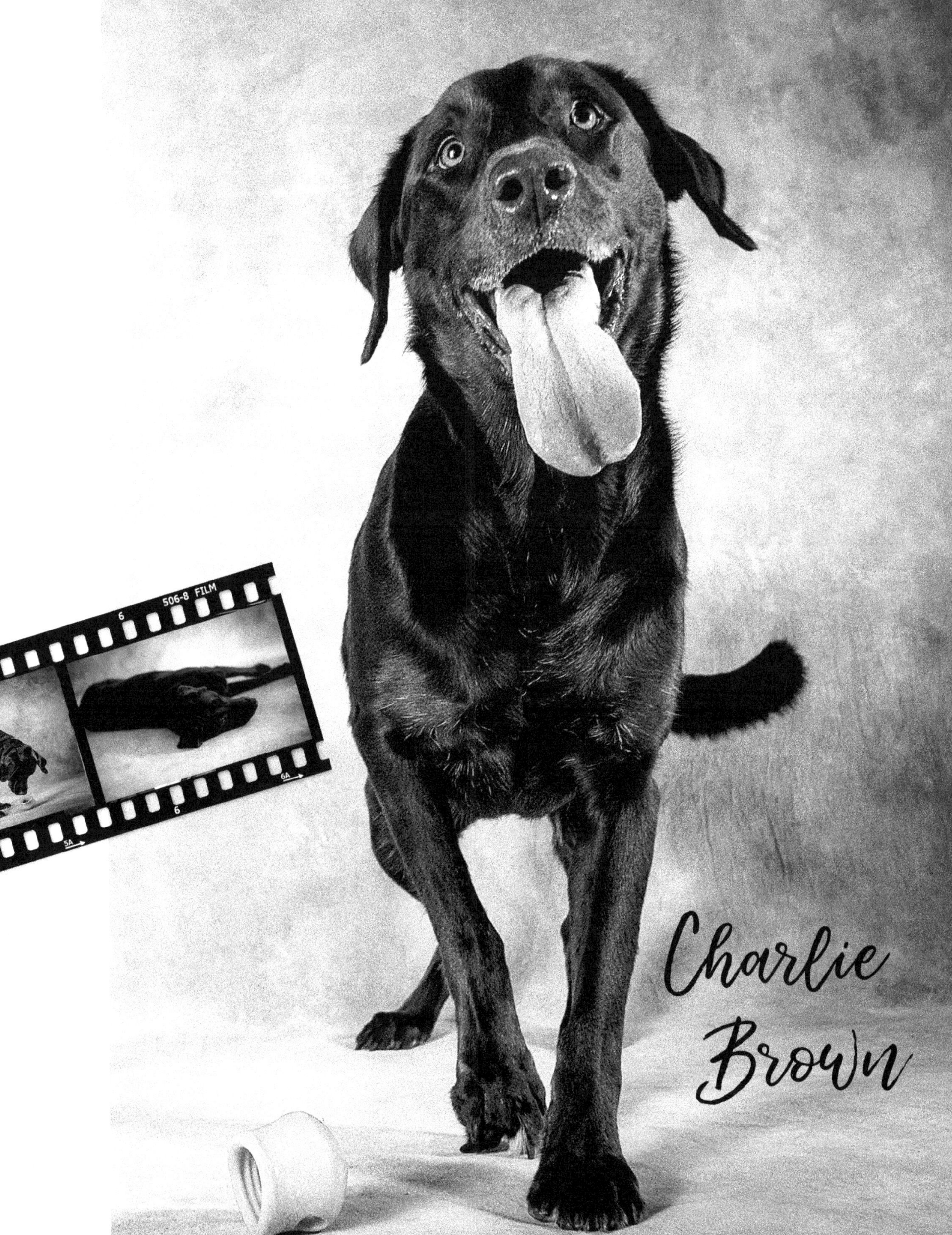

6
506-8 FILM
6A
6
5A
Charlie
Brown

CHARLIE , a purebred West Highland Terrier, is getting up there in dog years, but this fourteen-year-old is still full of life and spunk. He once belonged to a woman who wanted to have him euthanized when he was ten. Charlie's current mom learned about the dog and called the owner, volunteering to take the Westie. The woman demurred, saying she didn't think it would be a "good fit," and several days passed. Then the woman called again, and asked Charlie's current mom if she'd take him. Mom did, and Charlie has been happy at home ever since.

Charlie's favorite toy is the light from a laser pointer, and the most endearing thing he does is growl when his mom kisses him.

She'd stop kissing him, but he always comes back for more.

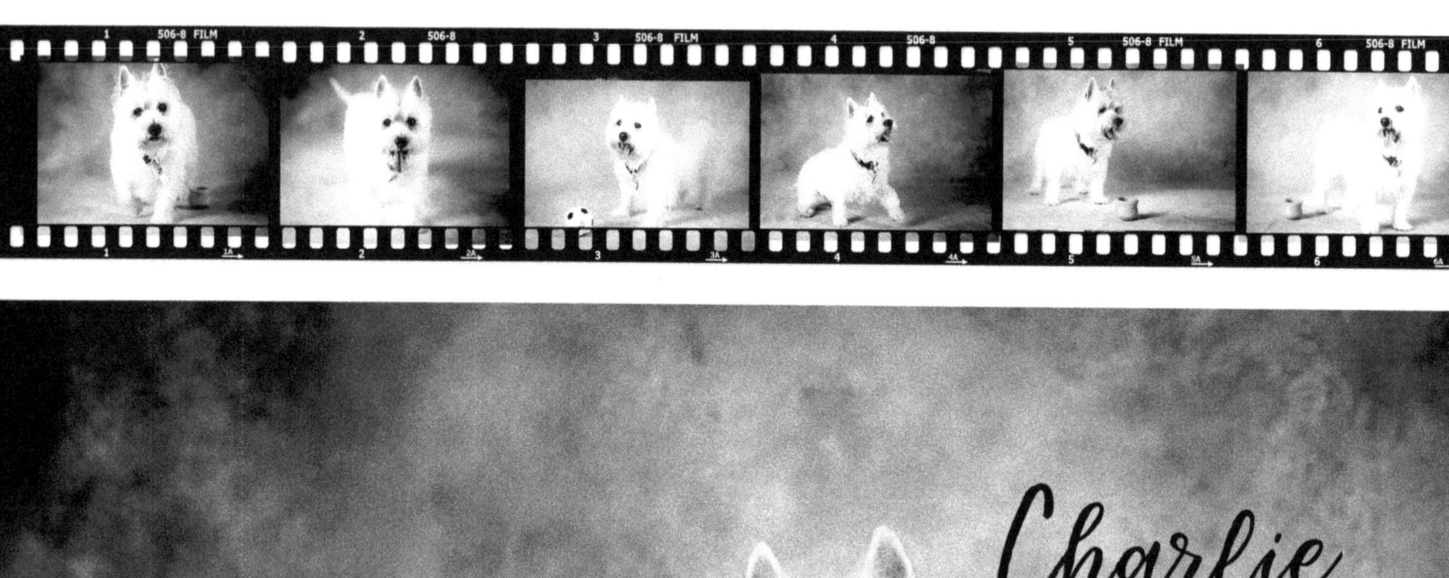

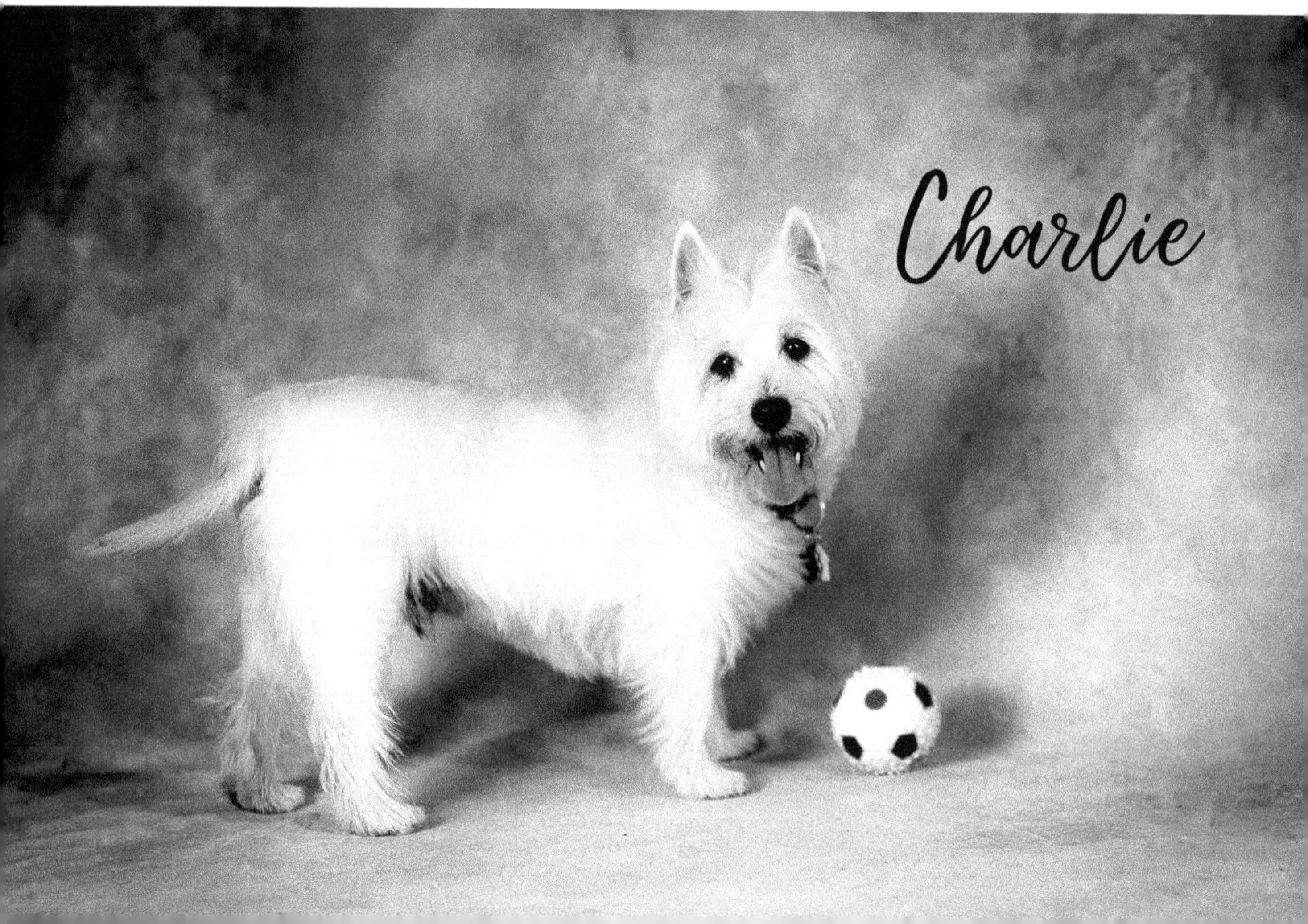

Charlie

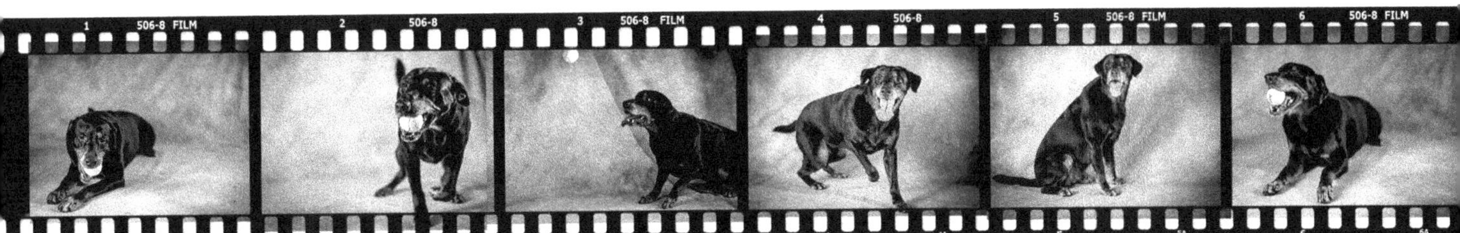

CHASE certainly lives up to his name . . . because this eight-year-old Labrador Retriever loves to chase, chase, chase, chase, chase, chase, chase, chase, chase . . . well, you get the idea. His boundless enthusiasm for chasing balls, swimming in the pool, and chasing anything else you might want to throw is exhausting, so maybe that's why his human mama says when he's not chasing, he's a "ninety-pound lap dog." He's a big sweetie, but he could wear out a less patient human . . . because this boy never stops until he collapses for a nap. He's also a swimmer, and his mom says he jumps in the pool every time the back door is opened.

It's good she keeps lots of towels handy.

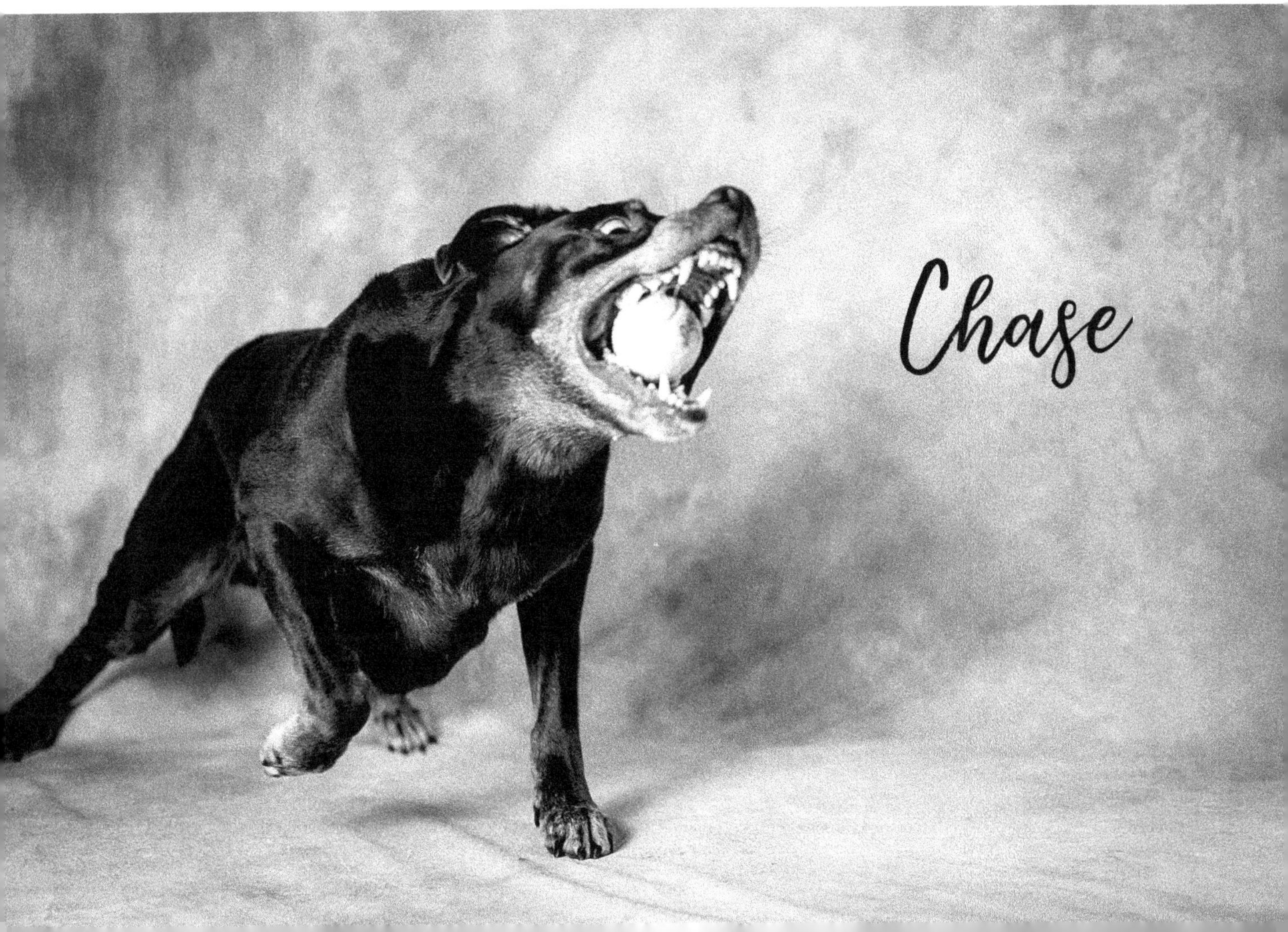

Chase

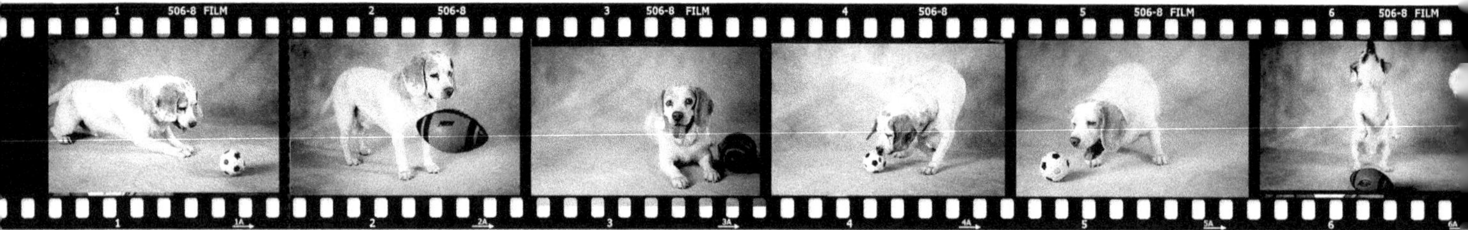

CLEMSON is a sweet dog, says her mom, who can "snore like a sailor!" The eight-year-old beagle came from a friend who had an unplanned litter. Clemson settled into her human family, and she loves her canine siblings, her human mom and dad, and her favorite stuffed butterfly. The worst thing she's ever done, her mom says, is eat seventeen pairs of shoes, two television remotes, and one camera.

Ouch. Bet that called for some Pepto-Bismol.

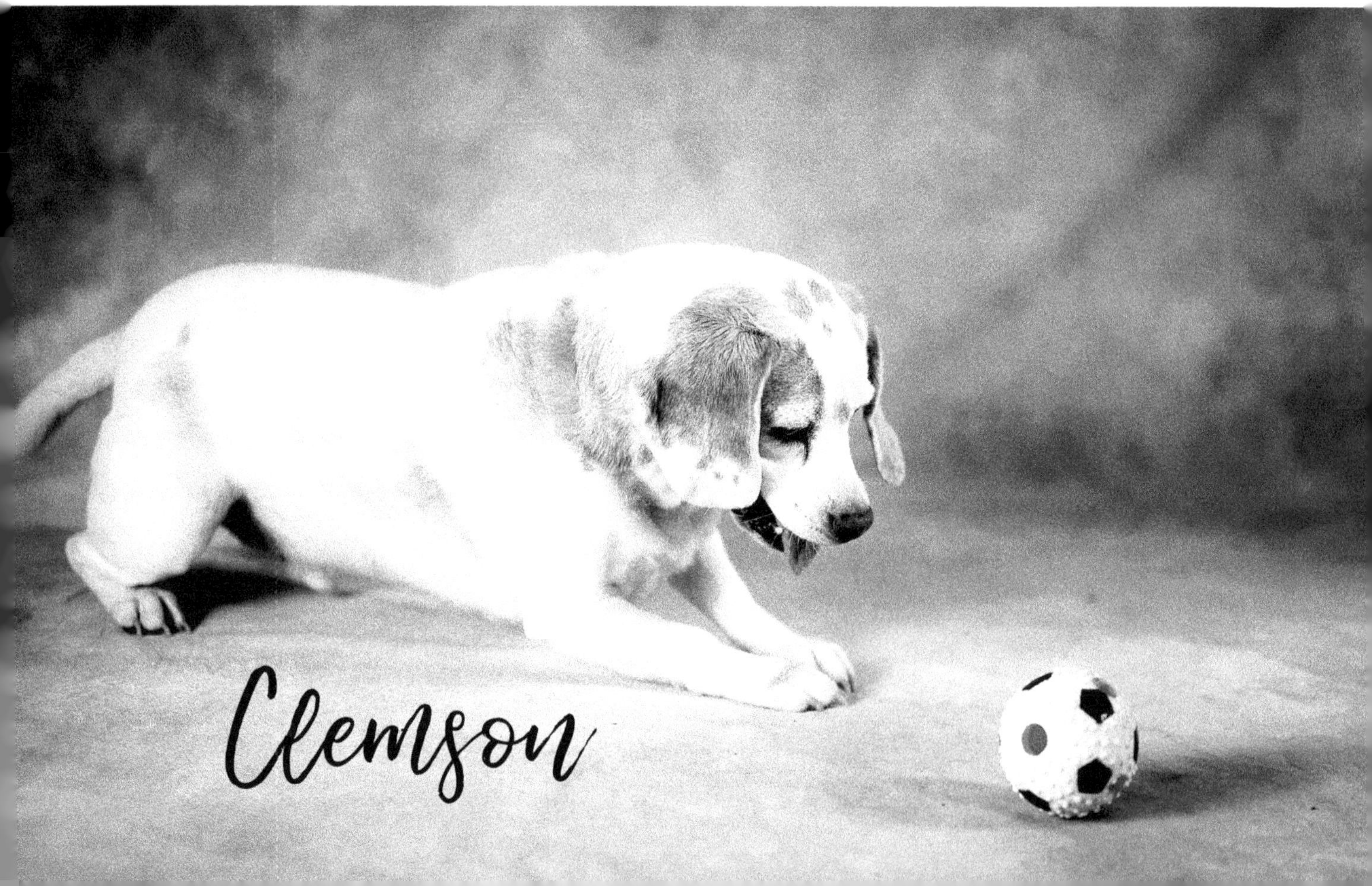

Clemson

COCO is a thirteen-year-old Shih Tzu whose human mama found her through friends. This lovely girl's favorite thing to do is snuggle--and receive belly rubs, especially after a long photo session. She's a very bright girl, but at thirteen, she'd rather plop down for a belly rub than chase a silly ball . . . unless it has treats in it, of course. Coco would do almost anything for a treat.
Or a belly rub, if you're willing.

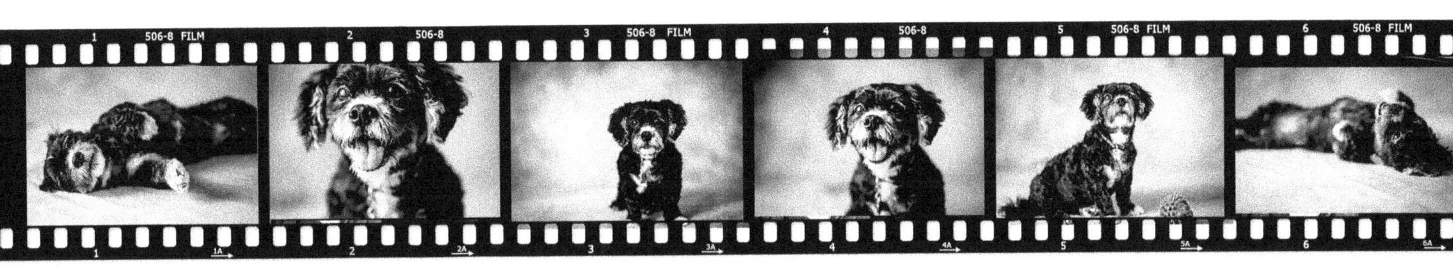

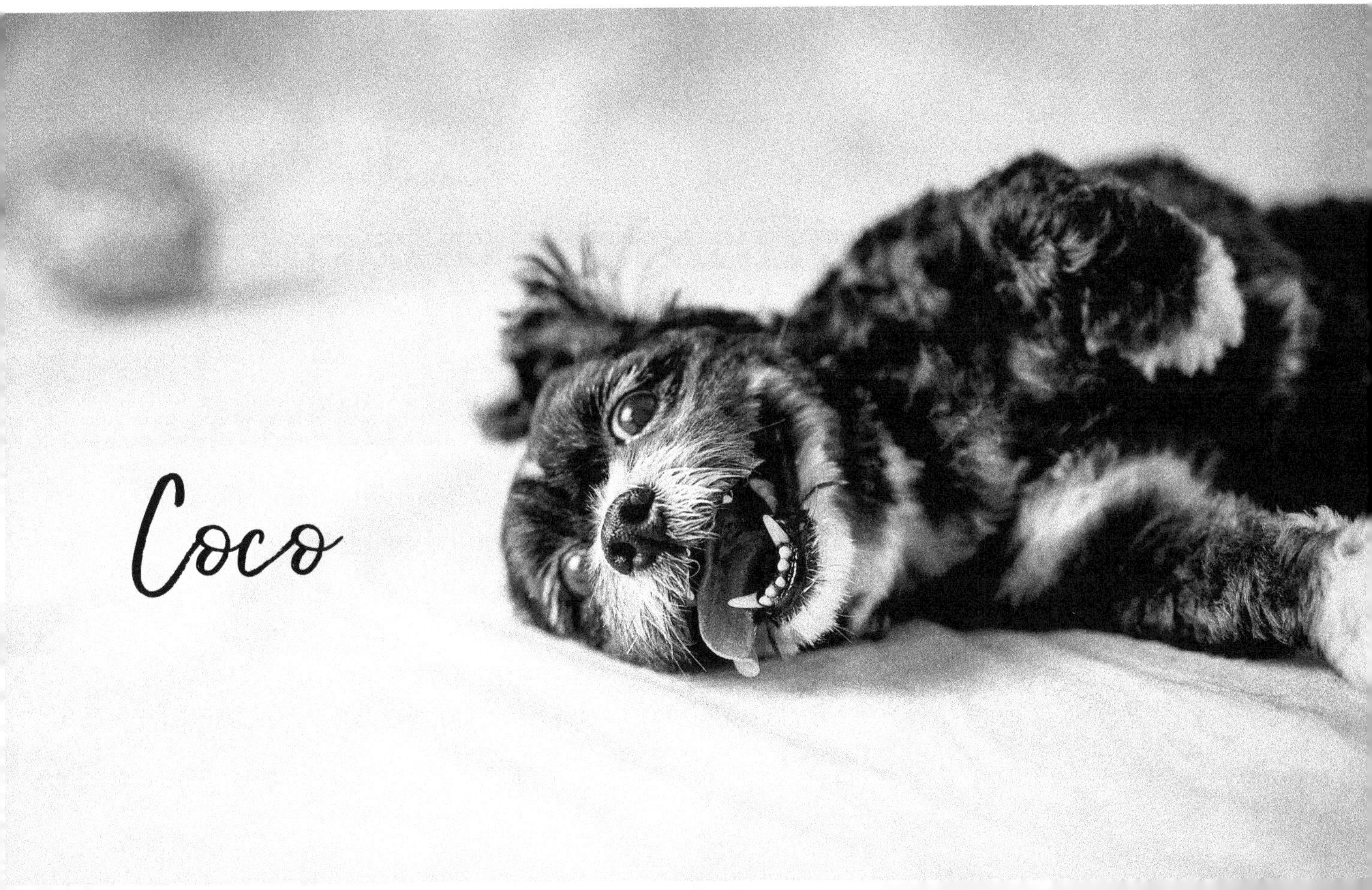

Coco

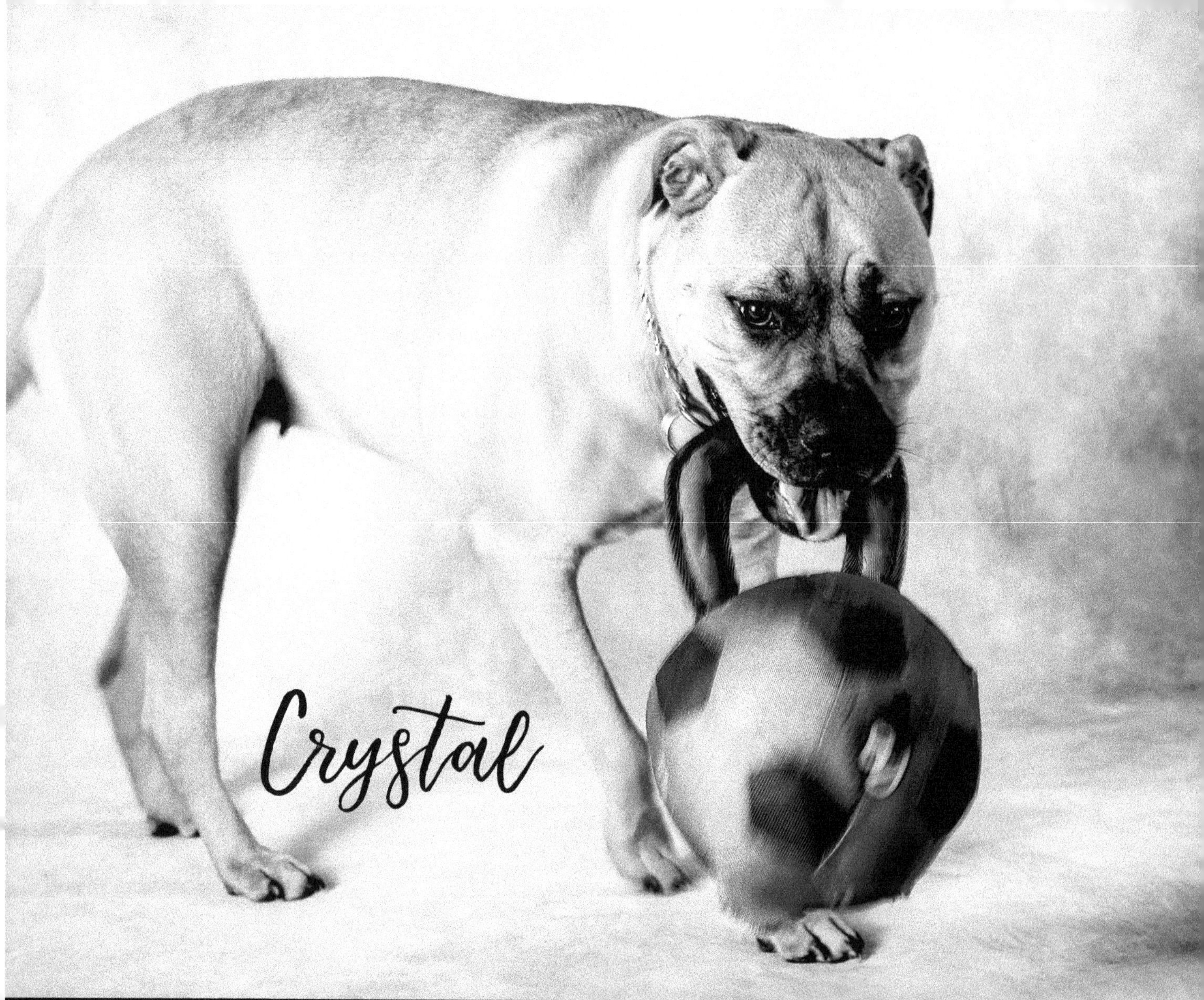

Crystal

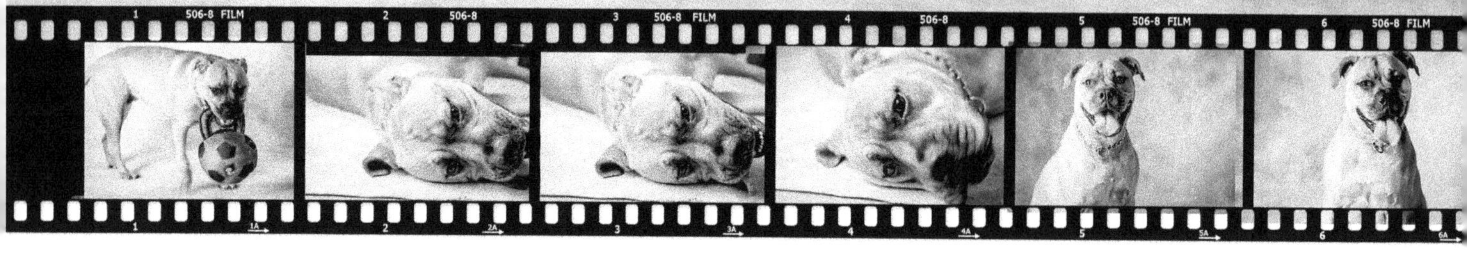

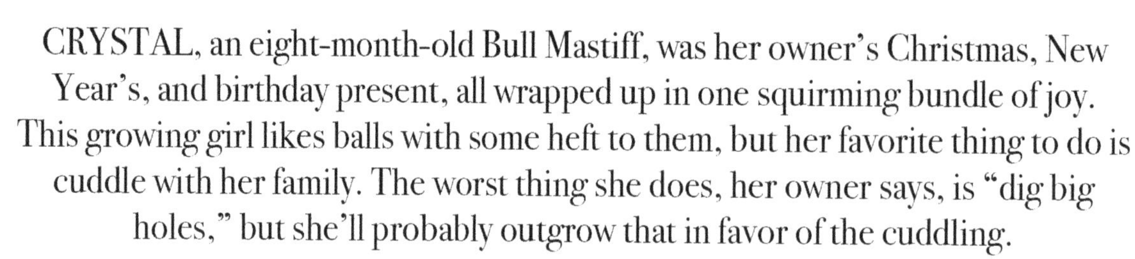

CRYSTAL, an eight-month-old Bull Mastiff, was her owner's Christmas, New Year's, and birthday present, all wrapped up in one squirming bundle of joy. This growing girl likes balls with some heft to them, but her favorite thing to do is cuddle with her family. The worst thing she does, her owner says, is "dig big holes," but she'll probably outgrow that in favor of the cuddling. Who wouldn't?

DAISY is a three-year-old Golden Doodle (a mix between a Golden Retriever and a Poodle) who came from a breeder. She loves playing with any child's toy, but her favorite things are SOCKS. Her human mom reports that Daisy "follows us at all times and loves the kids." But she's most excited when Daddy gets home. "She loves to please," says Mom. "And we love her!"

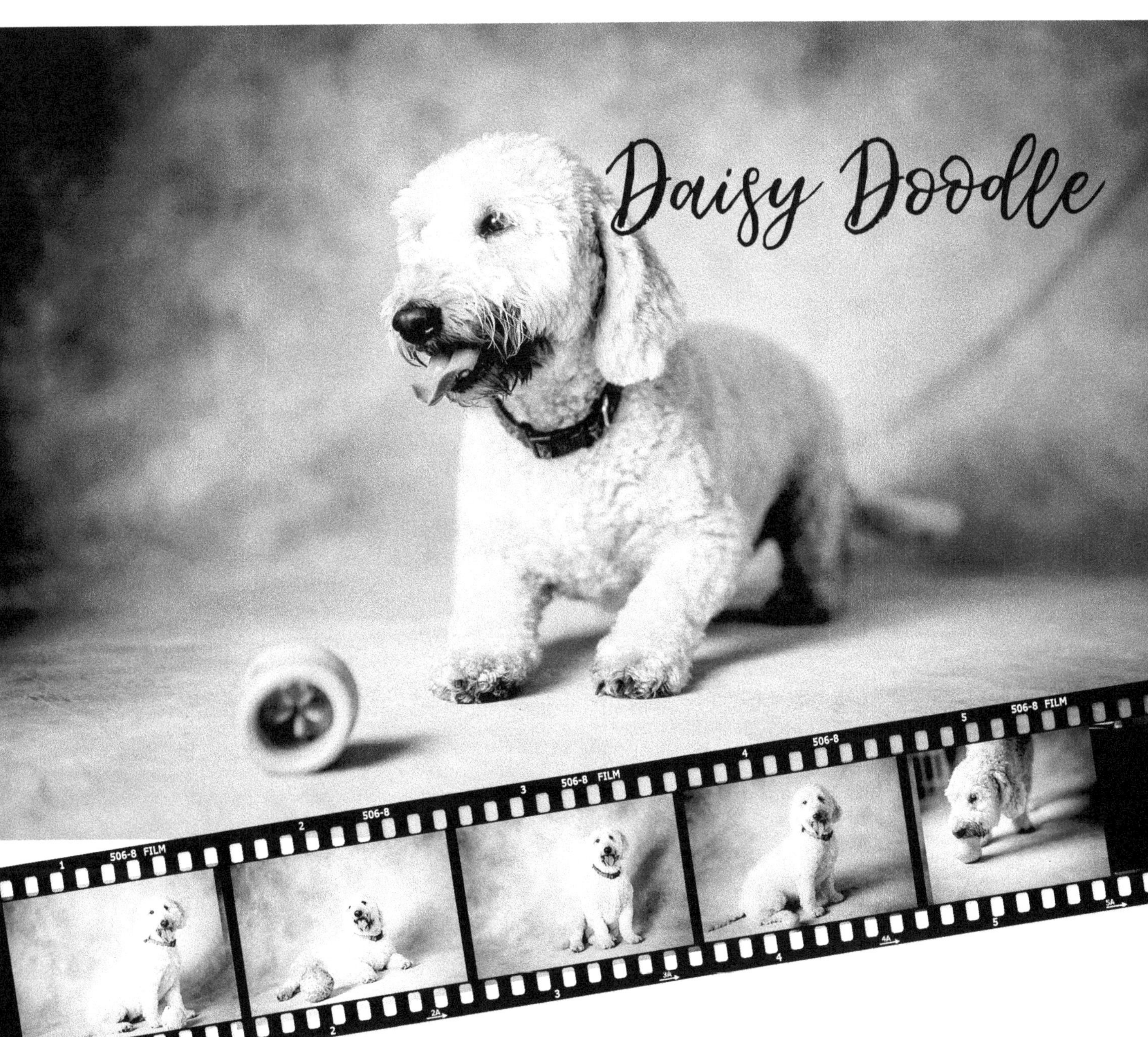

Daisy Mae

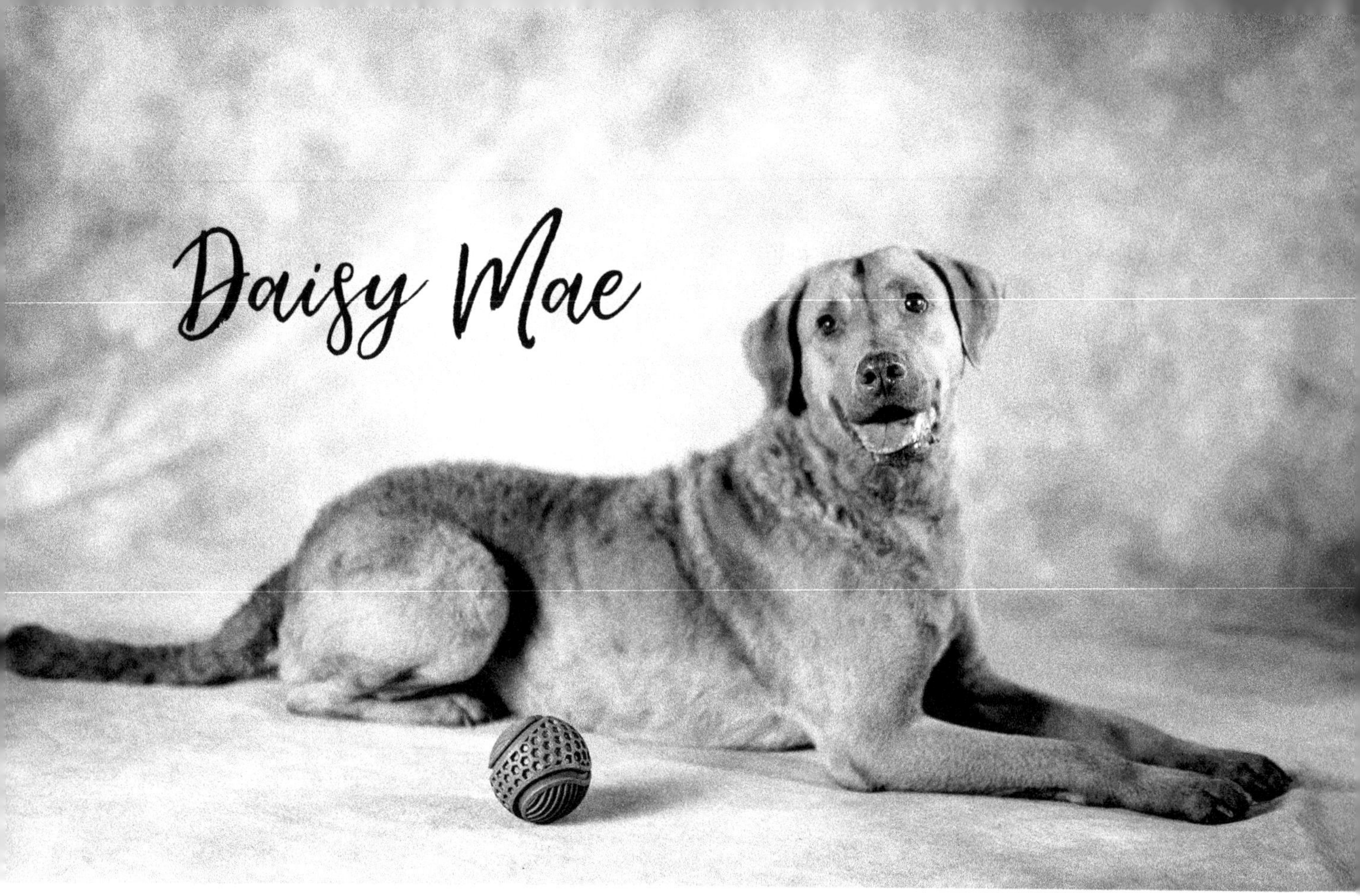

DAISY MAE is a champion on the dog show circuit, but she's a winner at home, too. A well-trained girl, she poses beautifully for the camera, and when her mama says "give love," Daisy Mae will place her head on her mama's chest for a hug. "She's a great snuggler," says her human mom, "and a perpetual scavenger!" If anyone leaves, say, a bag of chips unattended, Daisy Mae will find it and gobble down the contents in seconds. This six-year-old Chesapeake Bay Retriever came from a breeder in Pennsylvania, but she is loved equally with her adopted brother Teddy, who came from a Rescue.

Be sure to read his story on his page.

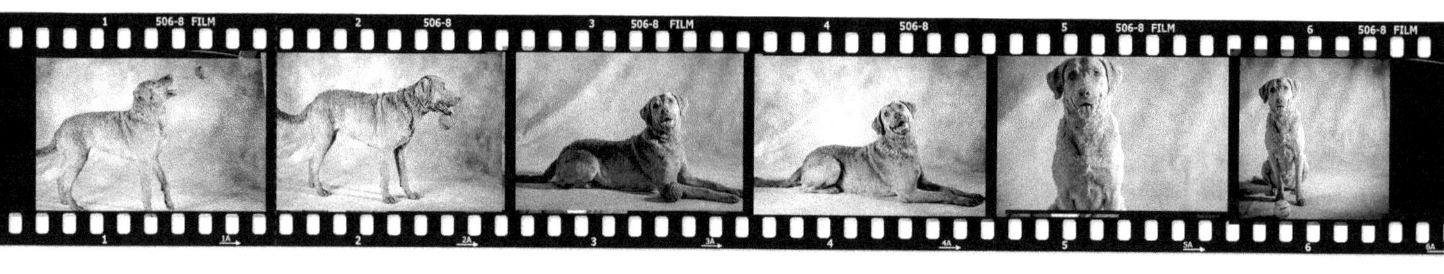

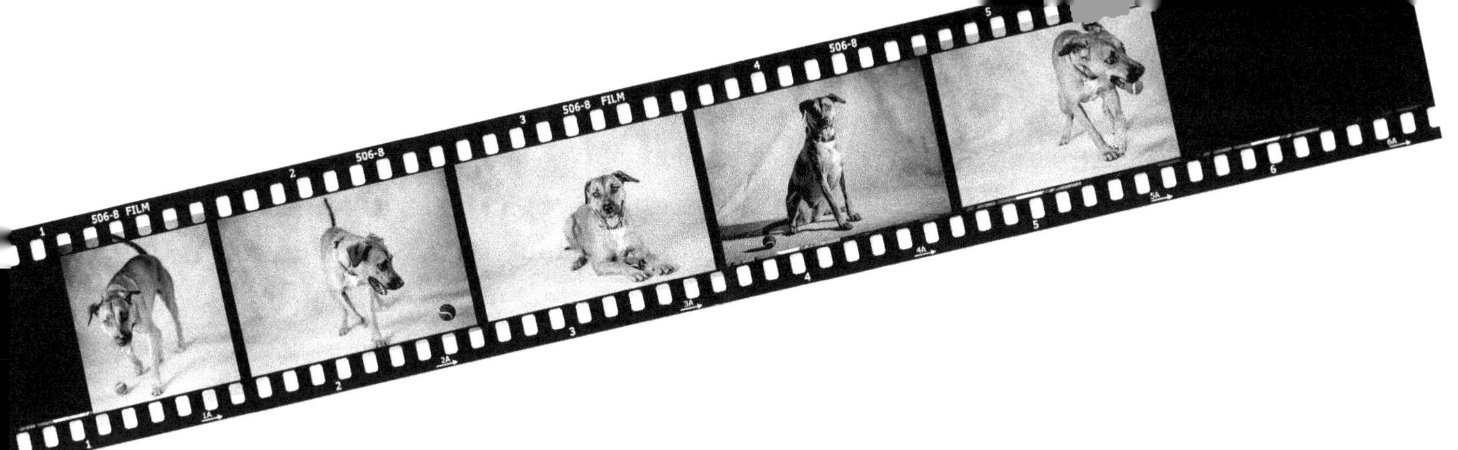

DAISY is a two-year-old German Shepherd/hound mix who loves to bring her mama a toy and drop it in her lap--she's a master of the not-so-subtle hint. Her favorite toy is a rope, but only if someone is tugging on the other end. Her mama found her at a county animal shelter, and Daisy has been with her mama and canine sibling Milo ever since. The worst thing Daisy ever did?
Jump out of a moving car and run away.
Daisy and her humans are glad she made her way home again.

Daisy

DALEK, a one-year-old beagle mix, loves his family. His favorite toy is a rope with a ball at the end, and he loves to lie down on top of his people, no matter where they are. His family found him online--his picture, that is, and they became convinced that Dalek was the dog for them. Their commitment is strong, because in his first year Dalek destroyed three dog beds, four blankets, three harnesses, two leashes, two pairs of prescription eyeglasses, a printer, and a pair of scissors. Take heart, friends. This stage usually passes . . . eventually.

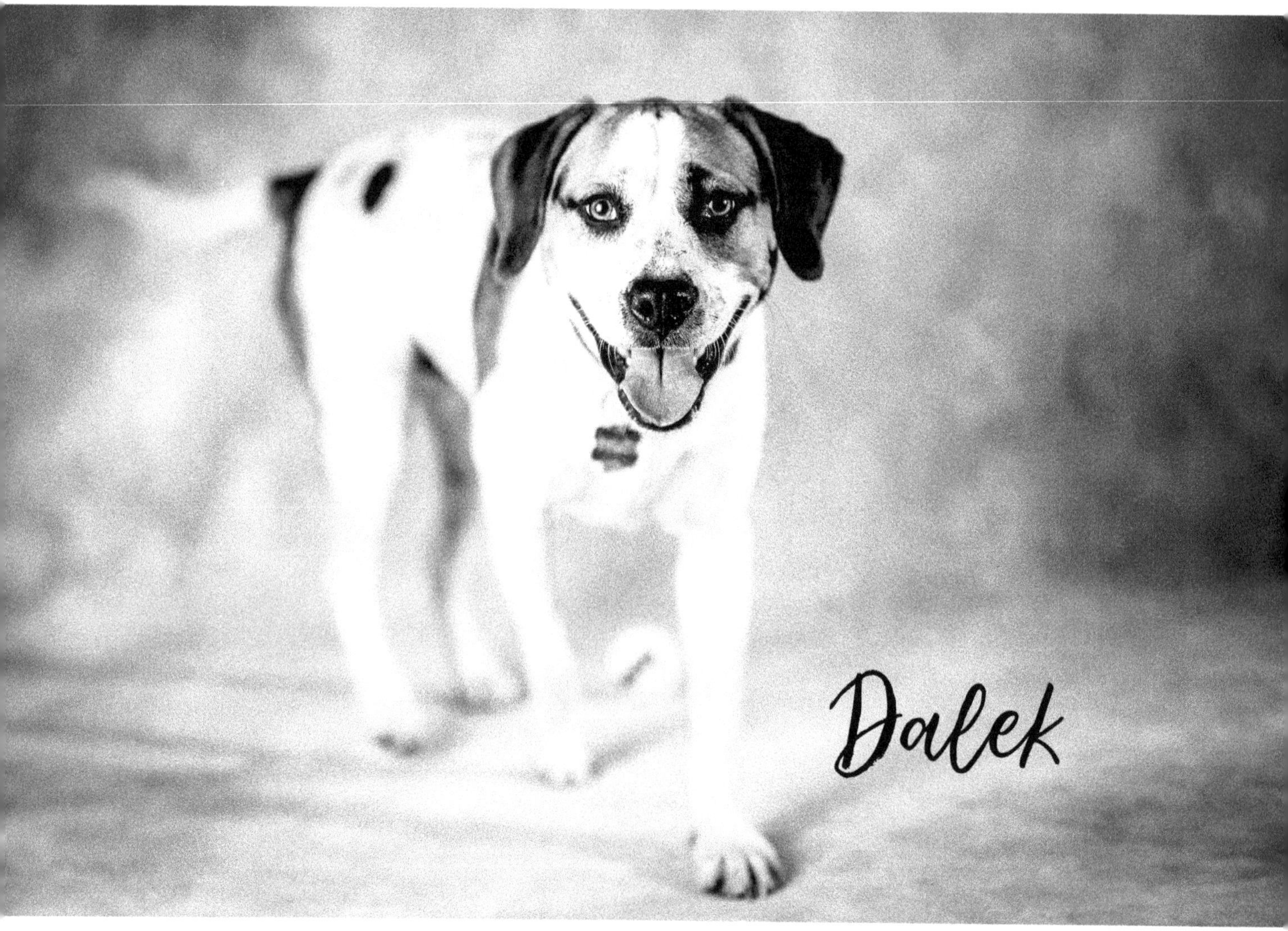

Dalek

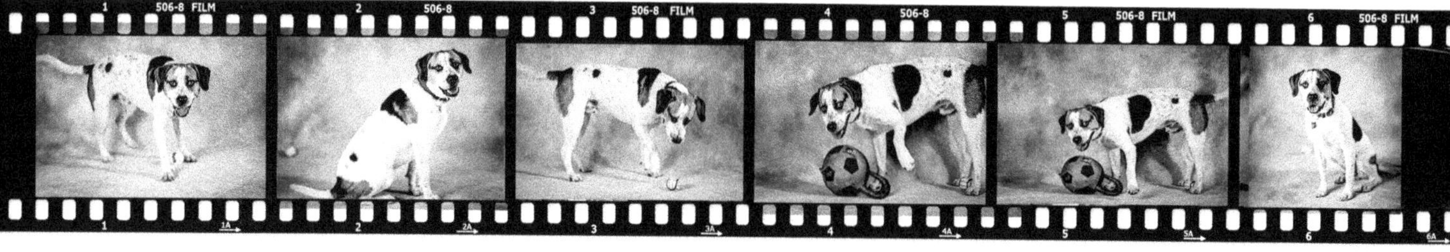

ELLA CRYSTAL is a seven-year-old Cavalier King Charles Spaniel. She came to her mom from a breeder. Ella is so special, says her mom, that she's the reason her mom became involved in rescuing other Cavaliers. Ella's favorite toy is a Lambchop puppet, and she gives free hugs. This friendly dog has never met a stranger and she's all sass. "Cavitude to the max!" says her mom. No wonder King Charles was so fond of this breed.

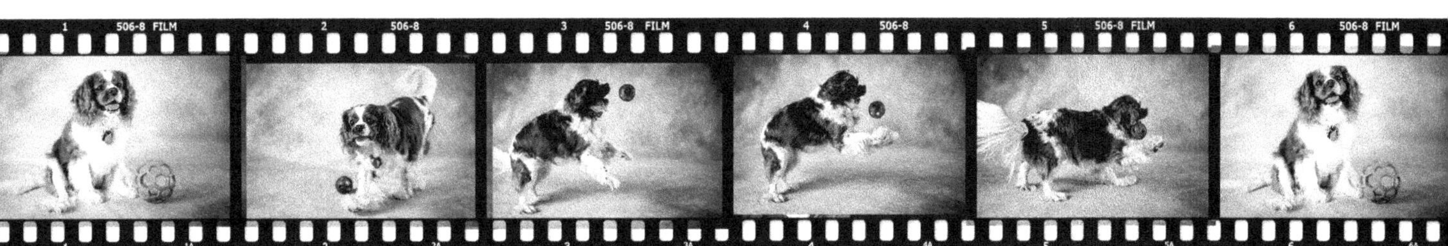

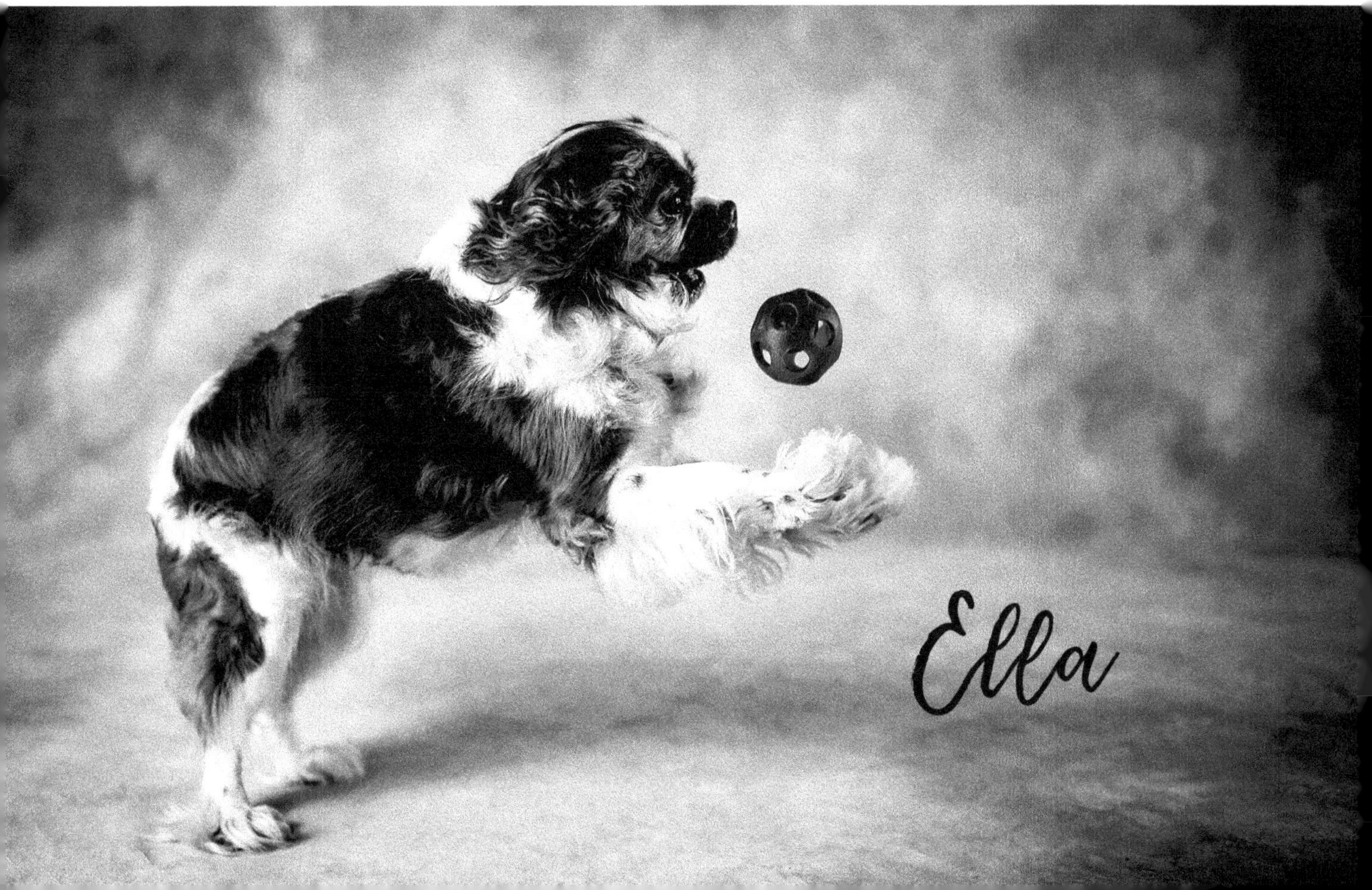

Ella

FINLEY is a two-year-old Golden Doodle who came to her forever home because her previous owner's health wouldn't allow her to keep this pretty girl. This fun-loving Doodle likes to play with her ball and her Kong doll. Finley has a cute tongue that hangs sideways and LOTS of energy. The worst thing Finley has ever done is eat a pen-- maybe she wants to be a writer?

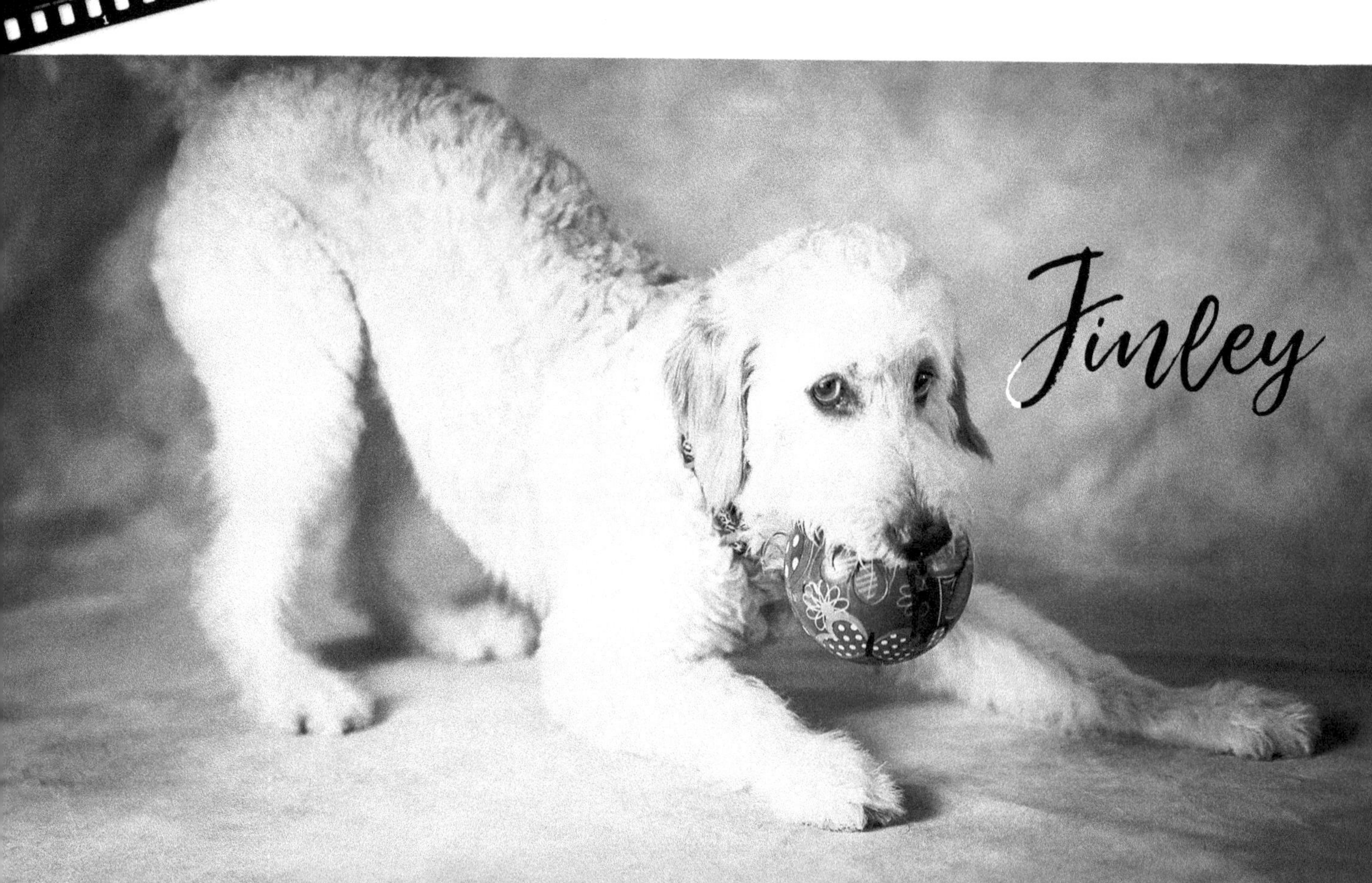

FLEUR DE LIS was a gift from a son to his mother--a gift intended to ease the pain of losing another dog. The human mama immediately loved this beautiful Siberian Husky, and Fleur, aka Flurry, loves her mama, her dad, and her stuffed rabbit. She snuggles and gives her mama lots of kisses, though she is an escape artist who often tricks people by sneaking through the doorway while they're talking or otherwise distracted. If you look closely, you can see the beautiful Fleur de Lis design on her forhead, hence the name.

A lovely, lively girl.

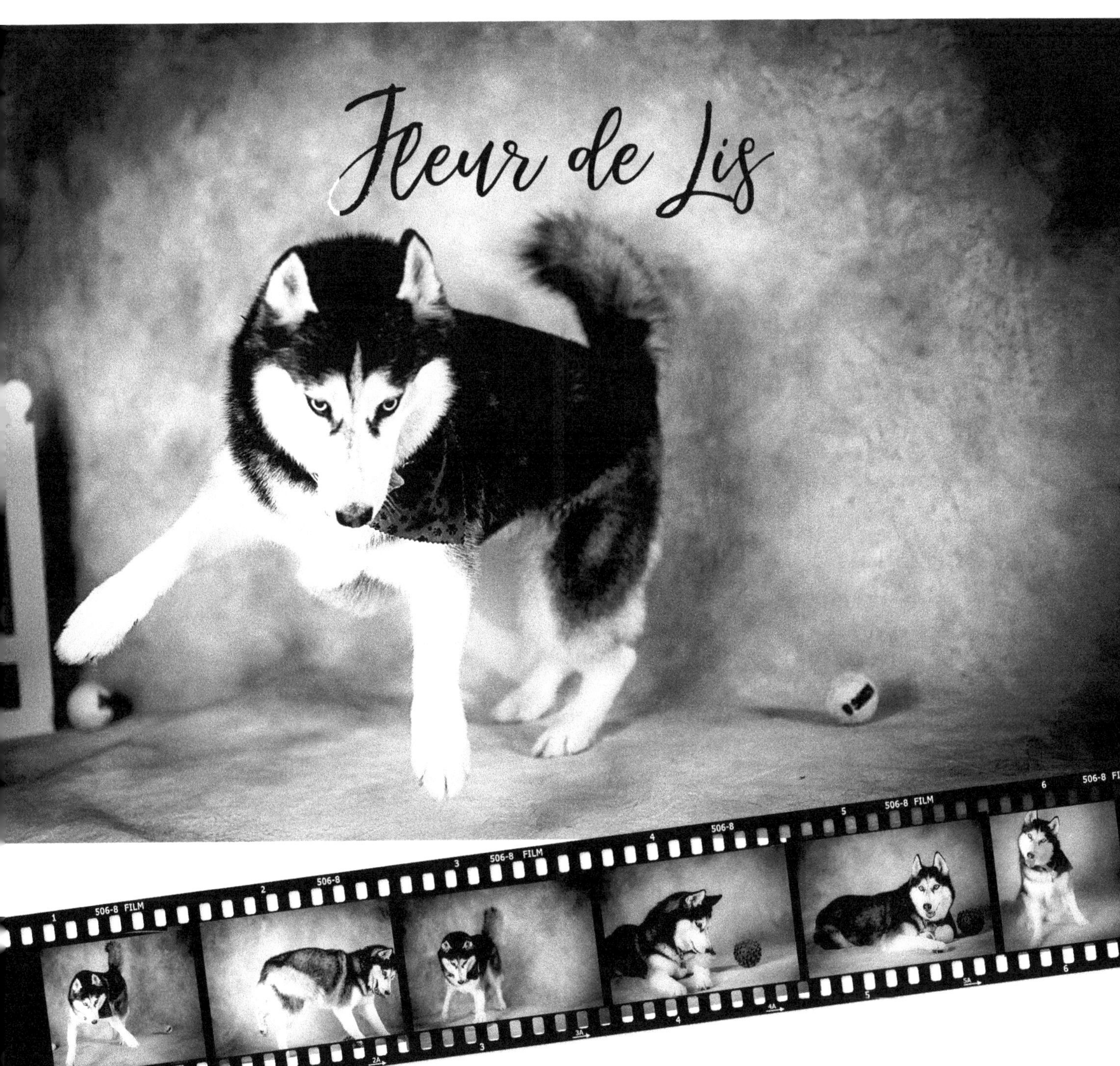

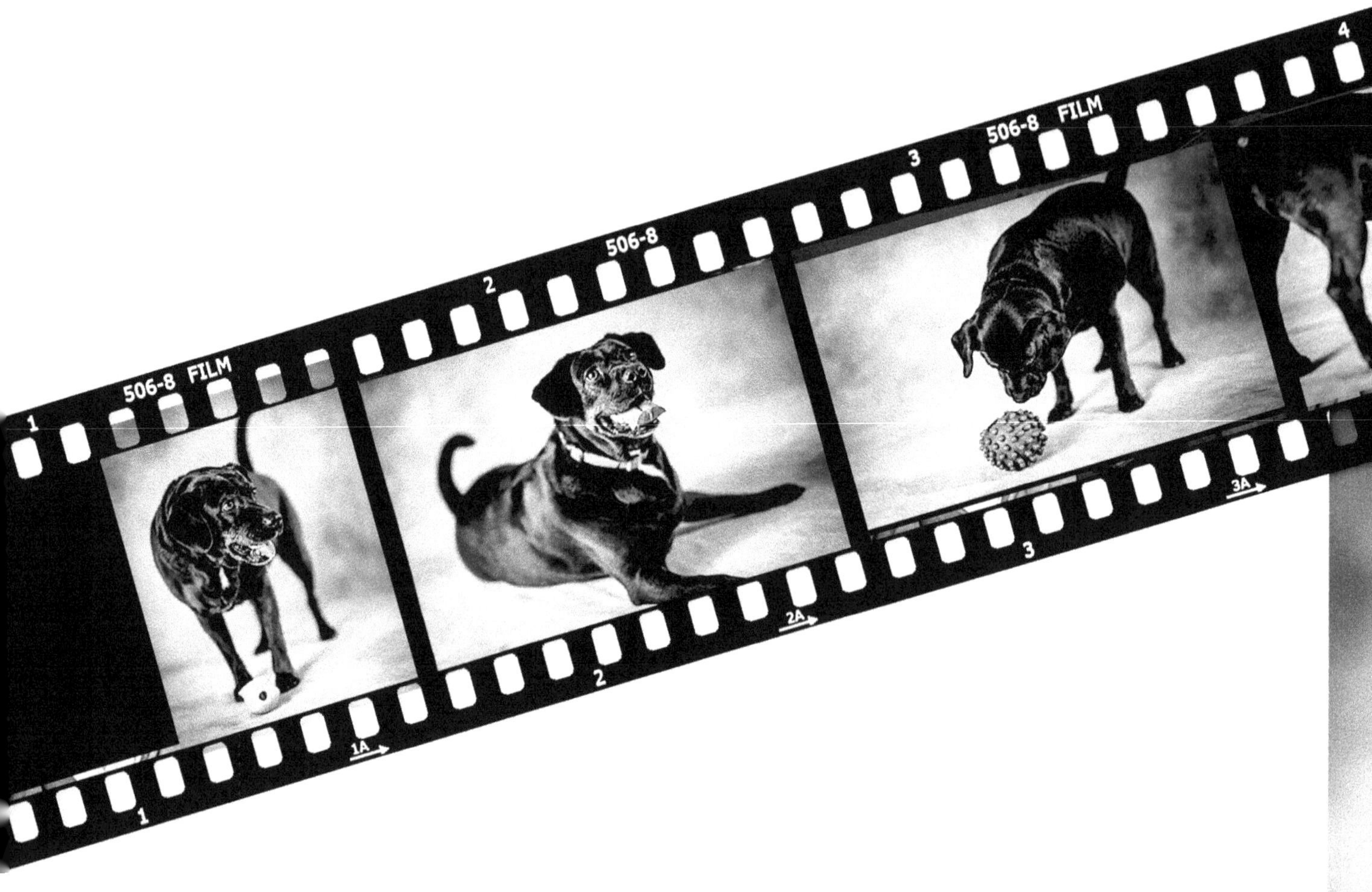

Sweet GADGET is a Collie/Lab mix whose favorite toy is a reindeer--a stuffed one, of course. The now seven-year-old was living with another family who had to find Gadget another home, so she moved in with her present mama.

The most endearing thing she does?

"She lets the kids dress her," says her mom. "And she has this surprised look that always makes me smile."

Sweet Gadget.

Proving that every dog deserves a second chance.

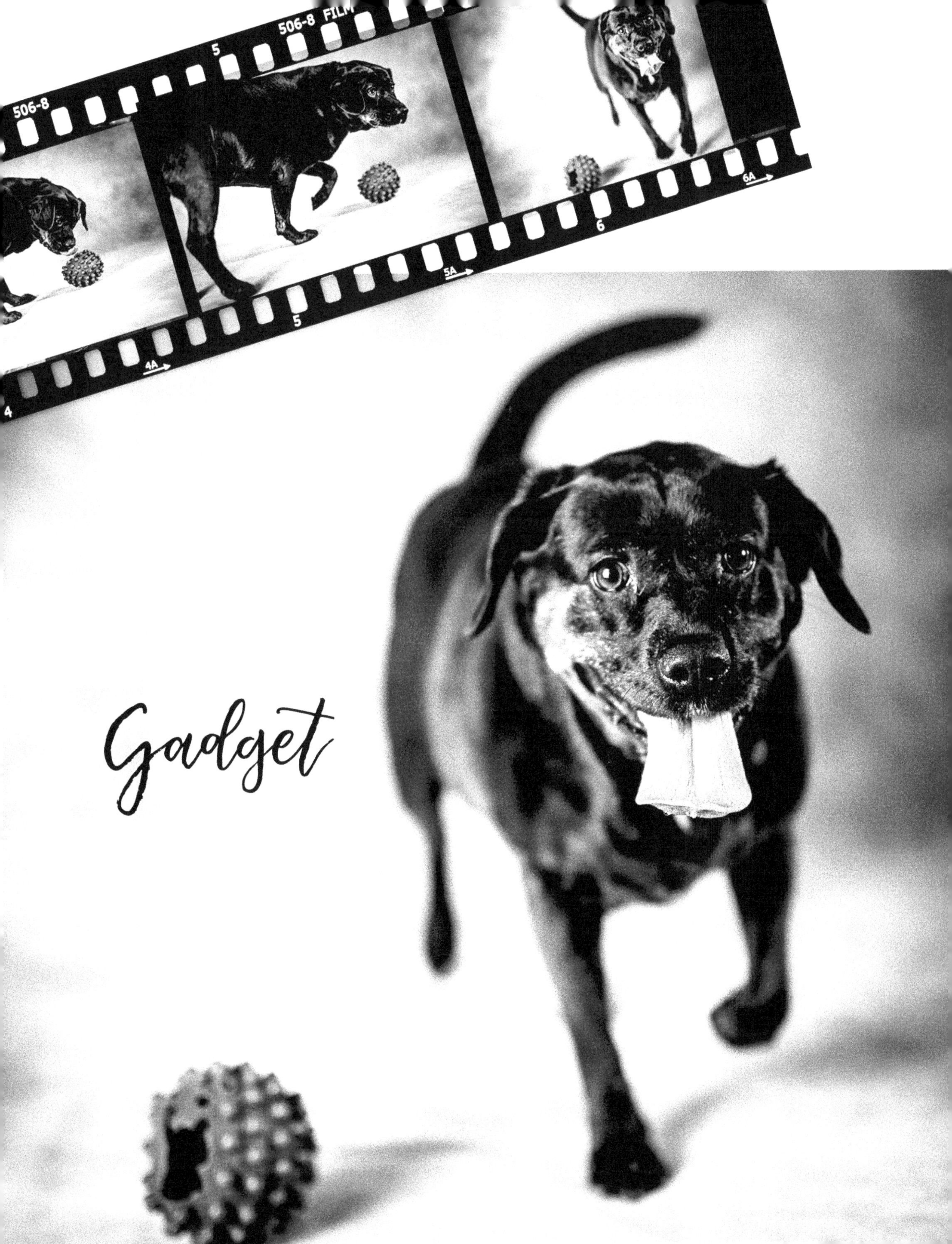
506-8
506-8 FILM
5
6
6A
5A
5
4A
4
Gadget

Glory

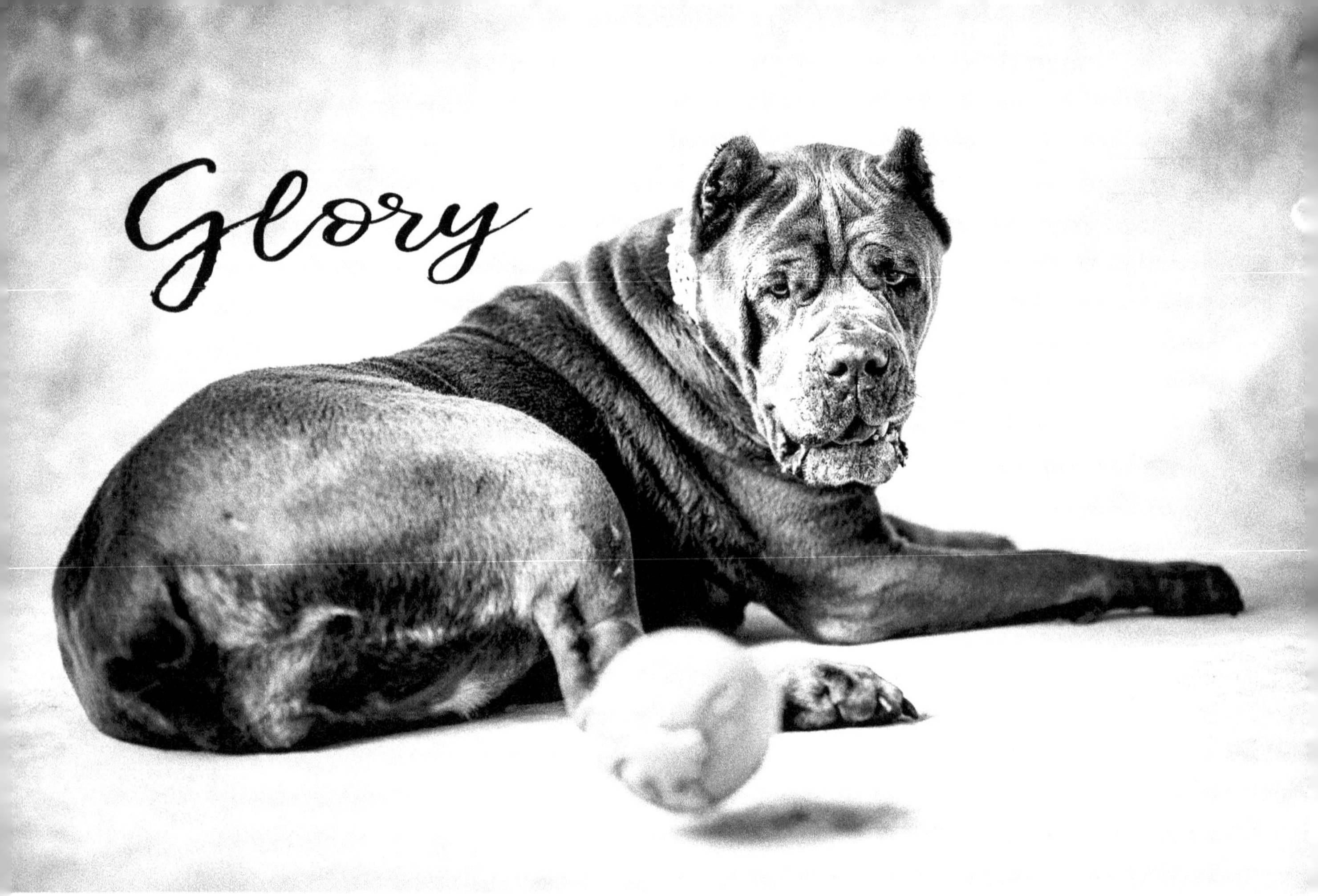

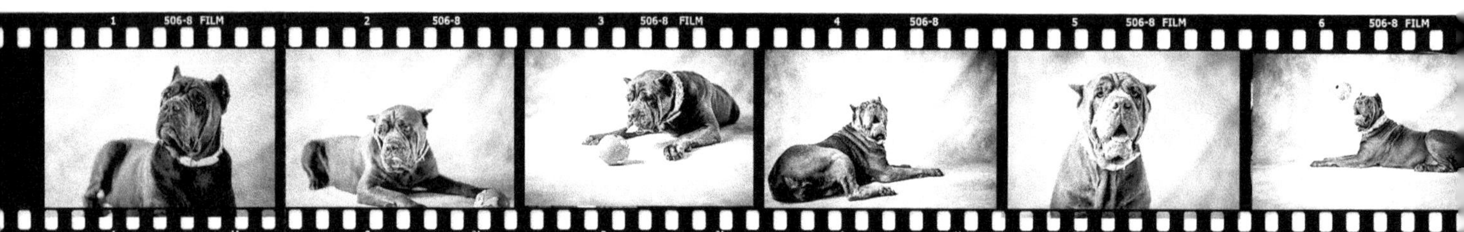

Beautiful GLORY, a mastiff mix, came to her family after they saw her picture online. They traveled to the Humane Society to pick her up, and she's been part of the family ever since. She loves to climb on the couch to sit with the family's nieces and nephews, and she chews up Dad's cookbooks when she's upset about something. In her previous life, someone cropped her ears, probably to make her look aggressive, but she's a sweetheart. "A chow hound," says her mom. "And she likes her ball only when there are treats inside it."

Epilogue: On July 17, 2018, Glory's mom wrote to let me know that Glory lost her battle with the "seizure monster."

Rest in peace, sweet girl. You will be missed.

GOOSE, a four-year-old Xoloitzcuintli (that's Mexican Hairless dog for the uninitiated) *loves* playing with balls and plastic bottles. His humans found him through a breeder because they love this unusual breed. Goose, says his mama, uses his "toes" to hold her hand and walks on his hind legs to hug her. The worst thing he has ever done? "He stopped in the middle of an agility trial," says his mom, "gave me a long look, and walked to the exit gate." Apparently, he didn't want to play. Goose's mom says he is simultaneously naughty, mischievious, pushy, sweet, and loveable. Sounds *just* like a Xoloitzcuintli.

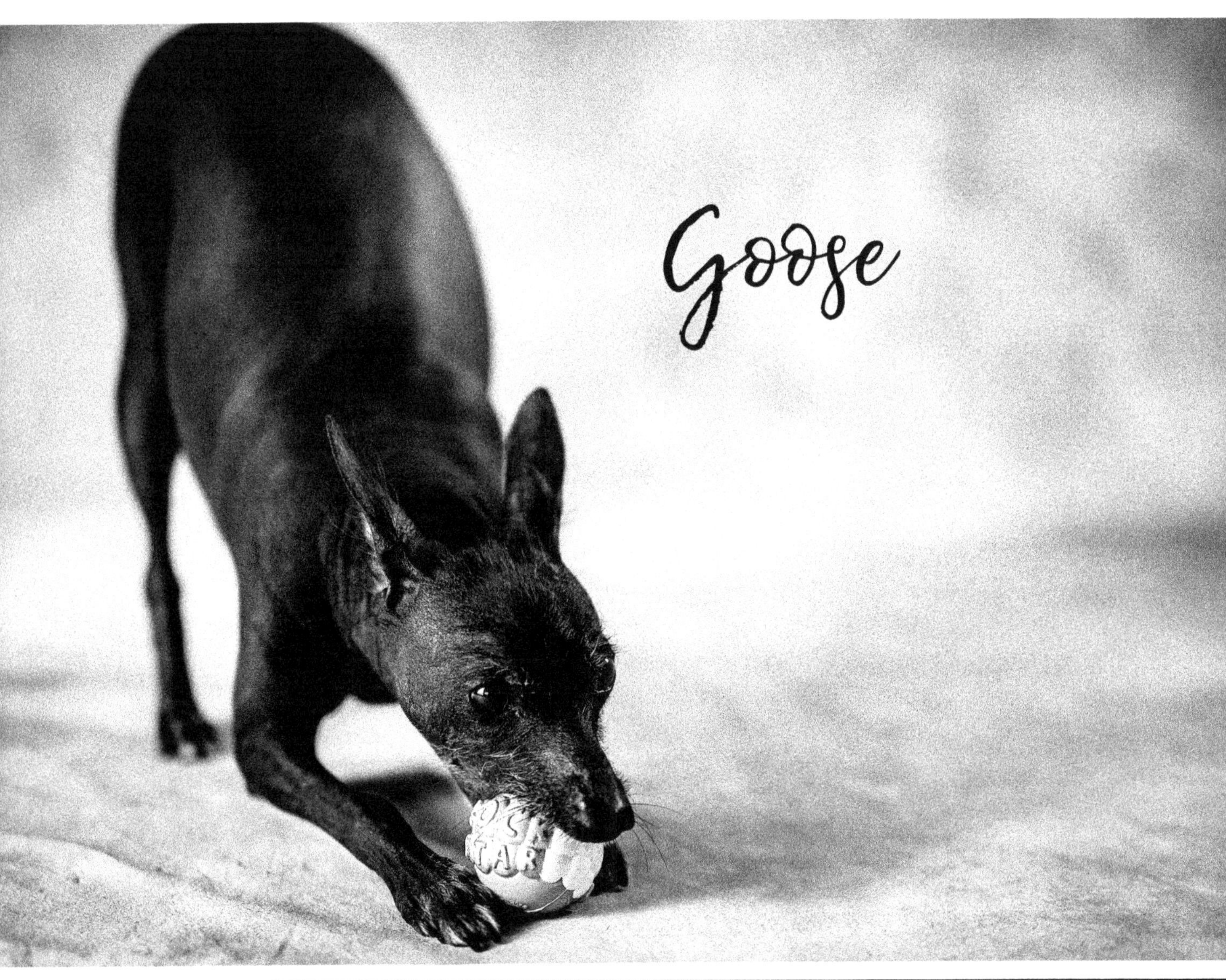

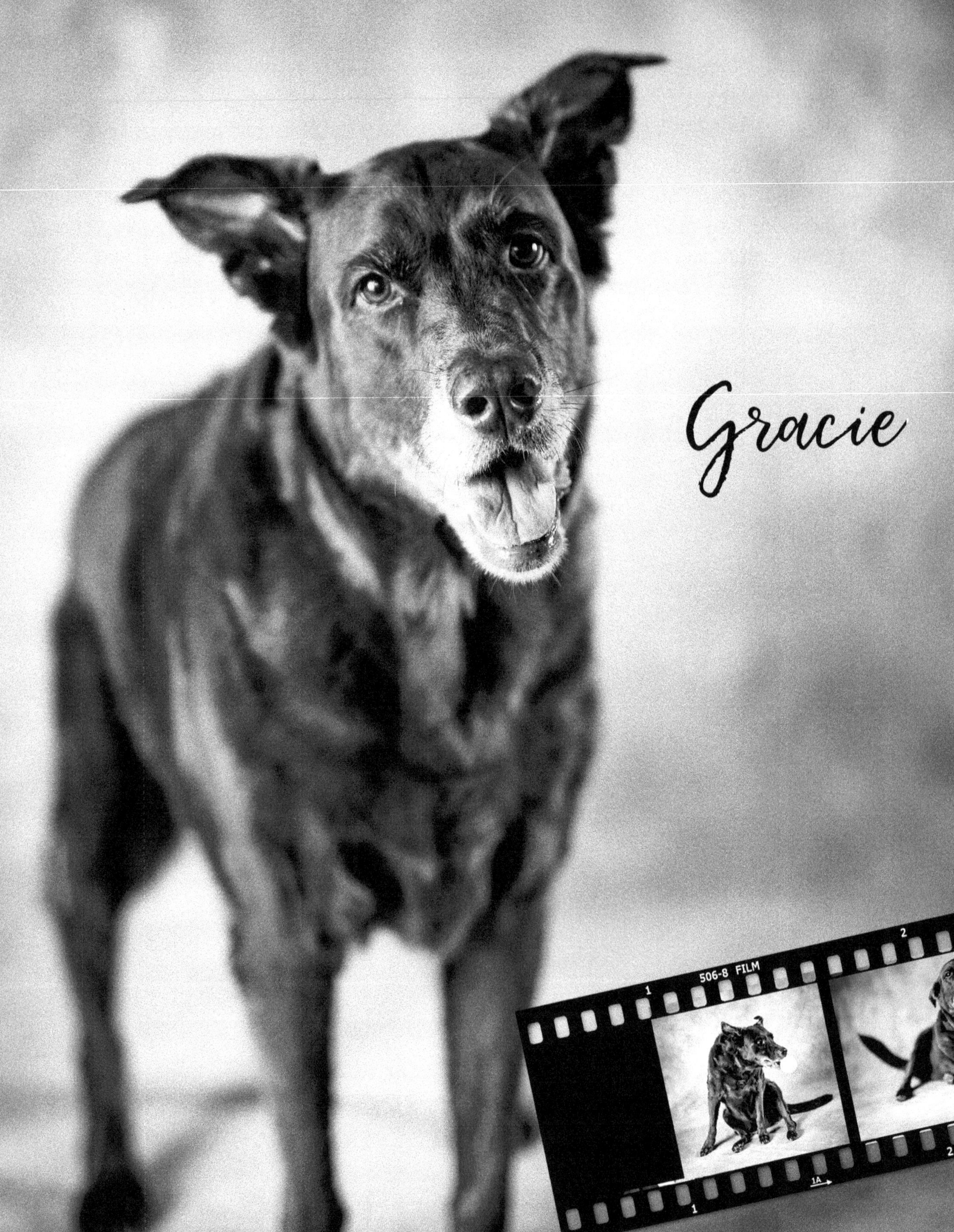
Gracie
506-8 FILM
1
2
1A
1
2

GRACIE found her forever home through the PAWS rescue group. The now-eight year old Chocolate Lab was one of four "parvo" puppies from a single litter. The nasty virus ran its course, and three of the pups survived, including Gracie. Gracie is the perfect example of a Labrador retriever: she loves to swim, she loves everyone she meets, and she is easy-going. The only thing she doesn't love, her mom says, is puppies, and who knows why?

Gracie suffers from hip dysplasia, almost certainly a result of the strong antibiotics she had to take in order to combat the deadly parvo virus. But she manages well, and her mom is patient with her. With a face like that, who wouldn't be?

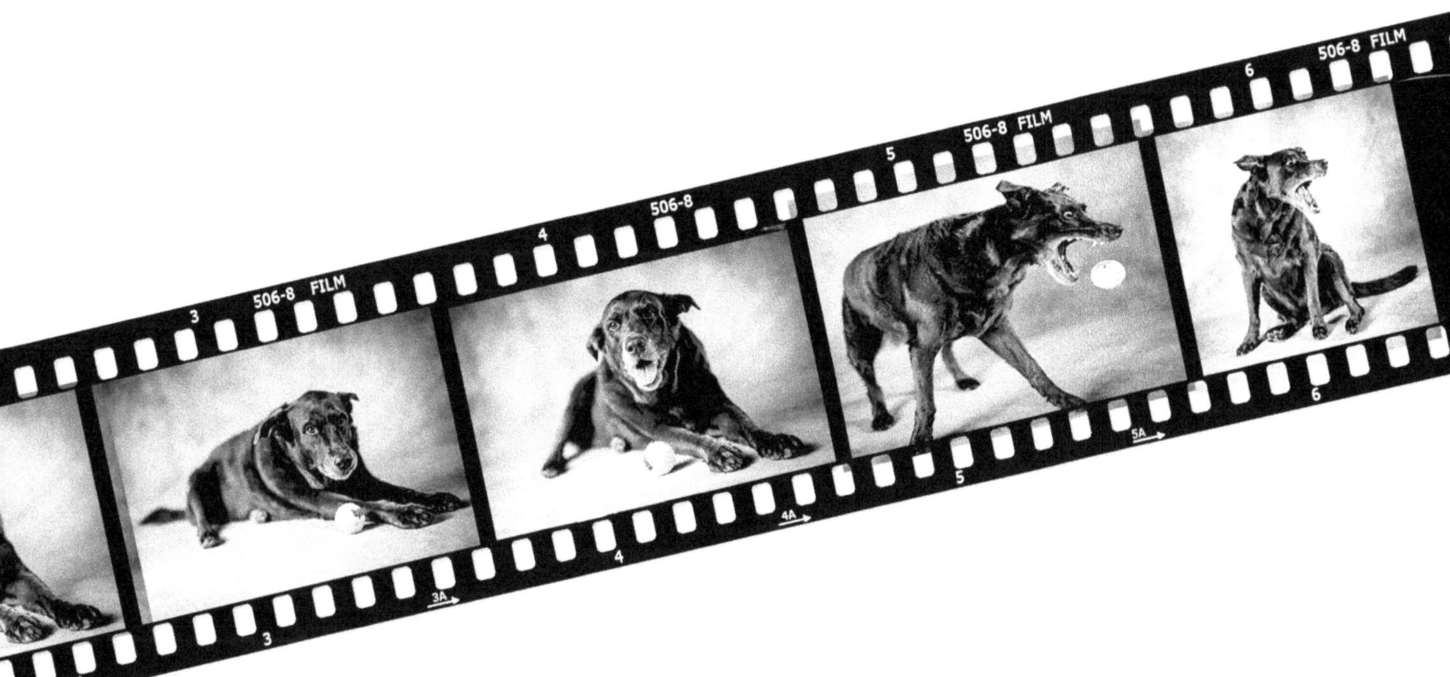

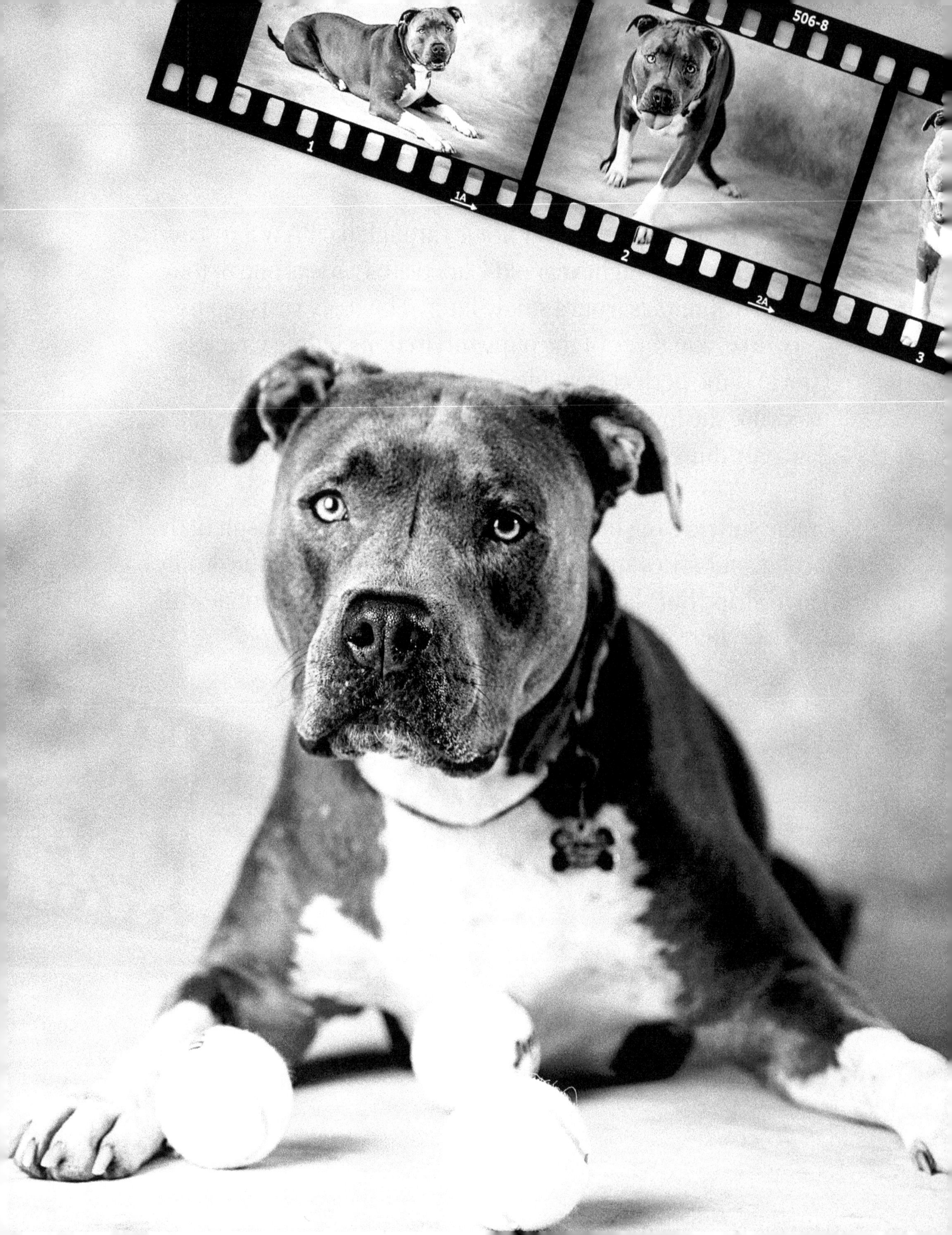
506-8
1
1A
2
2A
3

Gulf Coast Gunner

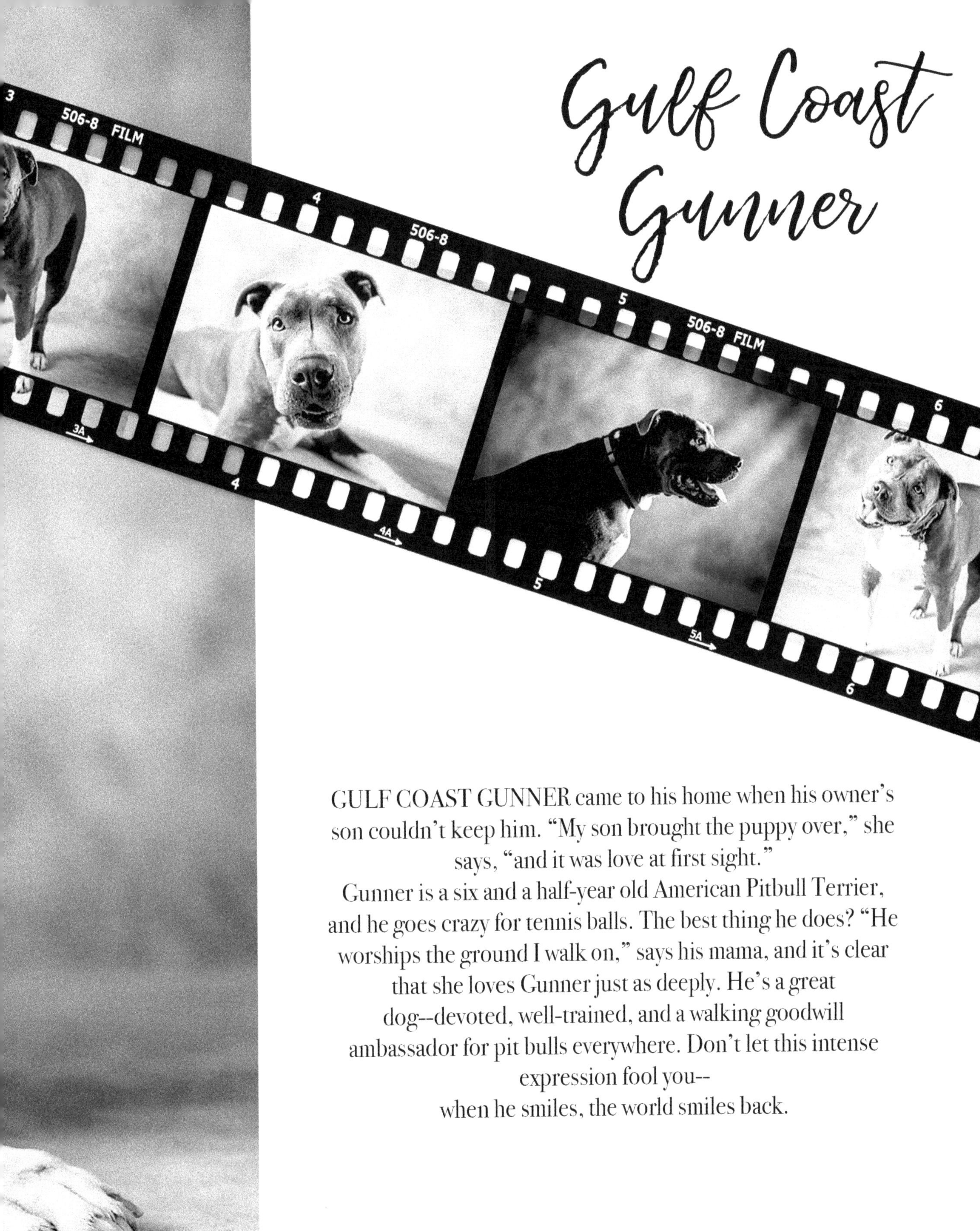

GULF COAST GUNNER came to his home when his owner's son couldn't keep him. "My son brought the puppy over," she says, "and it was love at first sight."

Gunner is a six and a half-year old American Pitbull Terrier, and he goes crazy for tennis balls. The best thing he does? "He worships the ground I walk on," says his mama, and it's clear that she loves Gunner just as deeply. He's a great dog--devoted, well-trained, and a walking goodwill ambassador for pit bulls everywhere. Don't let this intense expression fool you--
when he smiles, the world smiles back.

Gunny

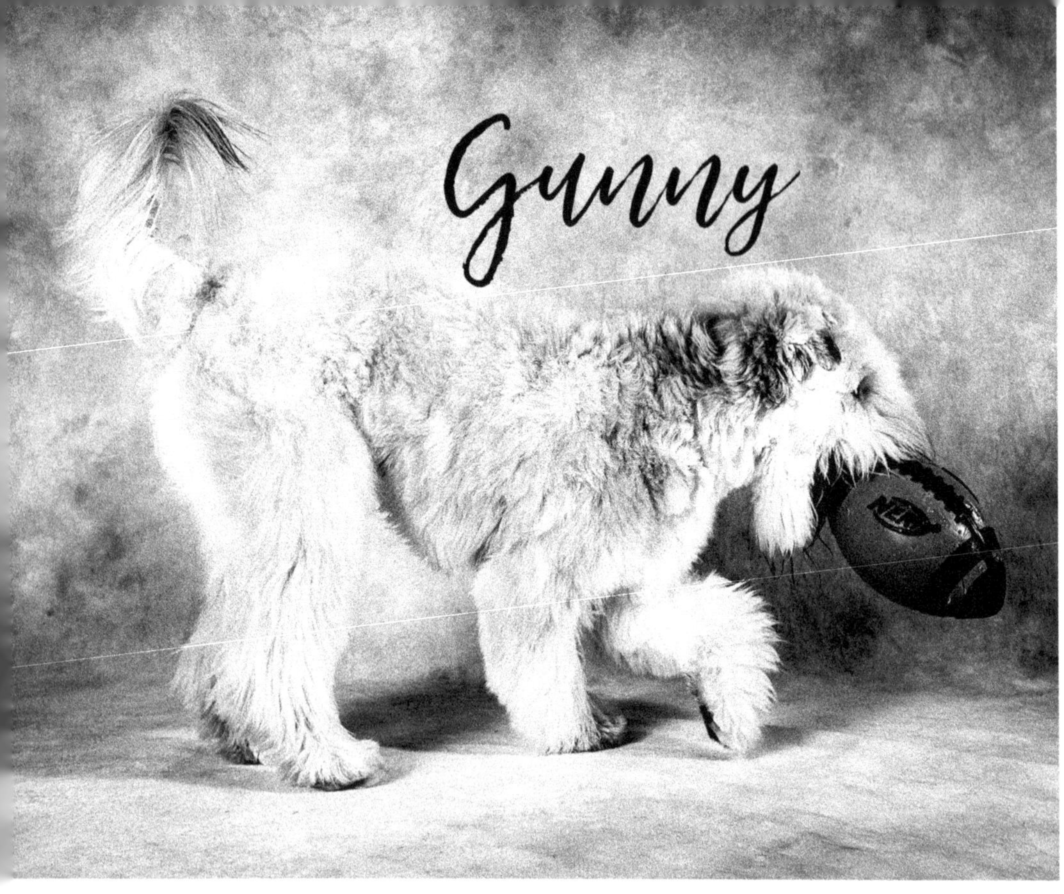

Eight year old BREEZEY and one-year-old GUNNY are Soft-coated Wheaten Terriers. Breezy found his forever home through the efforts of a Florida breed rescue group. Breezy is mature and dignified--he listens well and poses beautifully.
Gunny, on the other hand, is unbridled puppy-ness. He plays ball with gusto and loves his squeaky toys. When he's tired, he loves to rest his head in his mama's lap and watch his big brother.
They are a perfect pair.

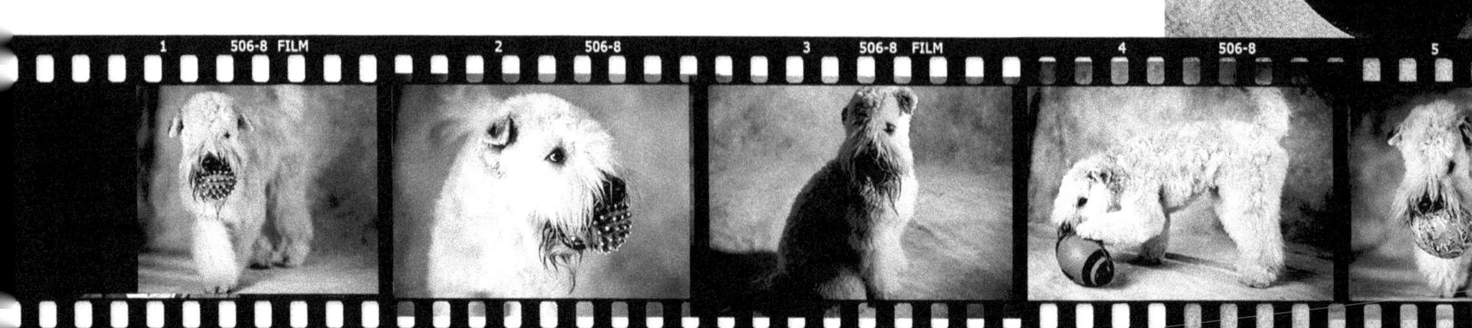

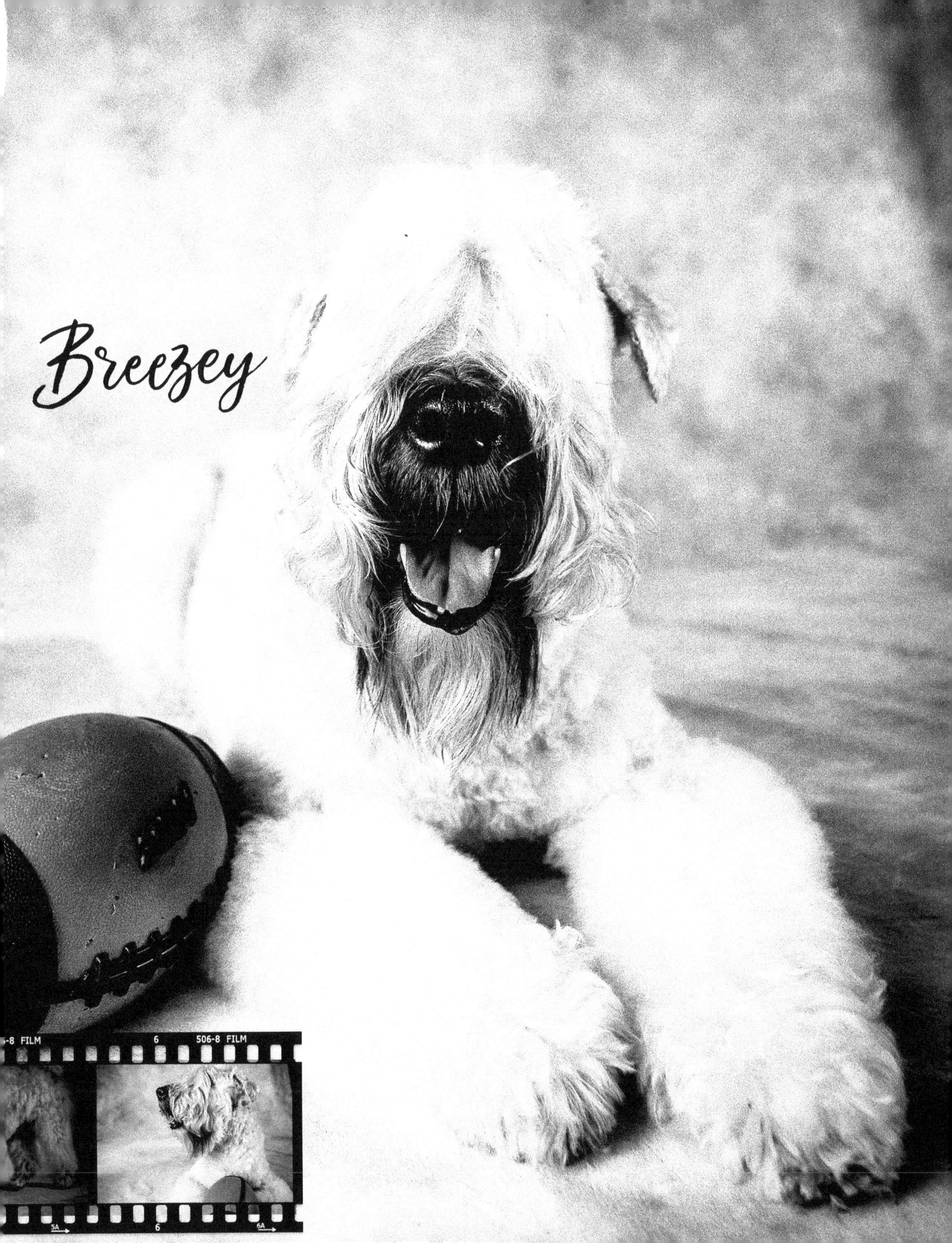
Breezey
-8 FILM
6
506-8 FILM
5A
6
6A

GRACIE B is a six-year-old American Staffordshire Terrier/Rottweiler mix. She was rescued from the Florida Everglades--and no one knows how long she was out there fending for herself. Gracie is now happily living with her mom, and she loves to snuggle in bed. She's a pro at convincing people to give her belly rubs, and her favorite toy is her Kong--preferably filled with low-fat wheat thins. After all, a pretty girl has to watch her figure.

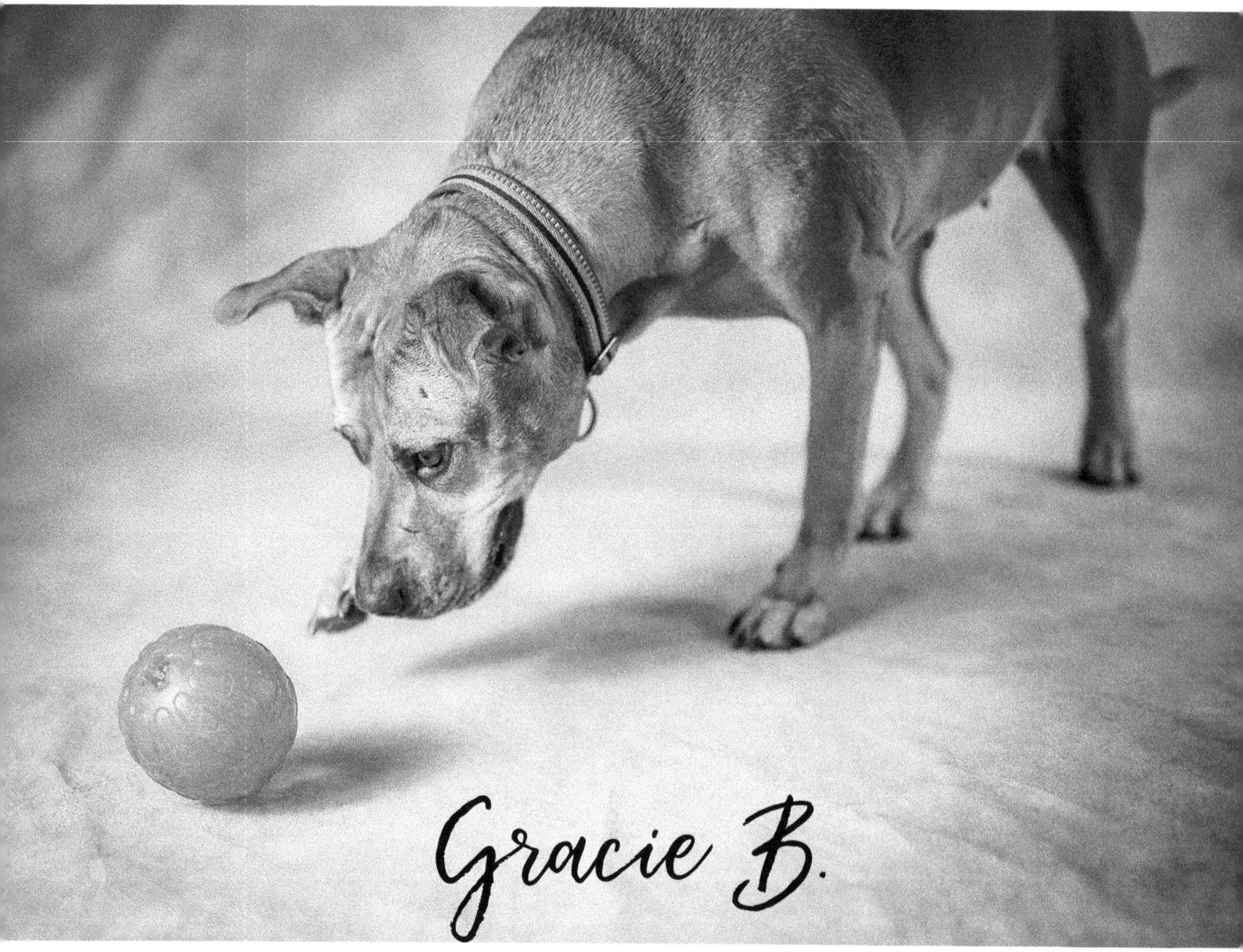

Gracie B.

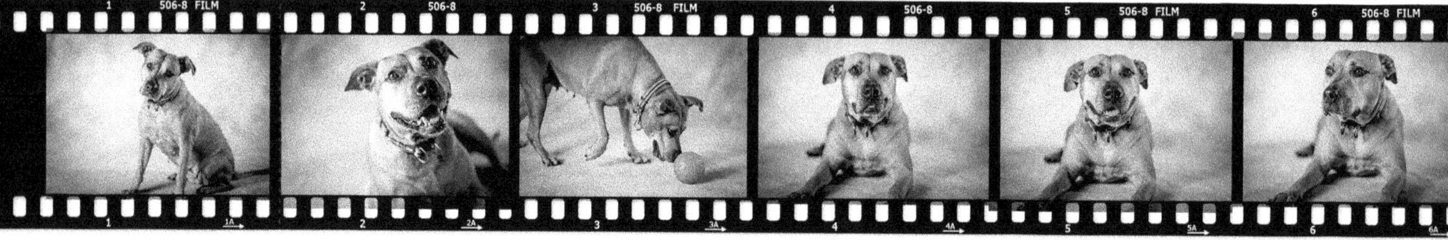

GWENYTH, now five years old, was being fostered by a woman who already had two dogs. Two dogs were her limit, she said. Only two. Then she heard about a woman who wanted Gwenyth to visit, to see if she would fit into their home. Gwenyth's foster mom took the terrier mix over, then went home and waited for news. "Come get your dog," the woman said when she called a bit later. "The minute you left, Gwenyth went to the door and she's been crying ever since."
Sometimes our dogs choose us. And that's okay.
Because the human heart can hold love enough for more than two dogs.

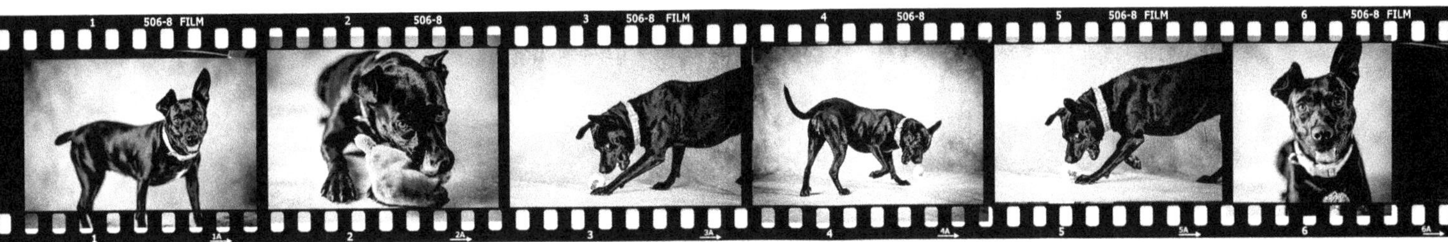

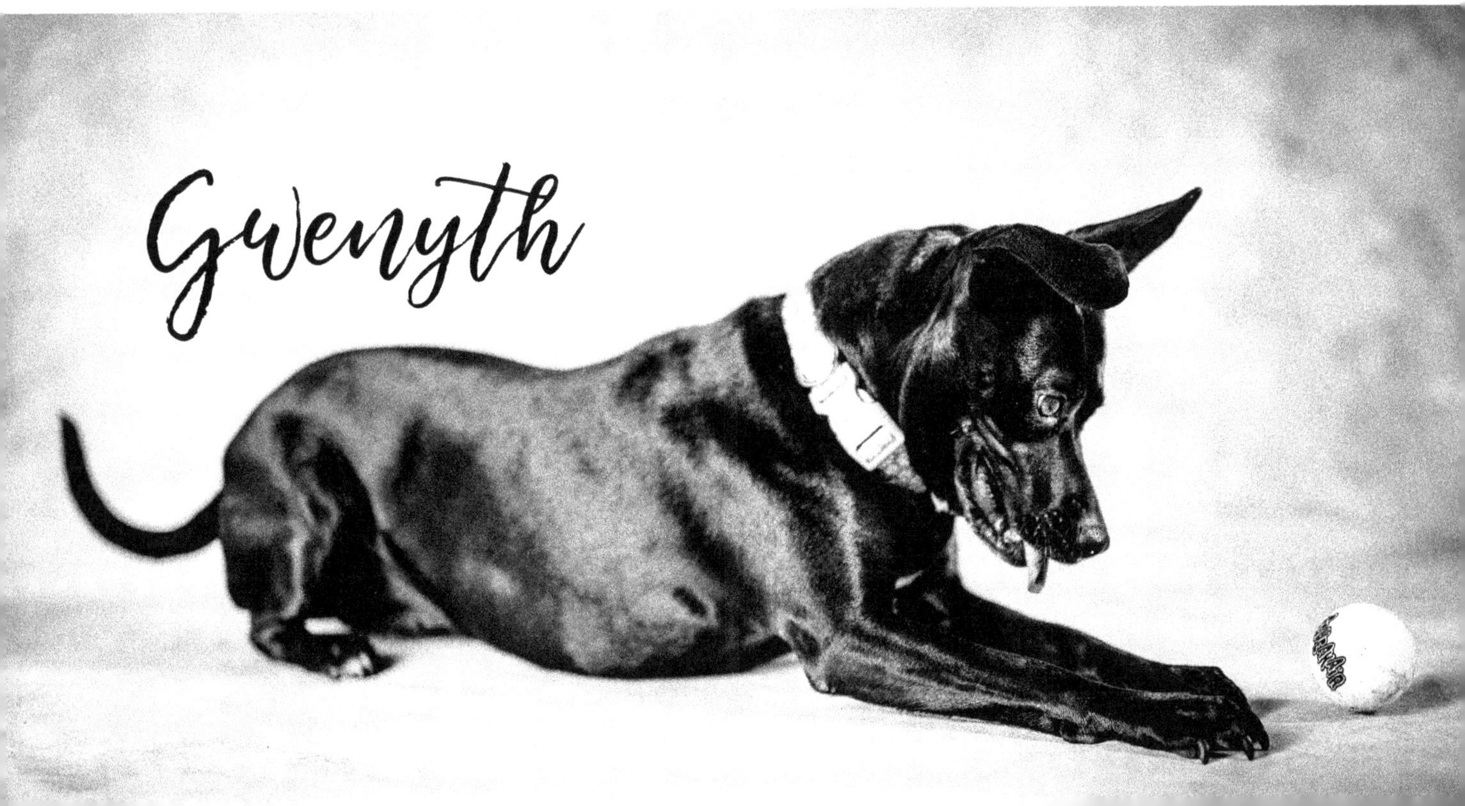

Gwenyth

HAPPI came from a private rescue in Florida. The black lab mix is three and a half years old, and her favorite toy is a tennis ball. She lives with her family which includes young children because Labs are perfect family dogs. Her human mom reports that Happi likes to “hug” family members when they are sitting, or she rests her head on their knees. The worst thing she’s ever done is run off to explore the neighborhood--and since they live in a rural area with large wildlife, that makes Mom nervous. After the installation of an electric fence, however, Happi has learned her boundaries and everyone is happy. For Happi.

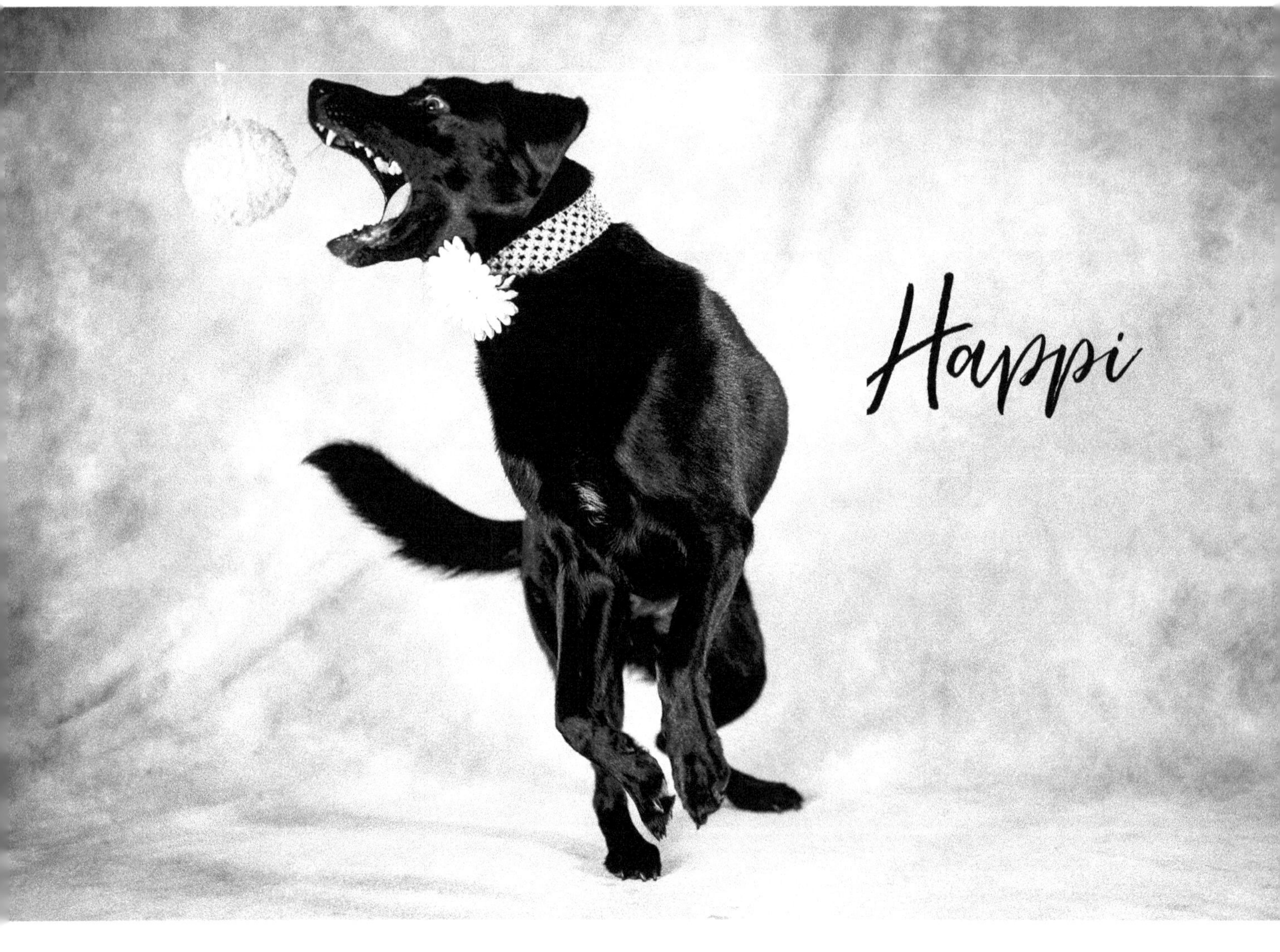

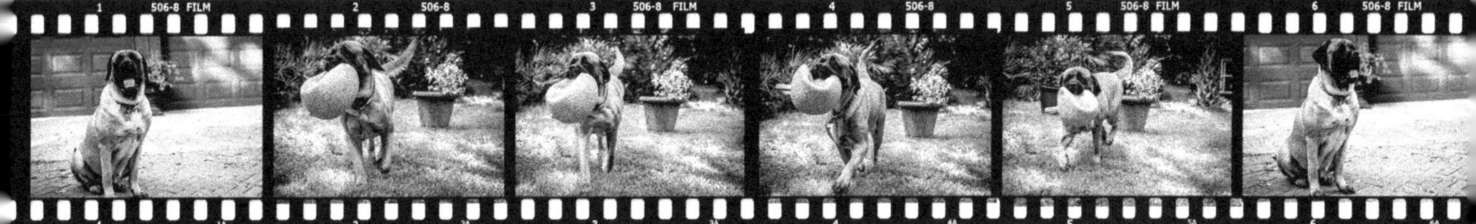

These photos of IVY, a 2.5 year old English Mastiff, are a last resort--she is *my* dog, you see, and all the while I worked on this book I tried to get her to come upstairs to my studio for photos, but she wanted no part of it. None. And when a mastiff doesn't want to do something, she is pretty much going to get her way.

Ivy *does* love to play with balls, though--balls made for horses. We've had eight mastiffs over the years, and she is the only one who will actually bring a ball back once you've thrown it. She's a perfect girl, a Canine Good Citizen, and my constant companion.

So forgive me for breaking convention for her, but I just couldn't leave her out.

--Angie Hunt

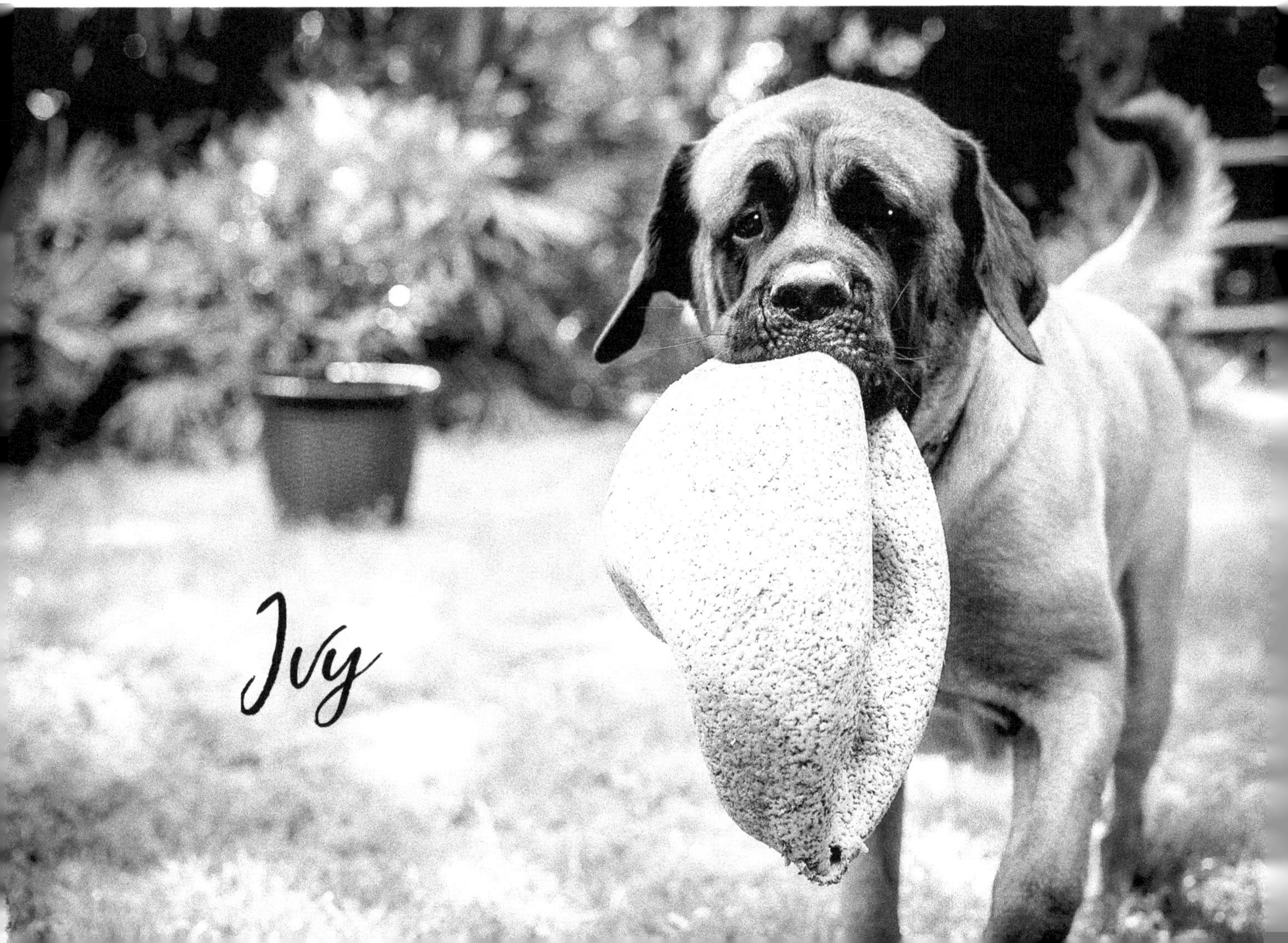

Ivy

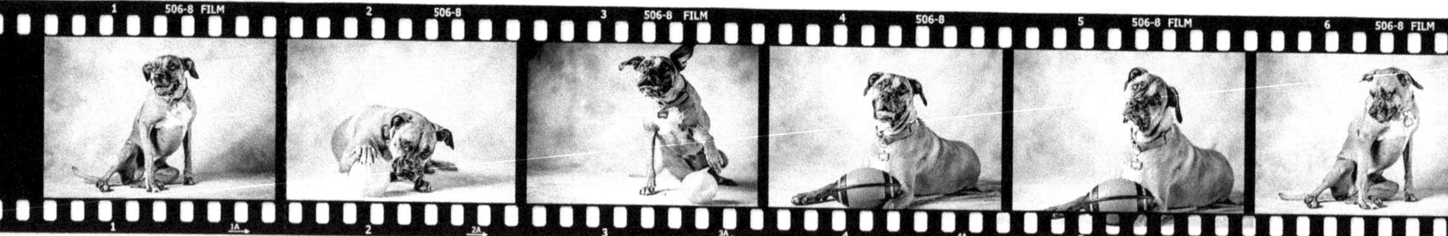

ISABELLE, or Izzy, is a three and a half-year-old Boxer/Rhodesian Ridgeback mix. When she was two days old, someone found her beneath the front porch of a house--she was all alone, with no mama or siblings nearby. She was taken to PetPal Animal Shelter, where she was bottle fed until she was old enough to eat on her own. Now she lives with doggie siblings and a mama who dotes on her. Her favorite toy, her mama says, is treats. She never does anything wrong, but she does do two quirky things--at night, she whines pathetically until she gets a special treat, and she loves to suckle on her special blanket as if she's nursing. Izzy is a happy dog and well-loved.

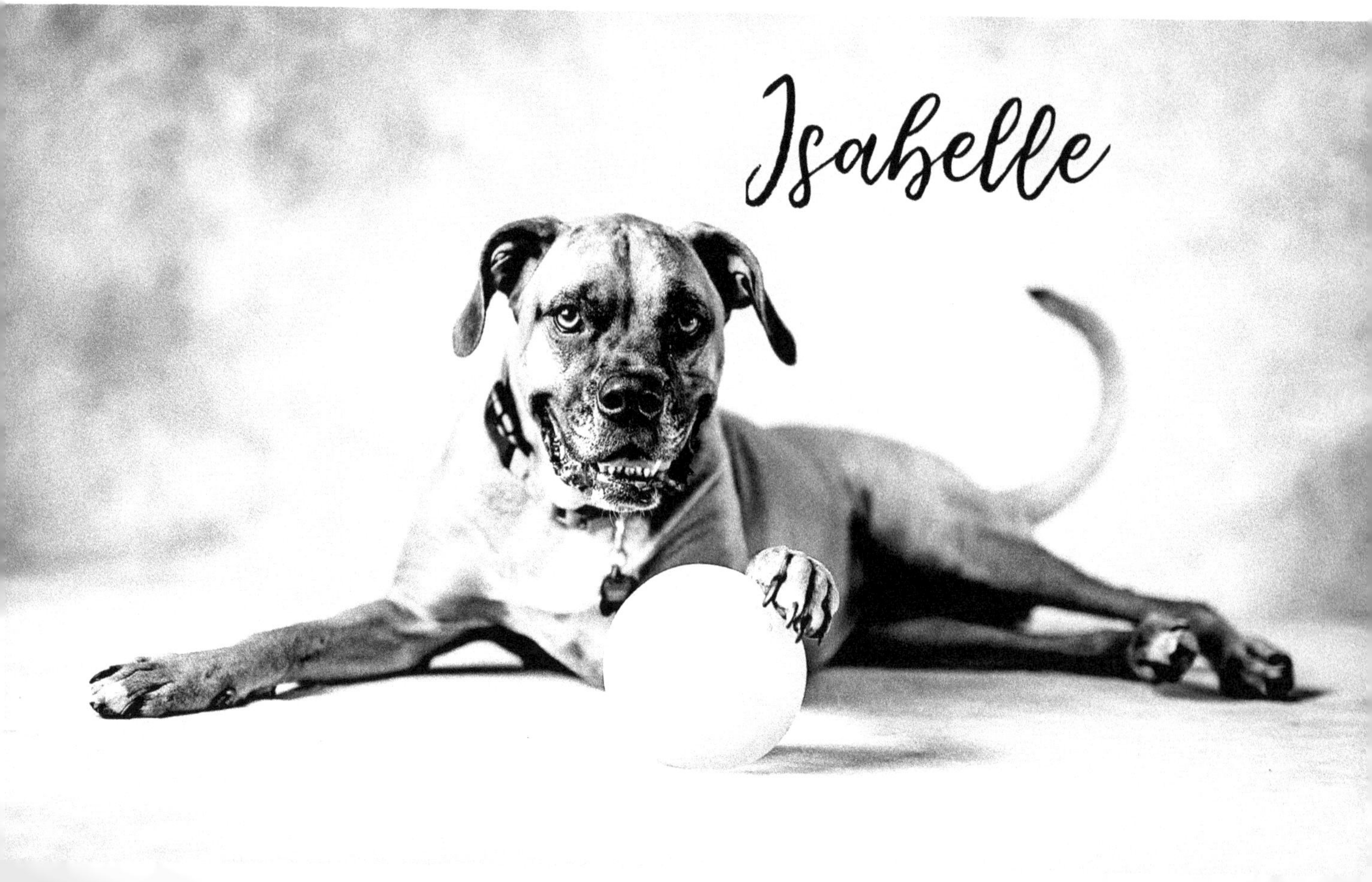

Isabelle

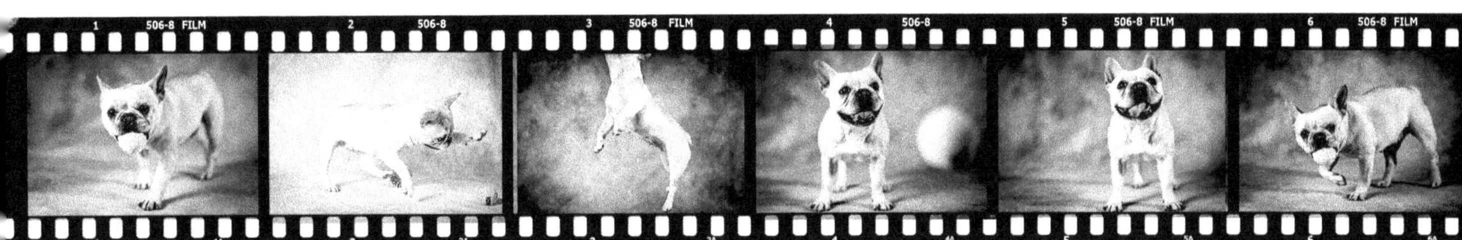

IZZY W. is a three-year-old French Bulldog who retired as a professional show dog at the grand old age of two. Her human mom says Izzy now lives a life of ease; her days are filled with chasing lizards, stretching in the sun, and playing with squeaky toys. She has a tendency to jump up and nip at people when she is over-excited, but she means no harm--she just can't contain herself. This adorable pup loves to jump and catch a ball, and she's more athletic than she looks. She has one quirk--because she was a show dog, she was taught to "stand and stack" at a young age, so she has never learned to sit on command. But this girl stacks like a champ.

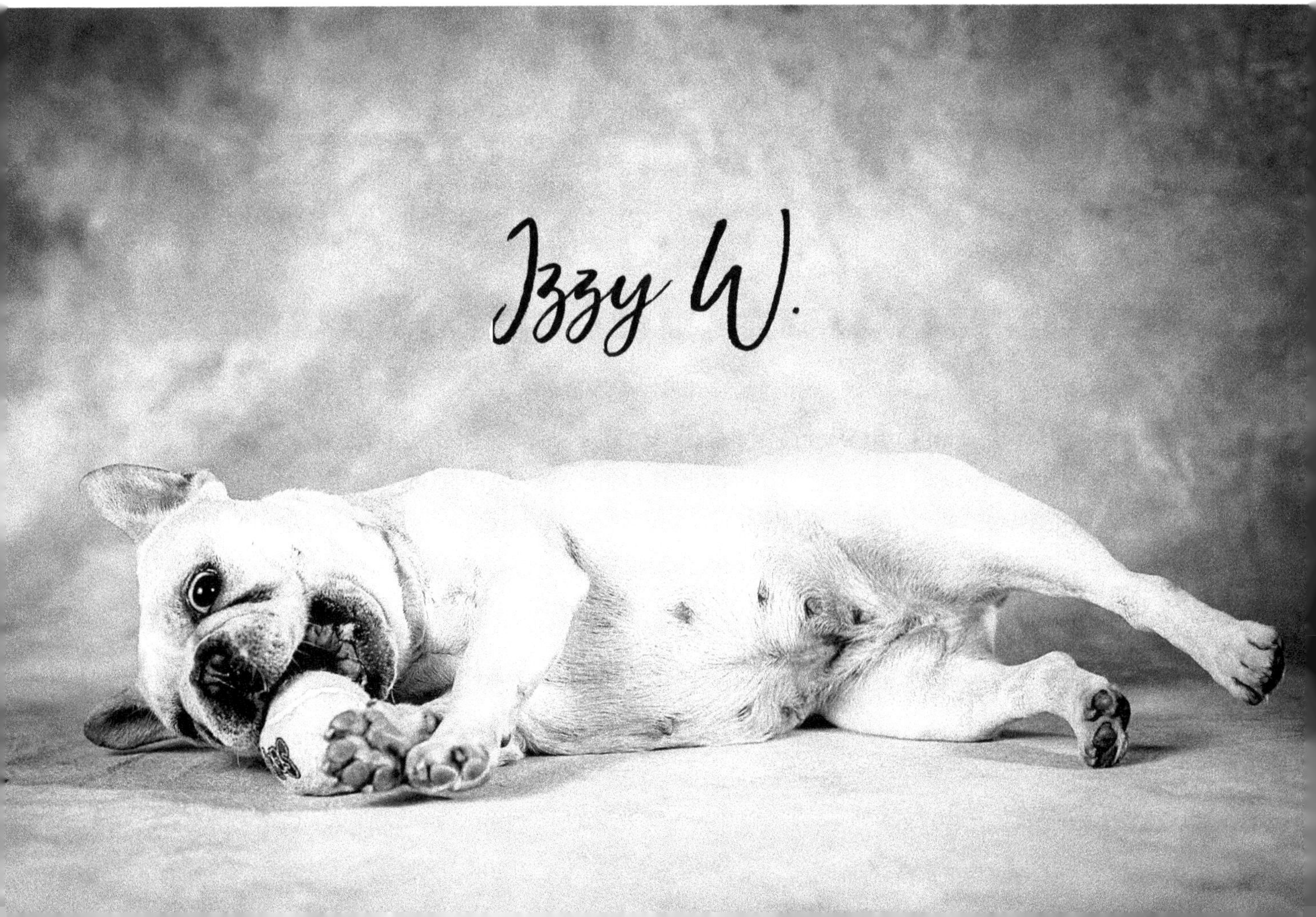

Izzy W.

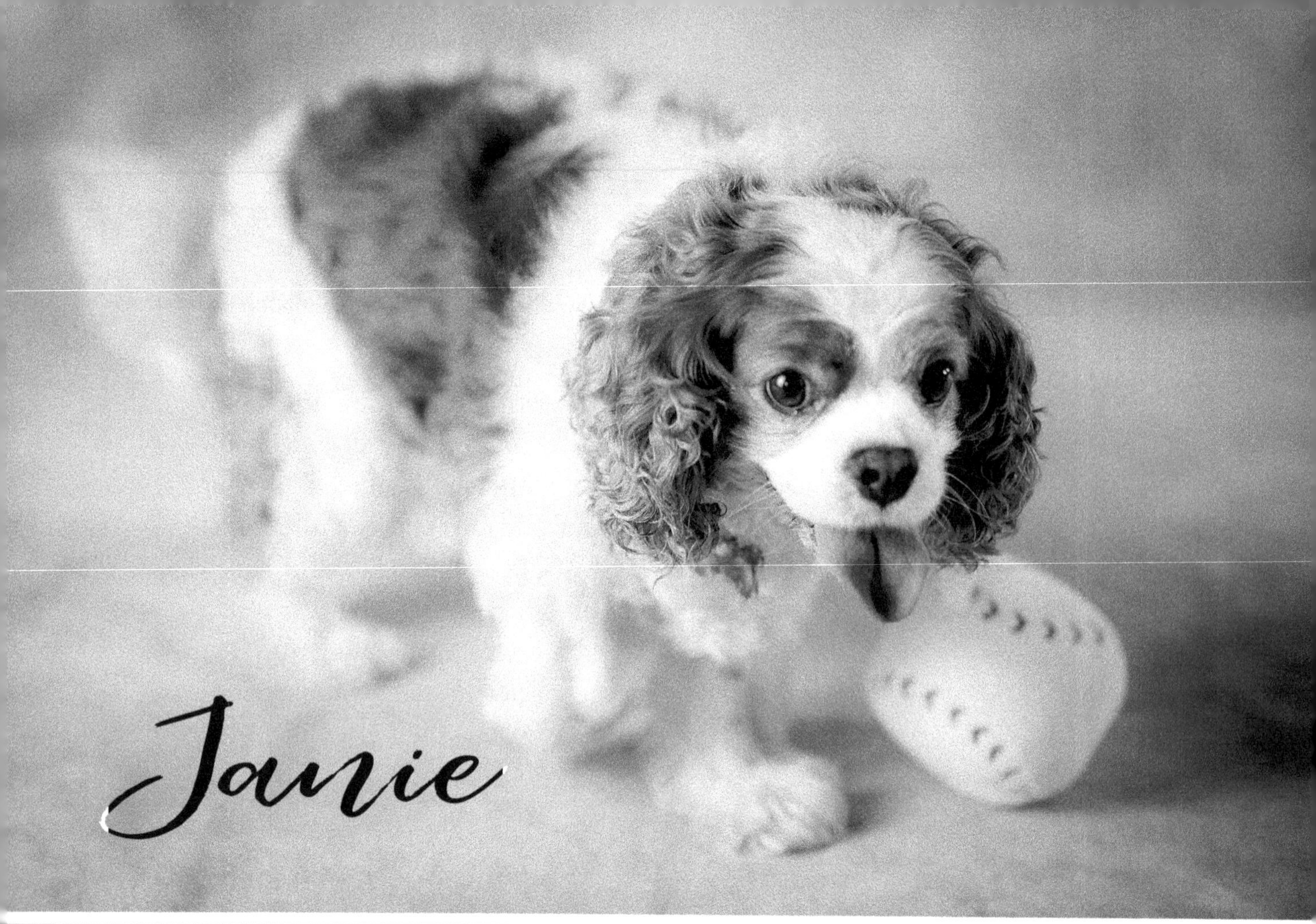

Janie

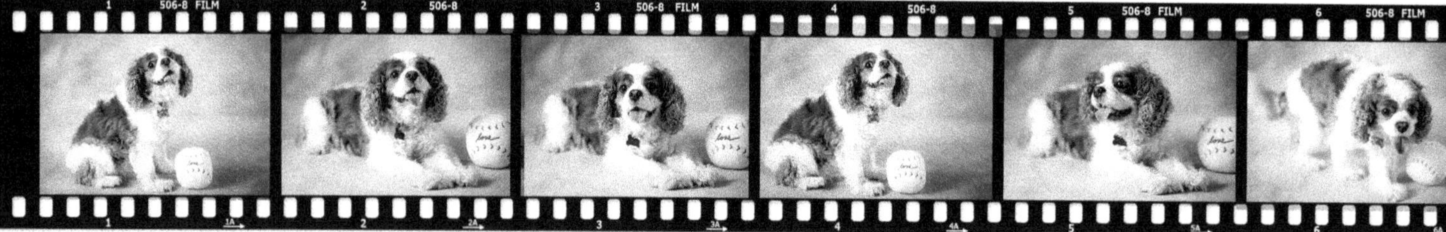

JANIE, aka Janie-Bear, is a six-year-old Cavalier King Charles Spaniel. Janie is deaf, and came to her forever home through a Cavalier Rescue group. Her human mom says Janie is a "huntress of geckos--hence the nickname Dora the Explorer!" She loves small stuffed animals and is a very quiet dog--except when she erupts into song, which is quite unlike any bark you've ever heard. The worst thing she's ever done? "Nothing!" says her mom.

This big-eyed girl is absolutely precious.

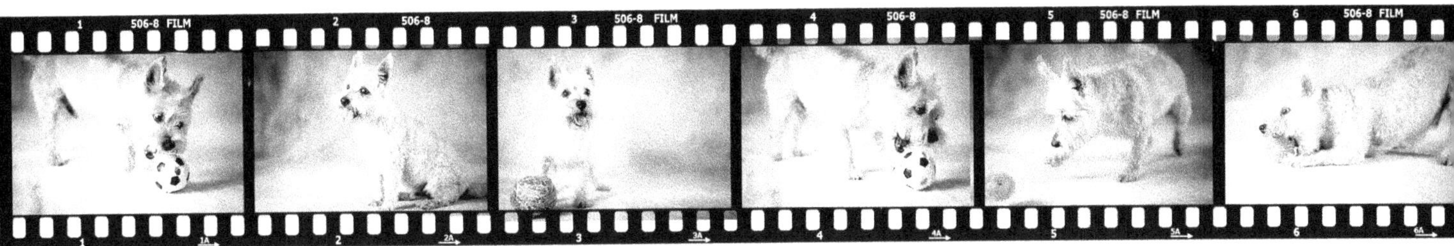

JASPER is an eleven-year-old Cairn Terrier who loves anything with a squeaky--or a treat--inside. He has no use for dogs his own size, but loves to run and wrestle with big dogs--maybe because that's how he sees himself. He likes to chase lizards and be held like a baby.

Jasper does have one little quirk--every night, without fail, he growls when his human parents watch TV. Why? "We think he's annoyed because we're not focusing on him," says his mom.

But no matter. As soon as the TV goes off, Jasper is his usual sweet self, ready to sleep and prepare for another day.

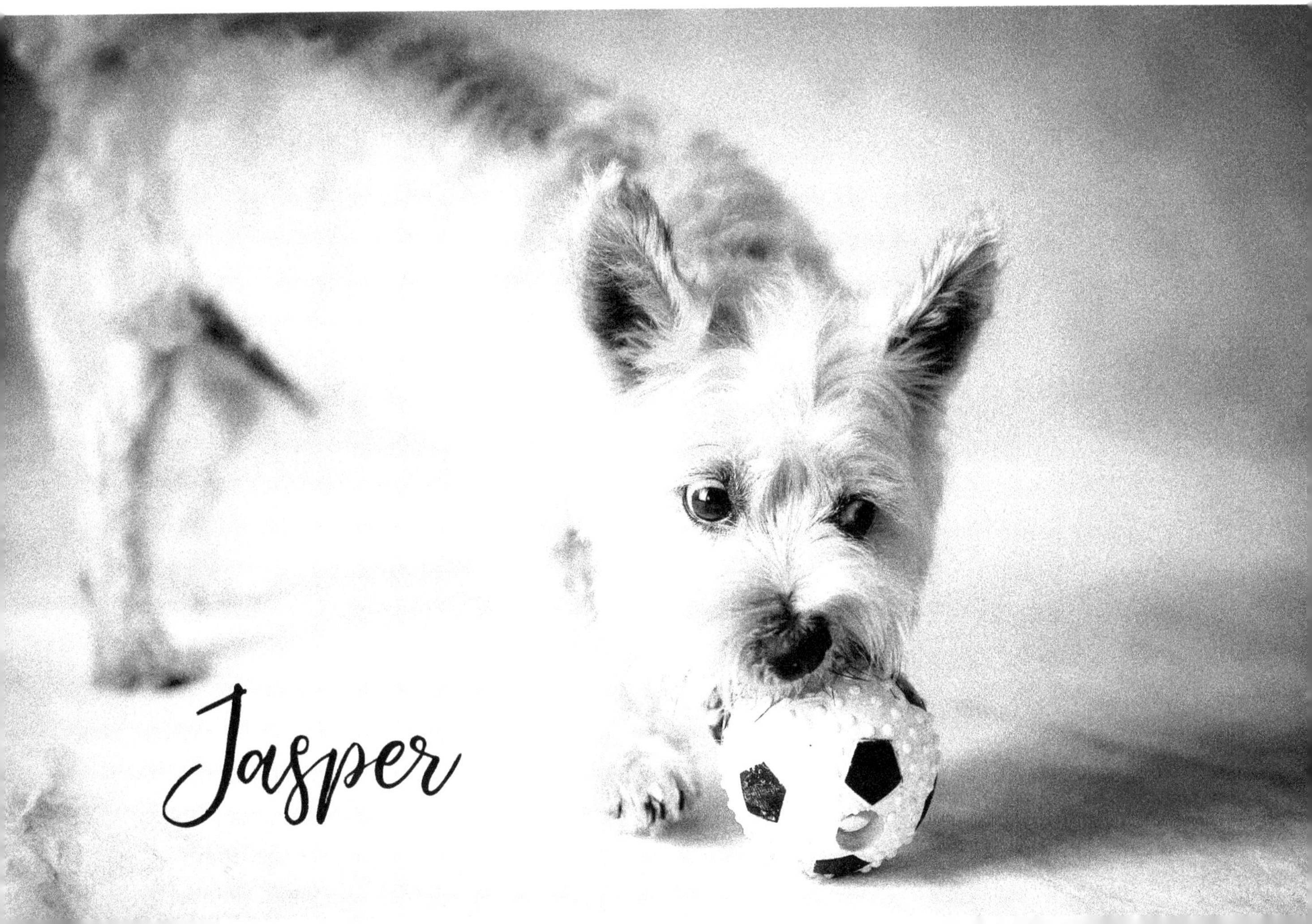

Jasper

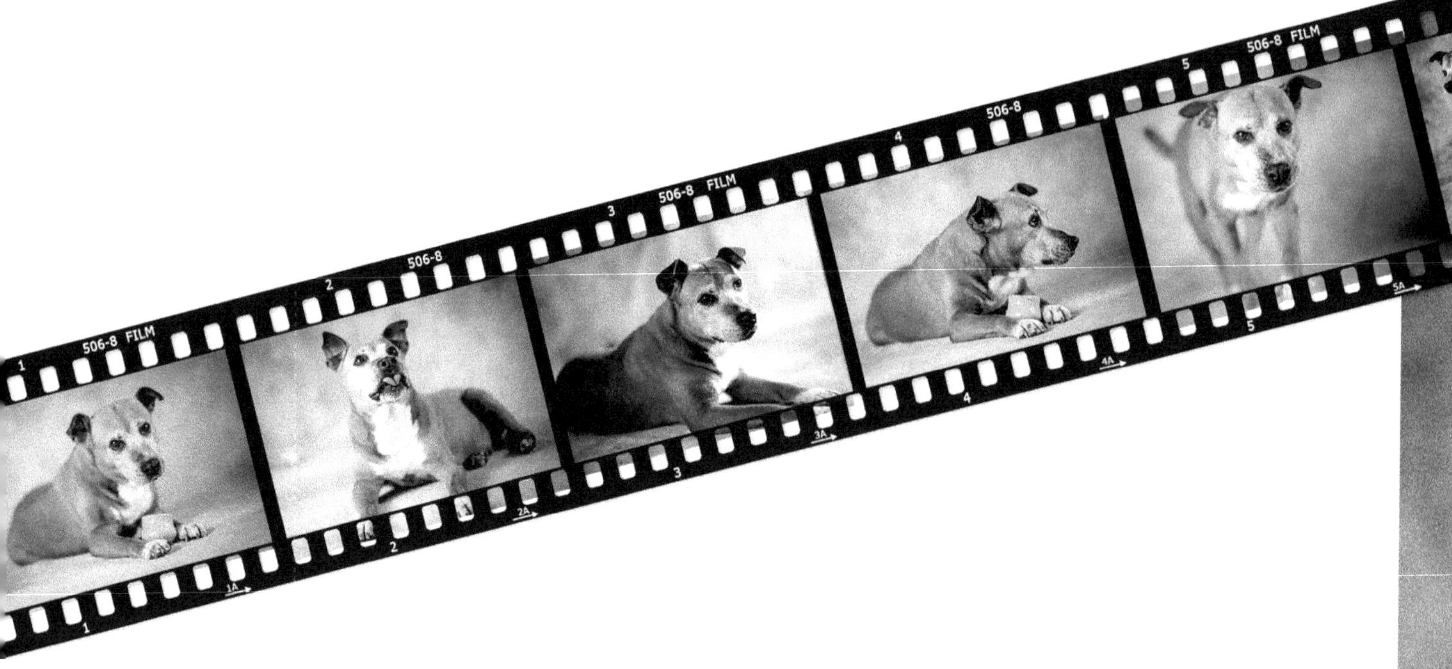

JESSE is another senior dog who still loves to play with balls. She's a ten-year-old pit bull mix who loves to lie in the sun. Her human mama found her at the SPCA when Jesse was two years old. They've been together ever since, along with the many animals her mama occasionally fosters to lend a hand at various shelters.

"Jesse," her mom says, "will lick you like there is no tomorrow." Maybe out of love . . . or gratitude.

In any case, Jesse is a happy girl, who gets as much affection as she joyfully gives.

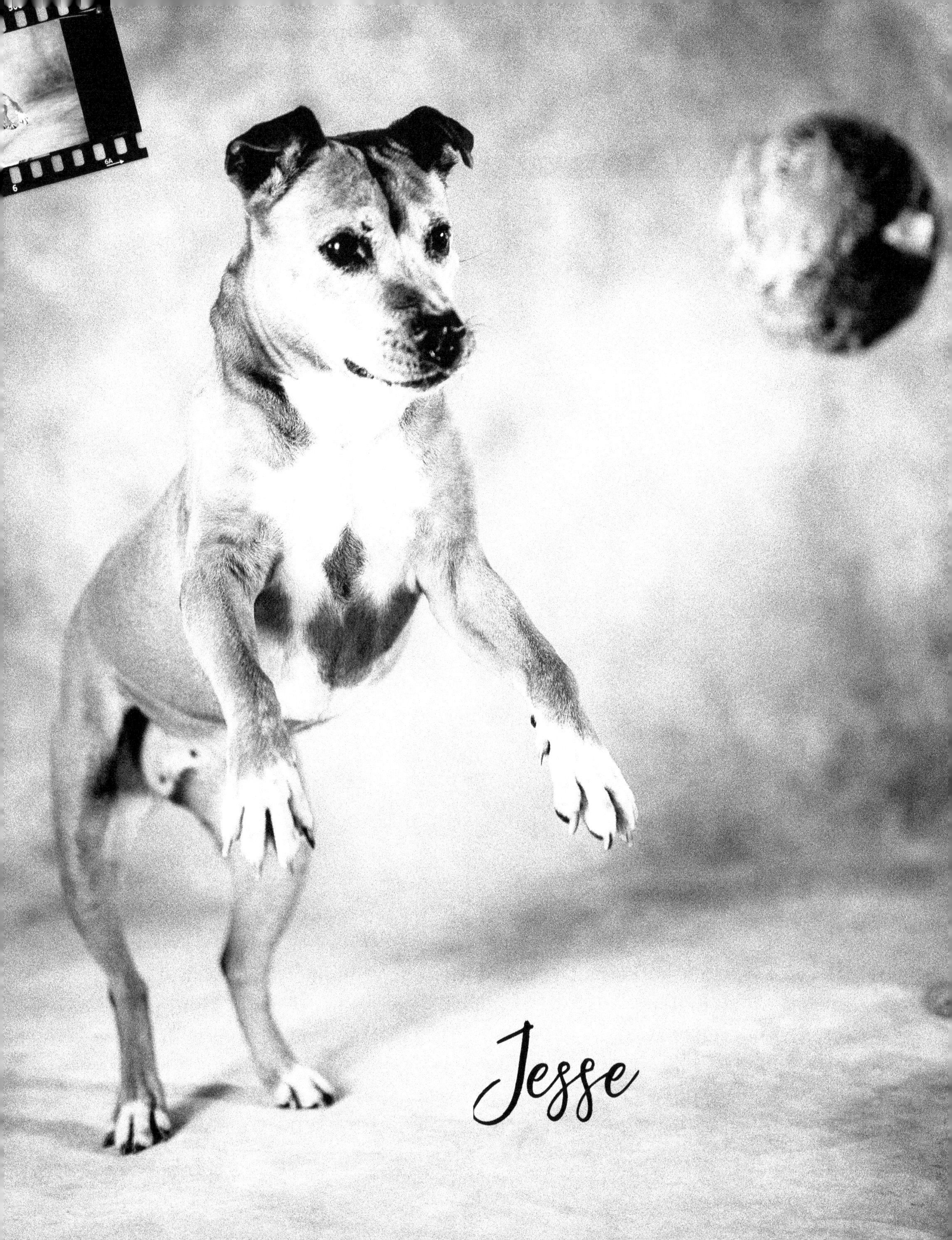
Jesse

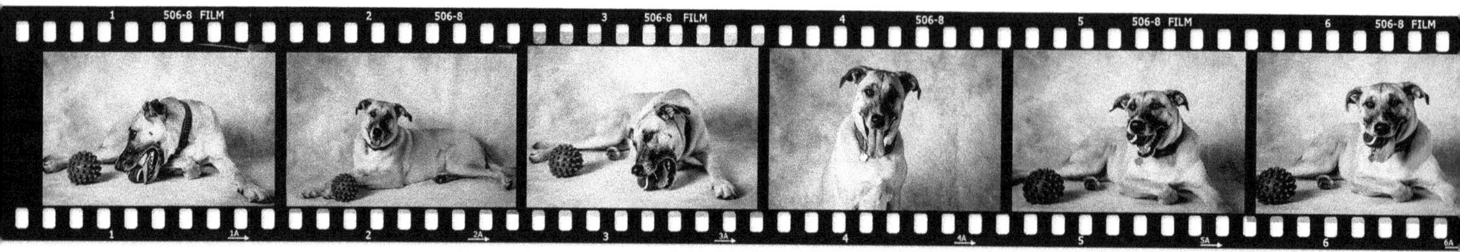

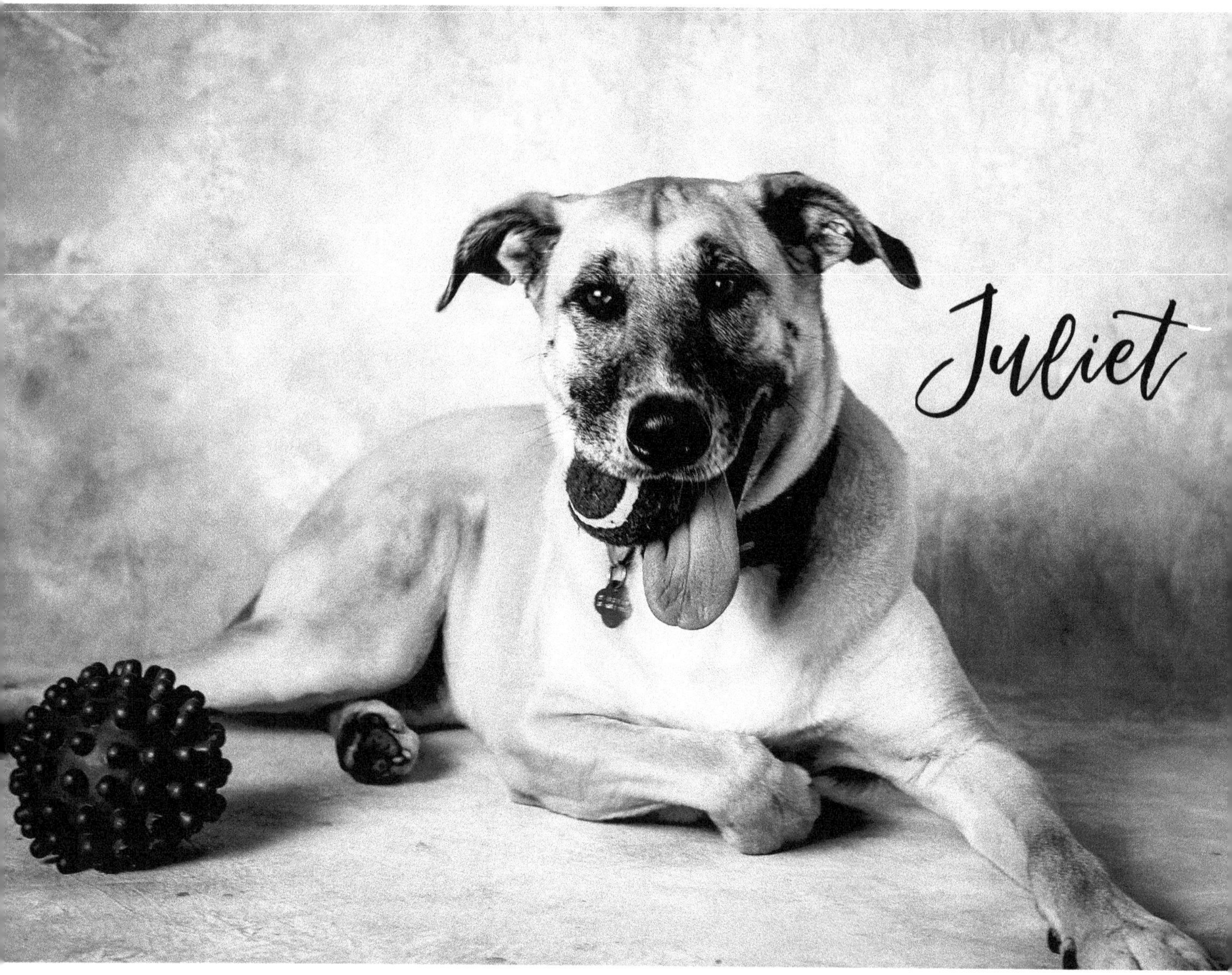

Juliet

JULIET is a four-and-a-half-year-old Anatolian Shepherd who found her home through Red Sky Rescue in Indiana. The most endearing thing about her, says her human dad, is that she greets her people at the door with a toy in her mouth while singing "the song of her people" in welcome. When a thunderstorm approaches, Juliet hops in the bathtub to hunker down, and her favorite activity s riding in the car with her head out the window, feeling the breeze on her face. Who doesn't love that?

KELLY is an 18-month old collie/lab mix that came to her forever family through the work of the Suncoast Animal League. She is extremely devoted to her human mama, and is always checking on her and helps out when her mama takes in foster puppies. The worst thing she's ever done is chew shoes, but that's entirely forgiveable. She was pregnant when she arrived at her forever home, and was a great mother to her two puppies, which soon found forever homes of their own. Kelly loves puppies and dances whenever new pups come into the house. "She saved me," says her human mama, "and I can't imagine my life without her."

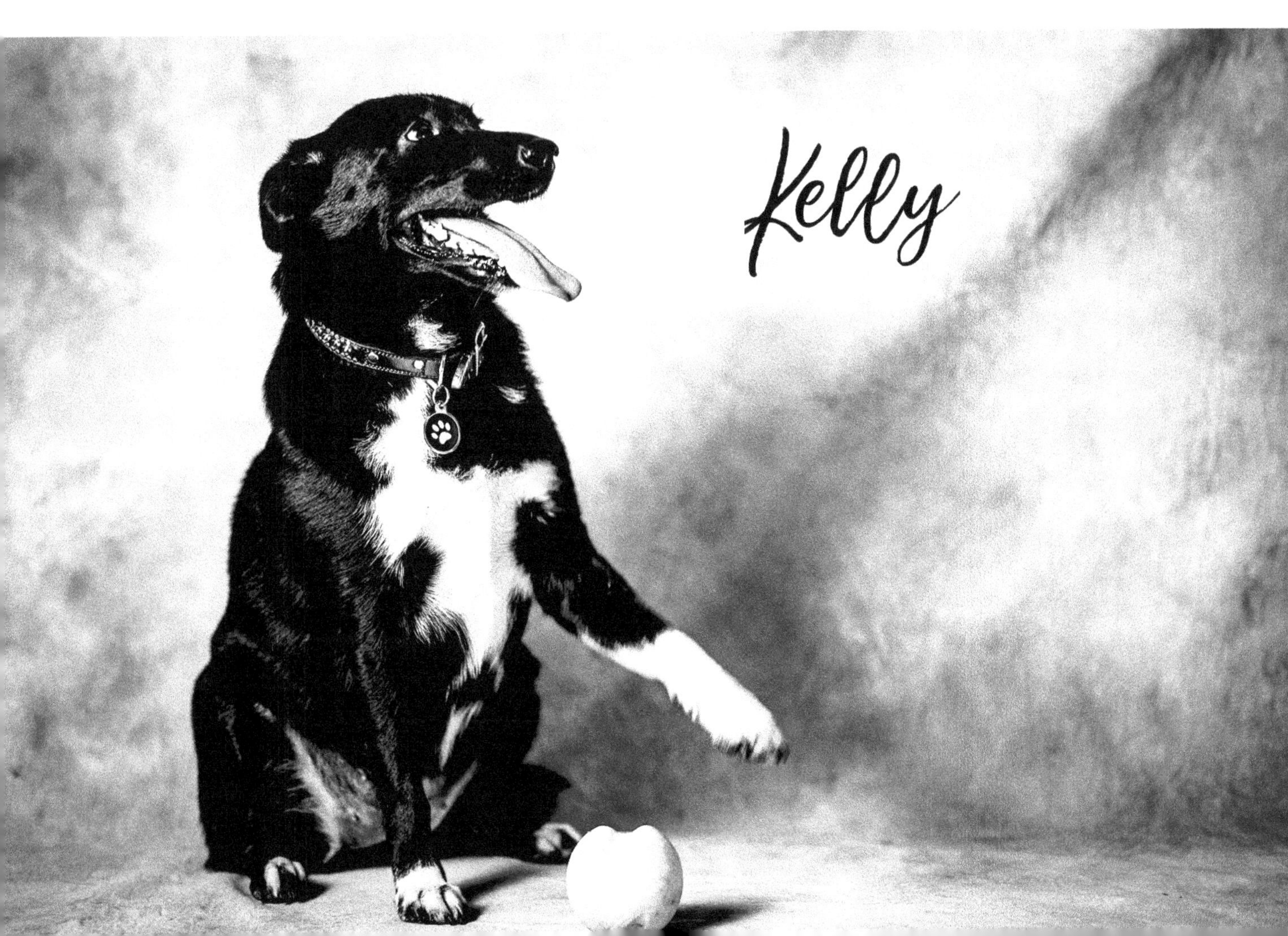

KEYLEE is a rock-star ball player. Look at that reach! Look at those tippee toes! This one-year-old Shepherd/Lab mix lives with Kiya and her humans, and she does a lot to keep life interesting. Keylee's mom once fostered a pregnant dog who had five puppies. After the dog gave birth, all the puppies were adopted but one. Foster mom became a "foster failure"--she couldn't bear to part with Keylee.

Keylee's mom smiles when asked what endearing thing Keylee does. "She makes me laugh," she says. "She loves water, and is very funny in the rain and in the pool."

Keylee can be a counter-surfer. "She can jump up and reach just about anything," her mom says. "She once ate a new pair of prescription glasses, and another time she ate the baked-from-scratch cake I was making for my sister's birthday party. I went outside for one minute, and when I came back in, half the cake was gone. Thankfully, I had a cake mix, so I whipped that together, baked it, and went to the birthday party. I ended up frosting a warm cake in the car."

But you don't get rid of a dog just because they ate glasses and a cake. You love them and teach them to do better.

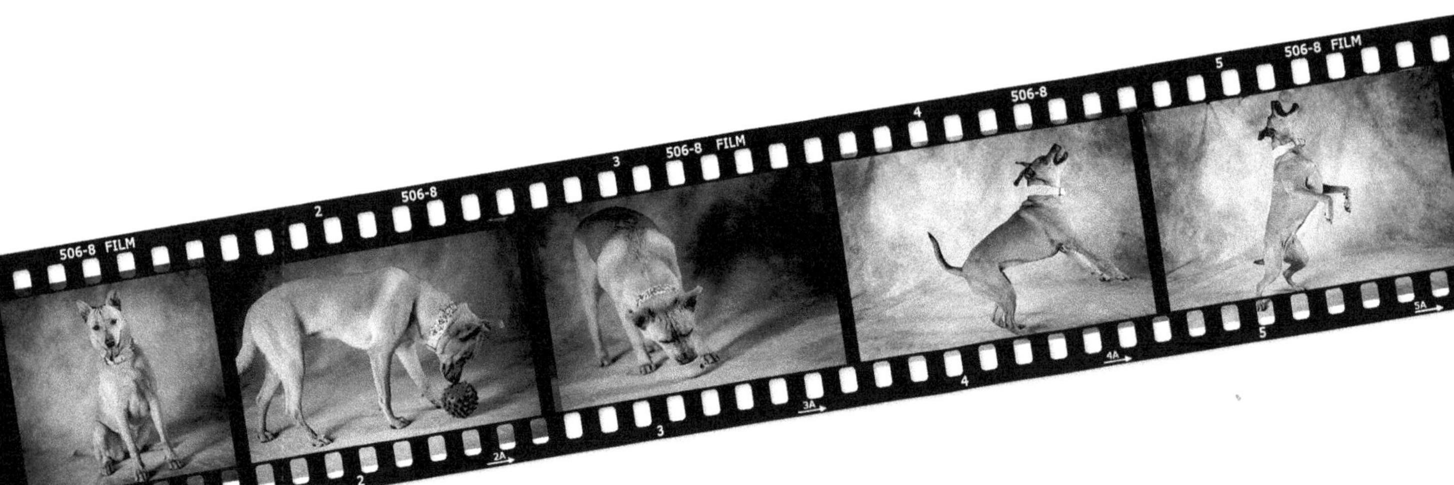

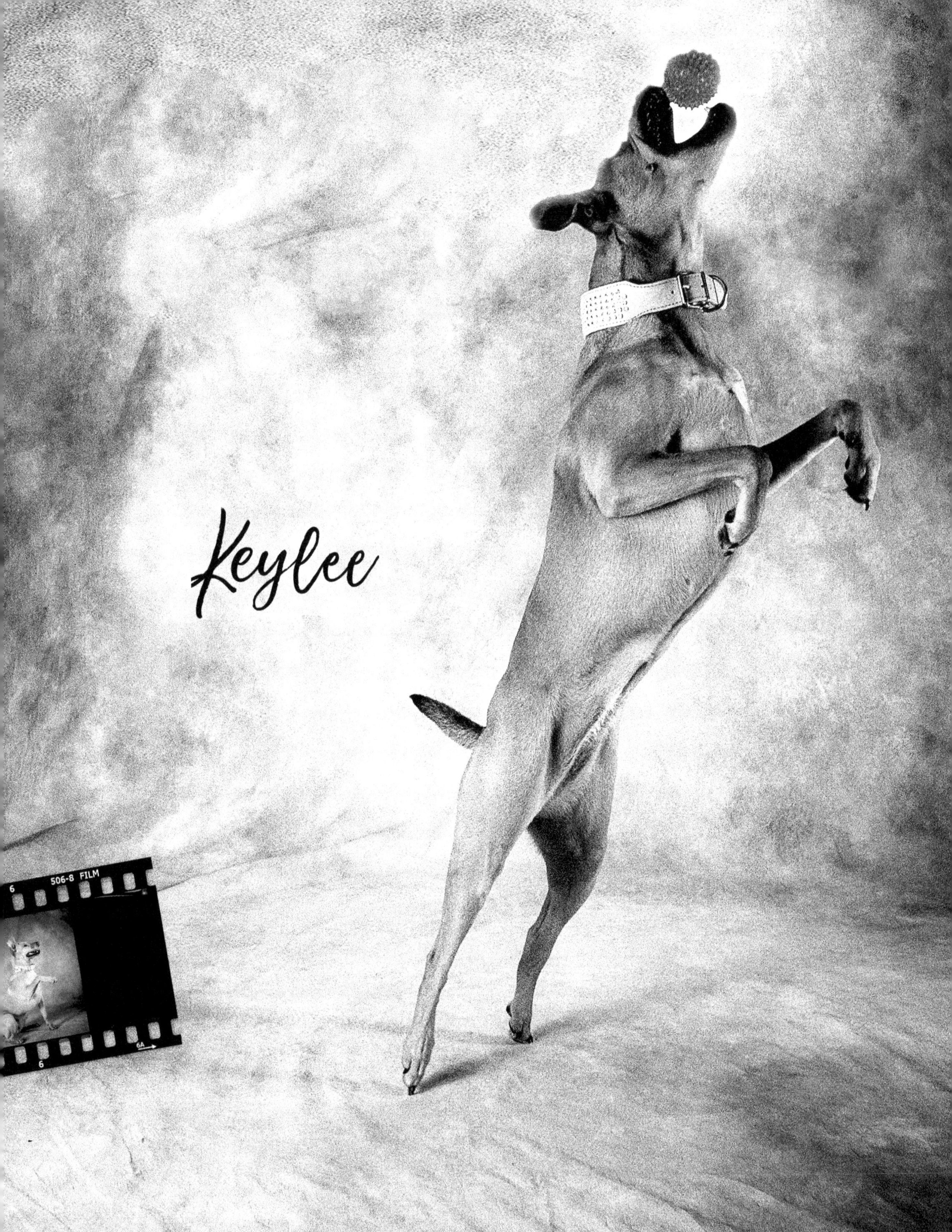
Keylee
6
506-8 FILM
6A
6

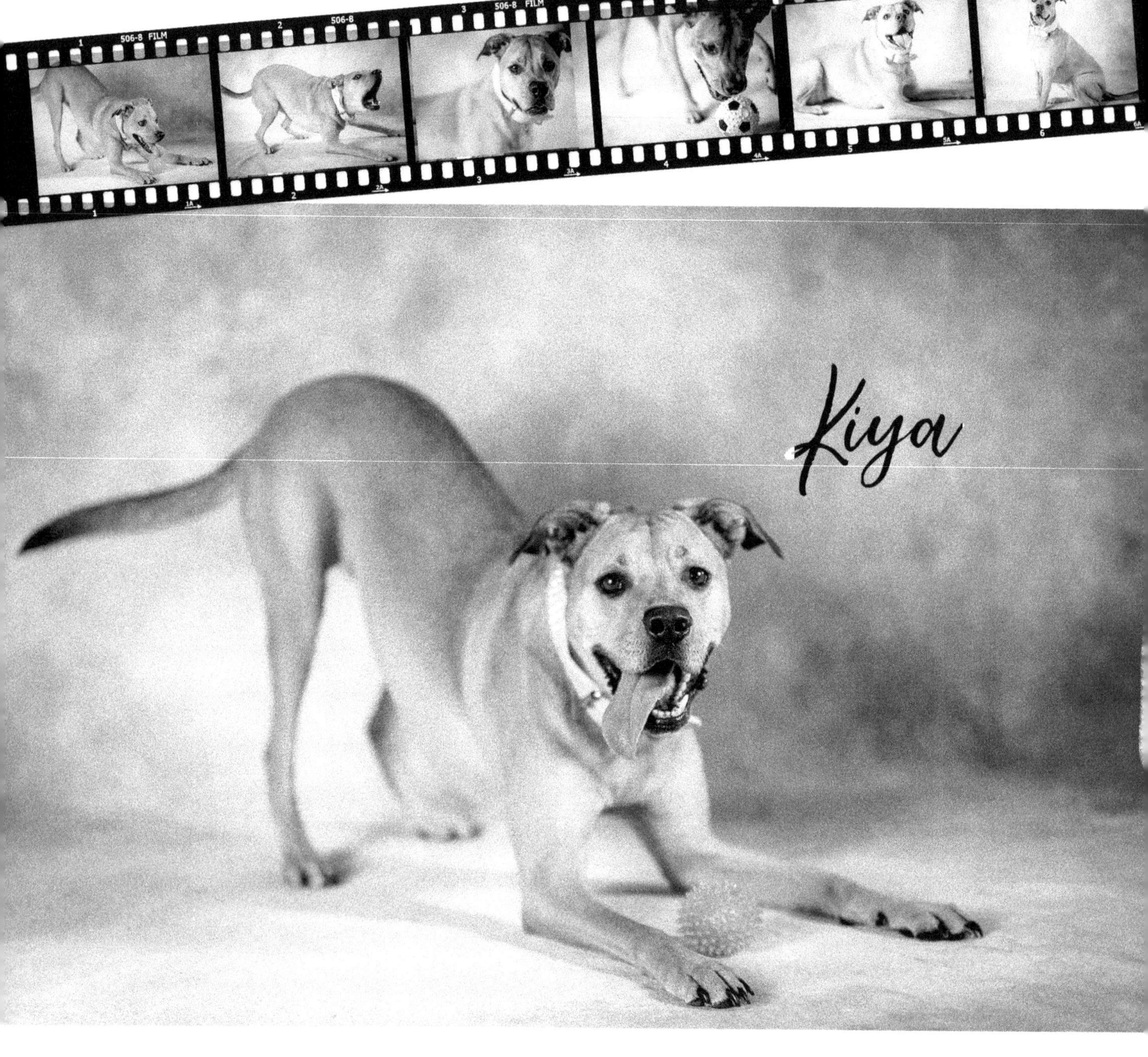

If you don’t speak dog body language, take a lesson from KIYA, who’s a master of the “play bow,” the posture that says “come on, let’s play!” The five-year-old Staffordshire Terrier mix was discovered online, when her human mom went looking for another dog to rescue. Kiyah’s favorite toys are balls of all kinds. “She could play fetch all day,” says her mom, “and she loves to swim.” Kiya is an angel in the behavior department, too. “She was even good as a pup,” says her mom. ‘Whenever I hear a suspicious noise, I always know it’s not Kiya making trouble, it’s her sister!”

LAINEY is a princess, pure and simple. Her family found her on the SPCA website, and she's been living the life of a princess ever since. The ten-year-old Pyrenees/Hound/Lab mix loves anything soft and fluffy, and can "groan" appropriately during conversation. She is the oldest of the family's three dogs, and reigns over the younger ones with grace and dignity. Always.

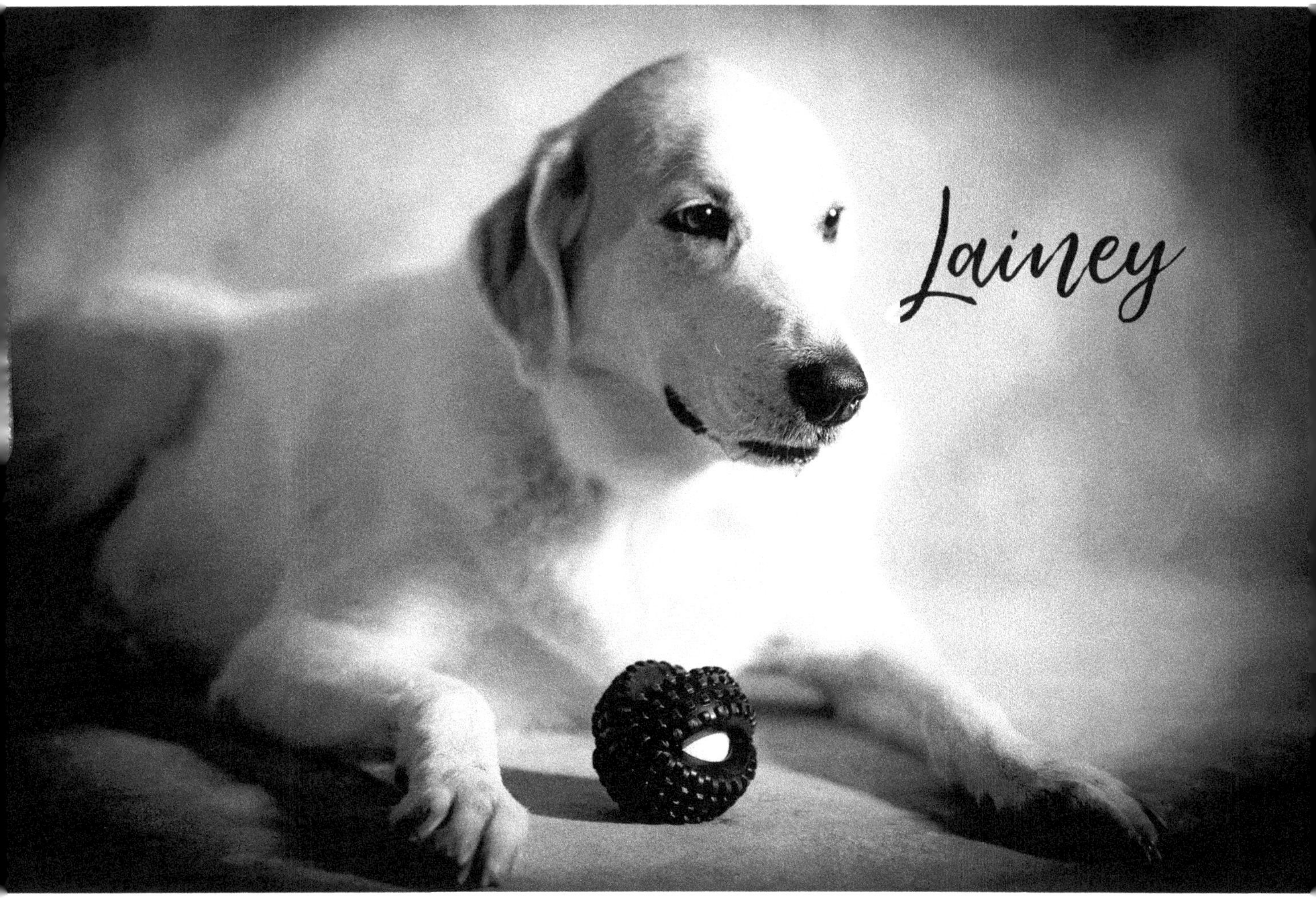

Lainey

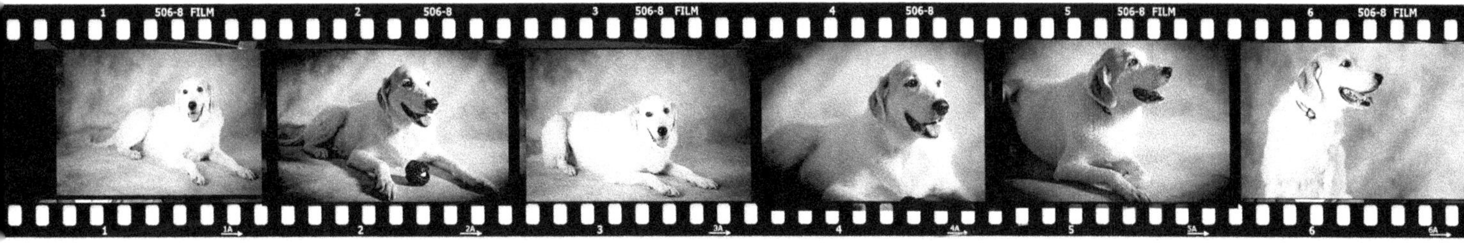

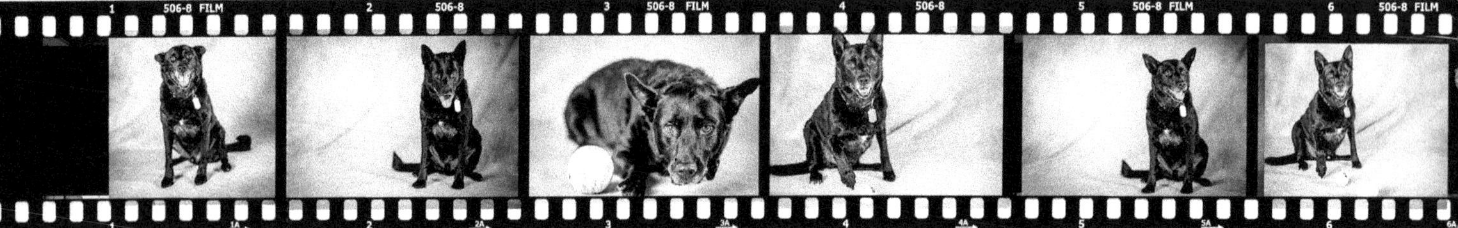

The great LEBOWSKI, aka "Bow-Bow", is a ten-year-old Shepherd/Akita mix. His current owner found him when he was working on an ambulance in downtown Indianapolis. They've been together ever since, except for a heart-rending couple of days in which the dog ran away--fortunately, his owner found him two days later, sleeping in his Jeep.

Bow-bow's favorite toy is "anything his siblings have." When he's not engaged in sibling rivalry, Bow-Bow loves to cuddle and lie on his back, looking like a gator. During his photo shoot, Bow-Bow would chase a ball, then run and plop down in the photographer's lap. Bow-bow knows how to have fun--and how to relax. And isn't that an important lesson to learn?

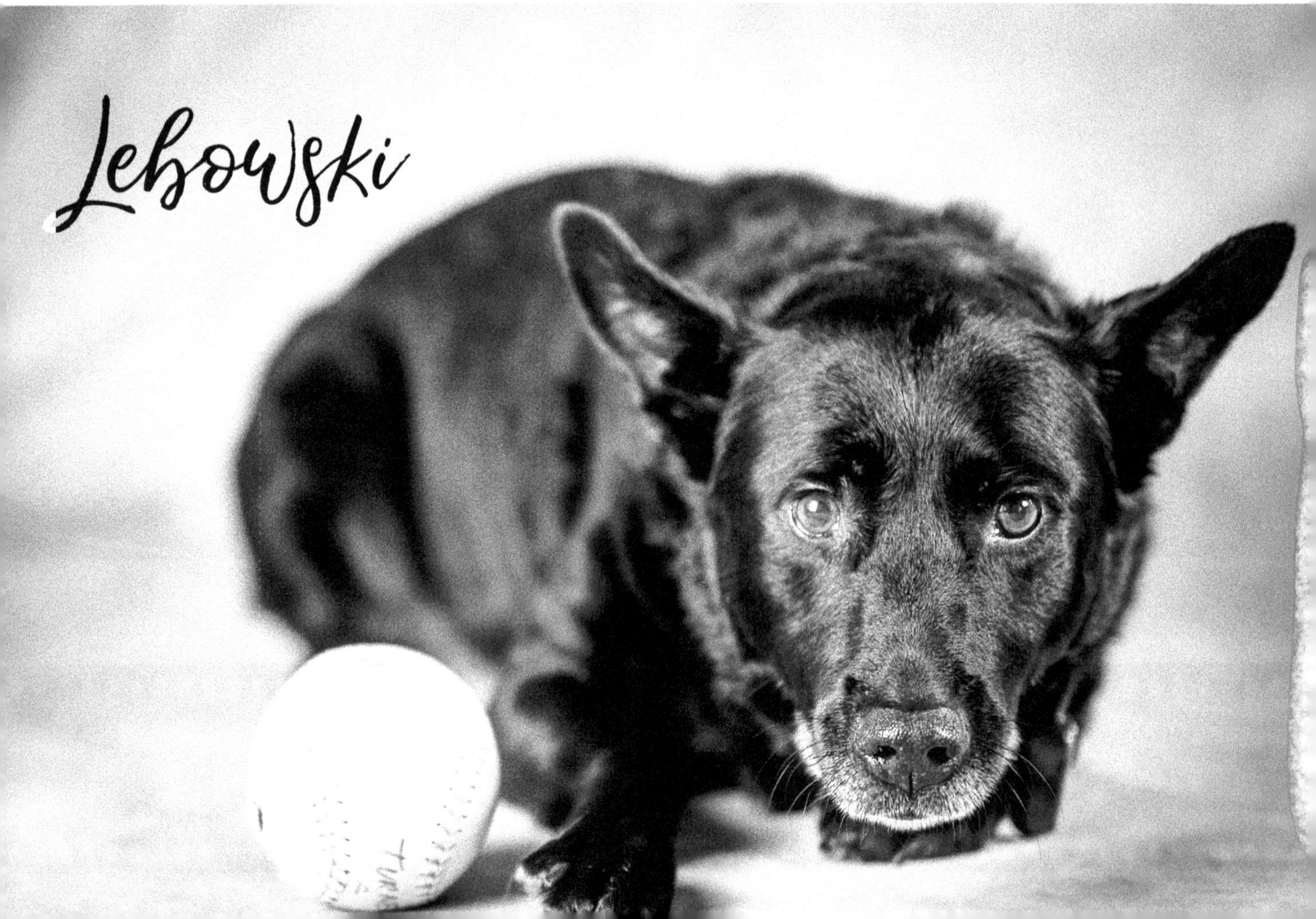

Lebowski

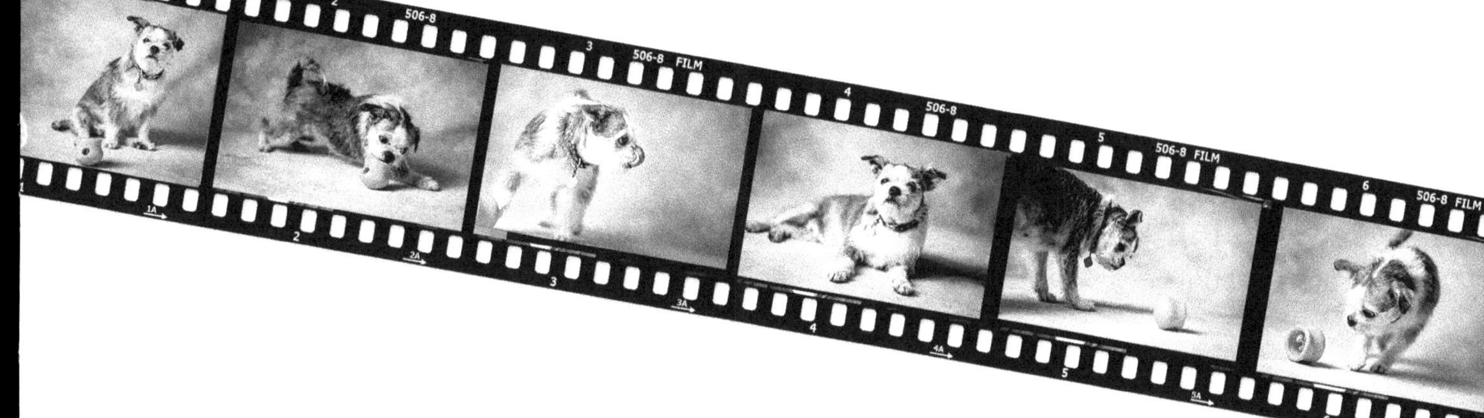

LILY was underweight and full of worms when she was found as a stray. A family volunteered to foster her until she could be adopted, but then they fell in love with her and couldn't let her go. She is a Terrier mix, about five years old, and her favorite toy is her big brother Andy, a Newfoundland. Lily is an affectionate cuddle bug--her human mother says she "loves to get up next to us and lay her head on us." Other than functioning as human pillows, her humans also provide other excitement. "She barks when we put on our shoes," says her mama. "She wants to go somewhere!" When she's out on her leash, Lily think she is the boss of the world--or at least every other dog she meets.

A lotta heart in one little dog--that's Lily!

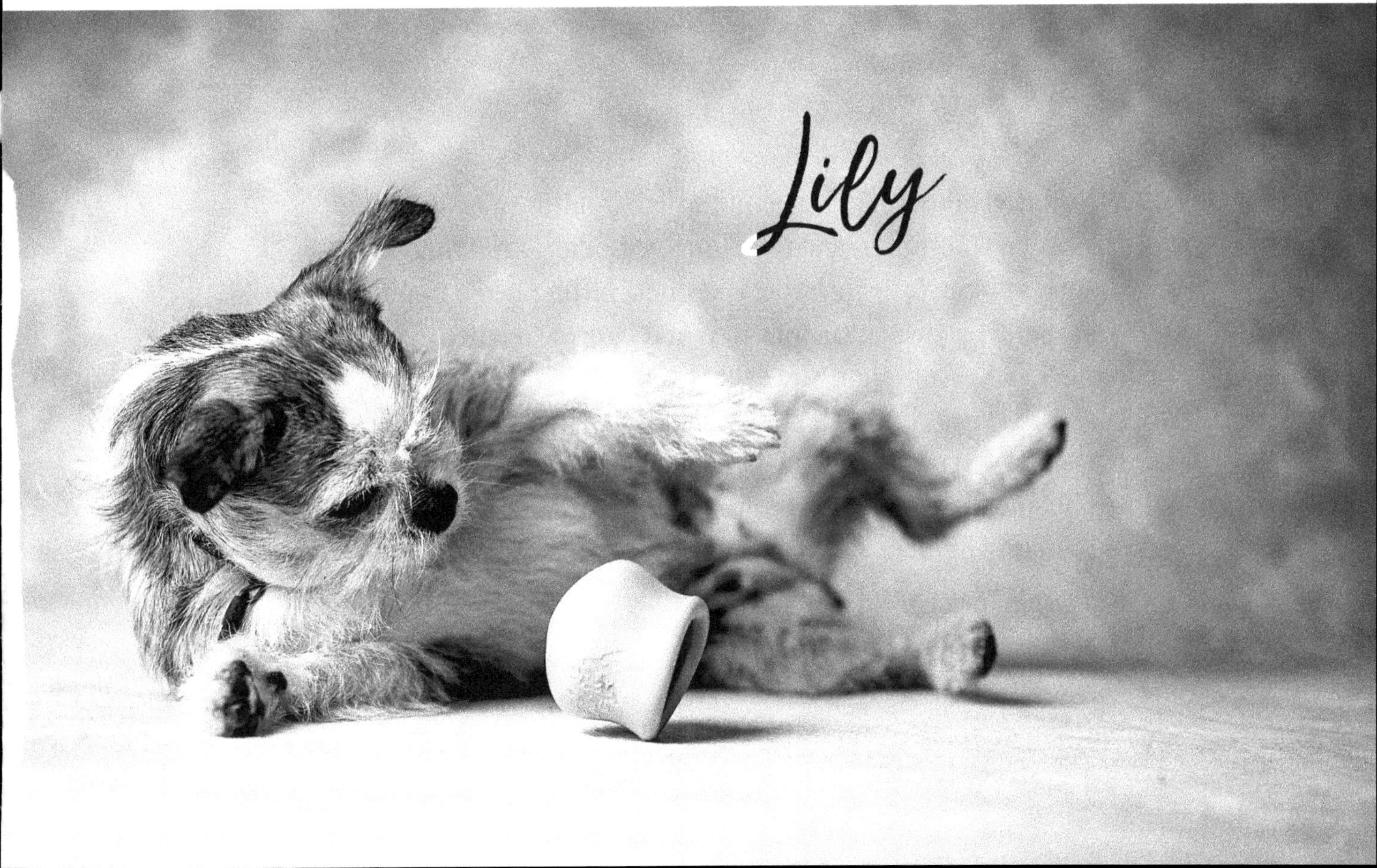

Lily

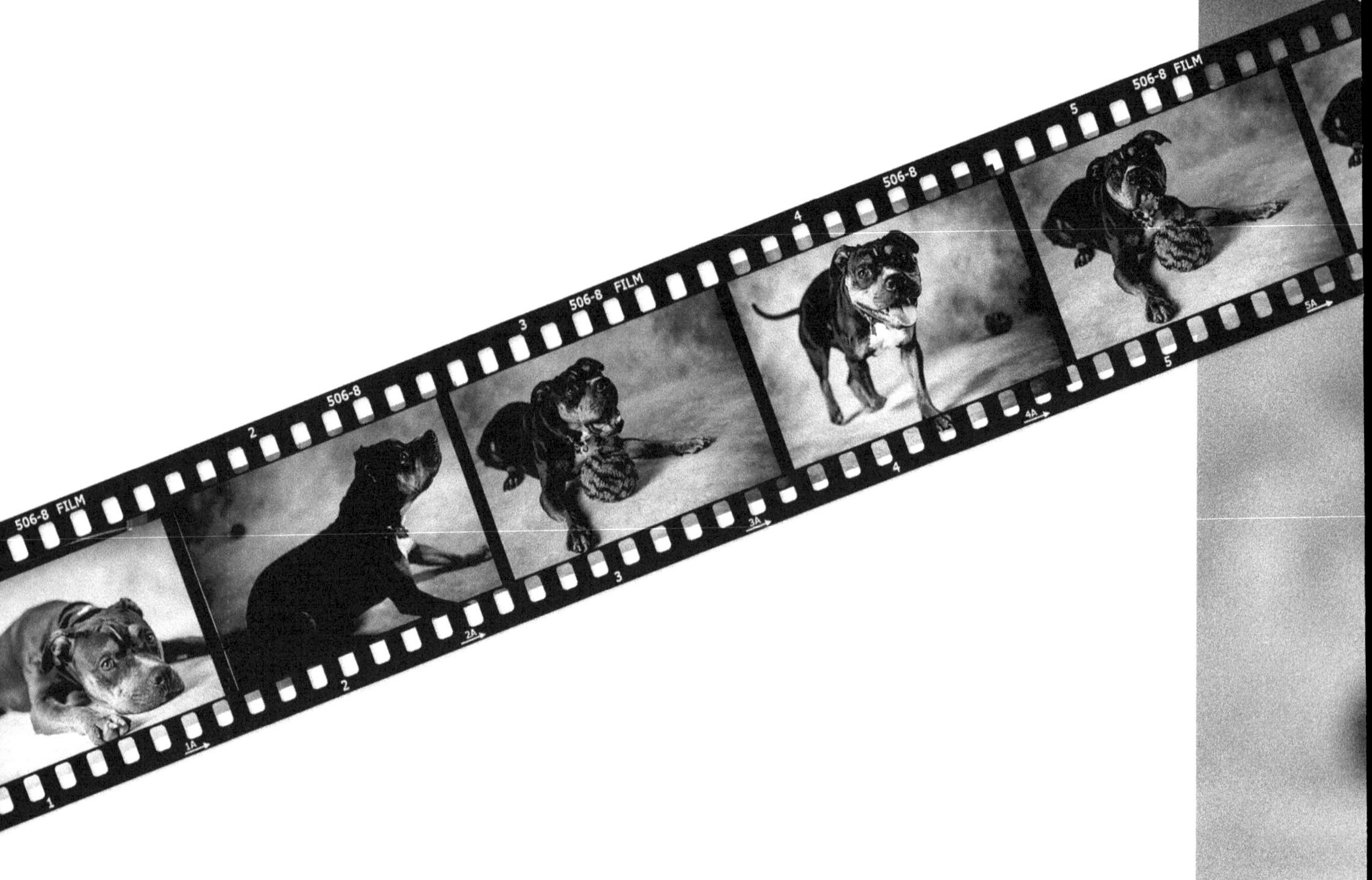

LUCHIA found her forever home in the late months of 2016. Her owner had been volunteering at the Humane Society, and there was something about the little girl whose kennel card reported that she was a Shar-pei. Her owner knew better, and later, when he ordered a doggie DNA test for her, she came back as mostly American Staffordshire Terrier. But no matter what breed label she may wear, Luchia is devoted to her human dad and her doggie sibling. She loves people, her hard chew bone, and any stuffed toy with a squeaker. Every night at bedtime, she rests her head on her dad's neck as they drift away and rest up for another busy day.

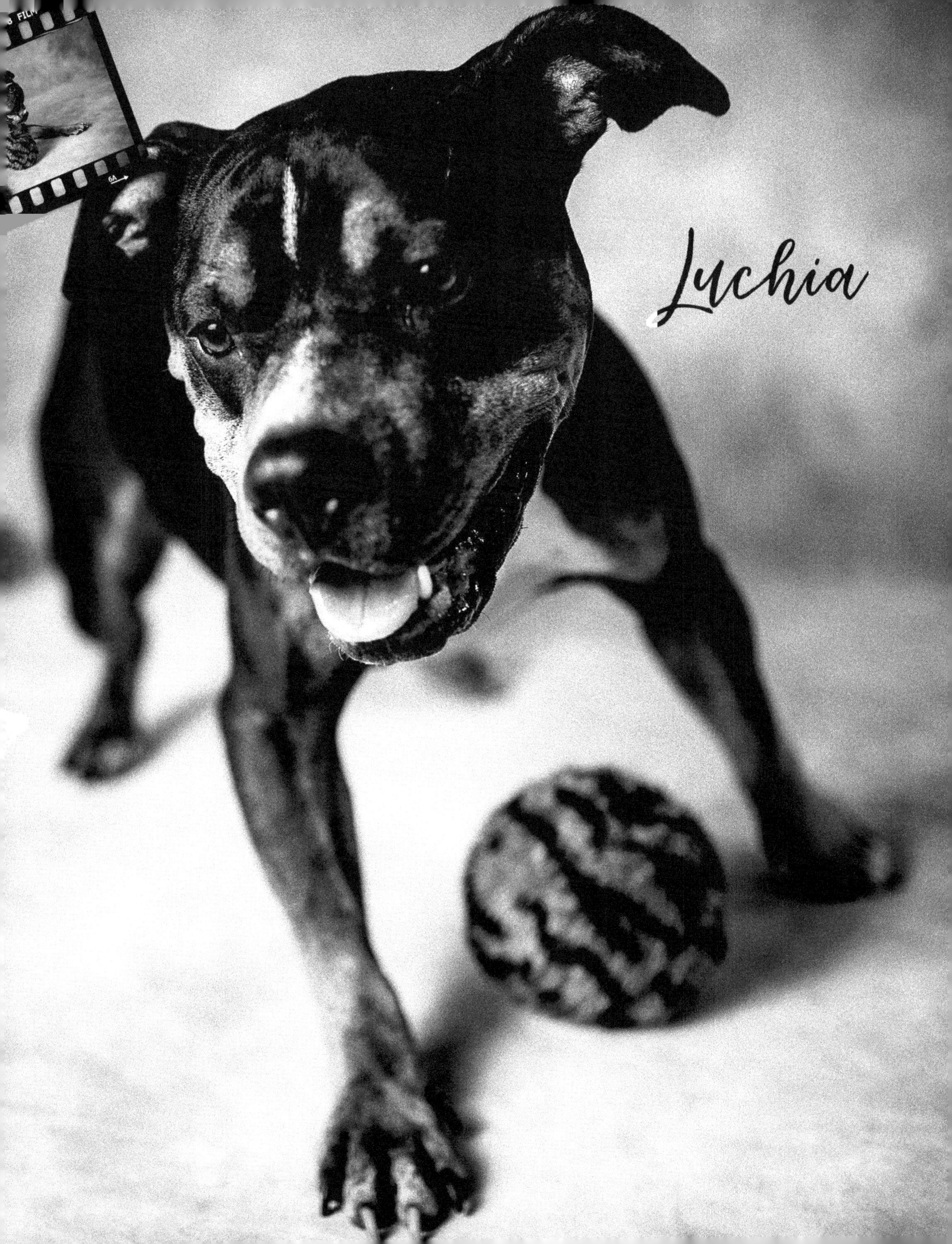
Luchia

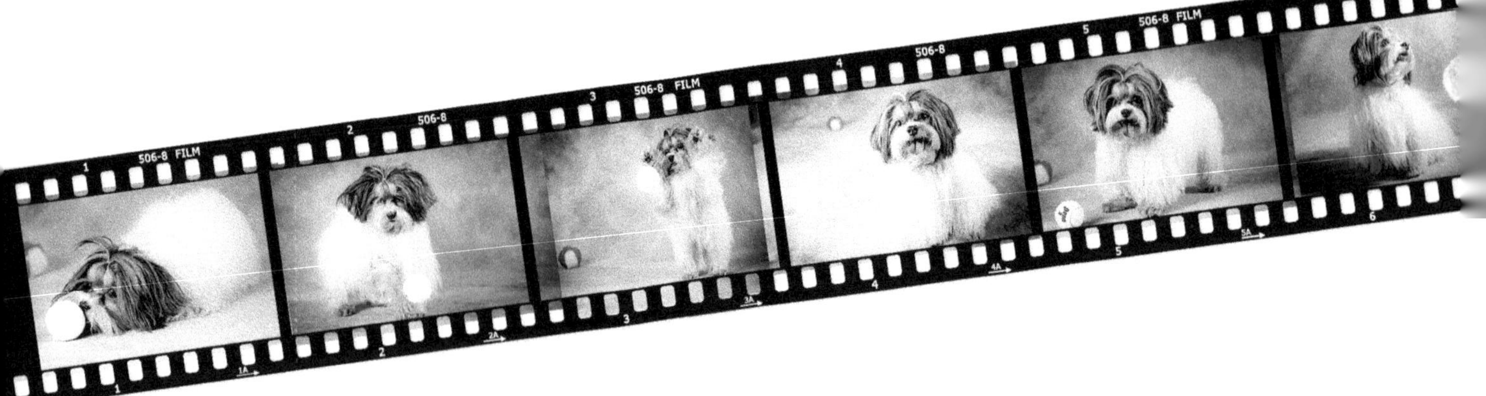

Don't let the ponytail fool you--LOLA, a four-year-old Havanese, may be a glamour girl, but she's got it goin' on. She knows how to roll over and retrieve the morning paper. She gives high fives, plays dead, and gives kisses--but no one had to teach her how to do *that*. Her favorite toy is her squeaky squirrel, but her favorite BALL is a rolled up ball of paper. She will go after it, torture it, and rip it until the paper surrenders. It's all part of a ritual she observes every night with her dad, and Lola is not ready for bed until the balled-up paper has been taught a lesson.

It's not the size of the dog that matters--it's the size of the *heart* inside the dog.

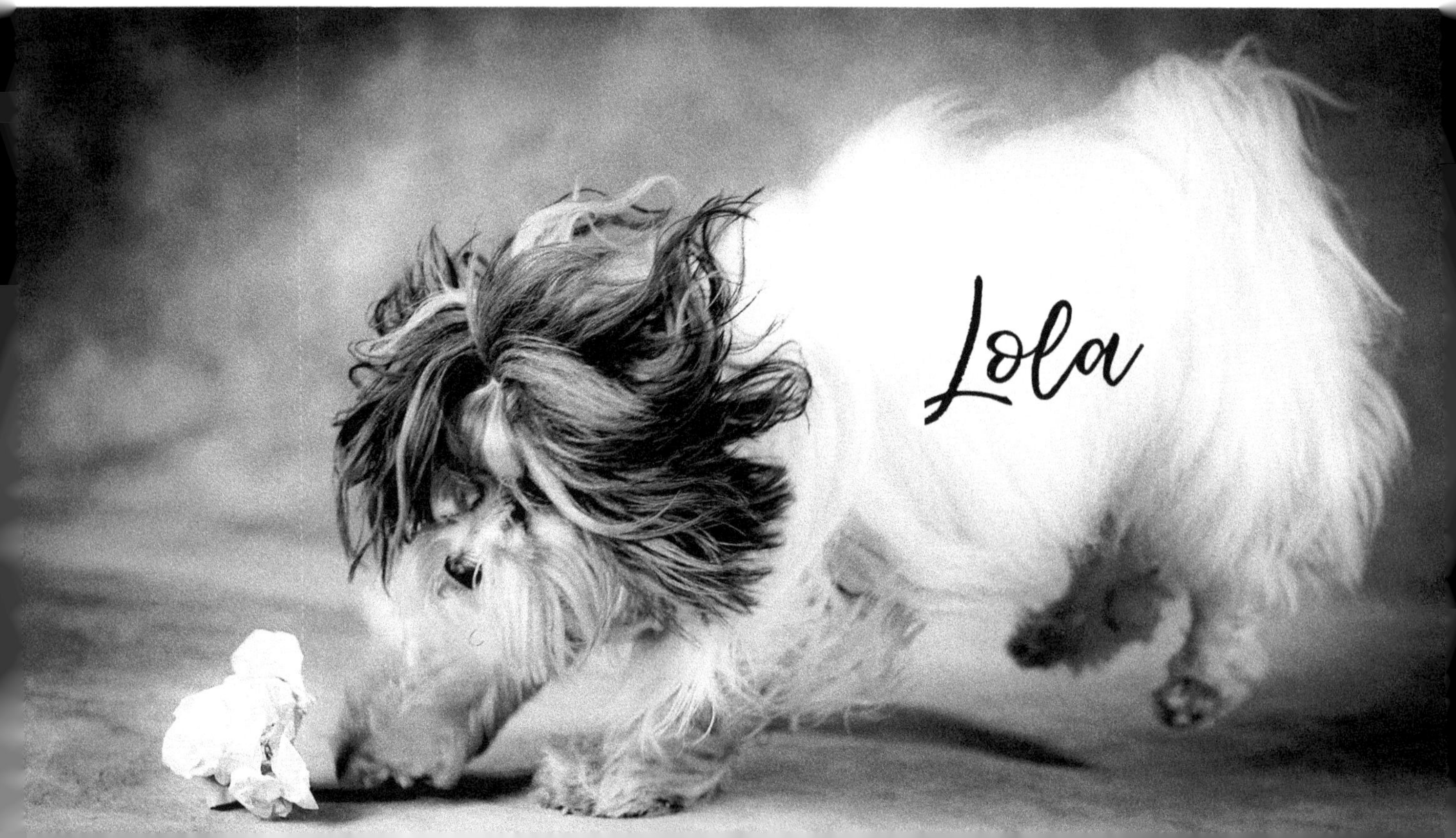

Lola

Eleven-year-old LUCKY found her forever home through the SPCA. The Lab mix had been surrendered to the shelter twice before reaching her second birthday. Lucky's mom isn't sure why people kept bringing her back, but she's glad they did. "She has been one of the most loving dogs I've ever known," her mom says. "She's content with just your hand touching her, knowing you're nearby. She loves tummy rubs and will roll over and rest her head on you while you rub her belly." Sounds like the third time was the charm for Lucky *and* her family.

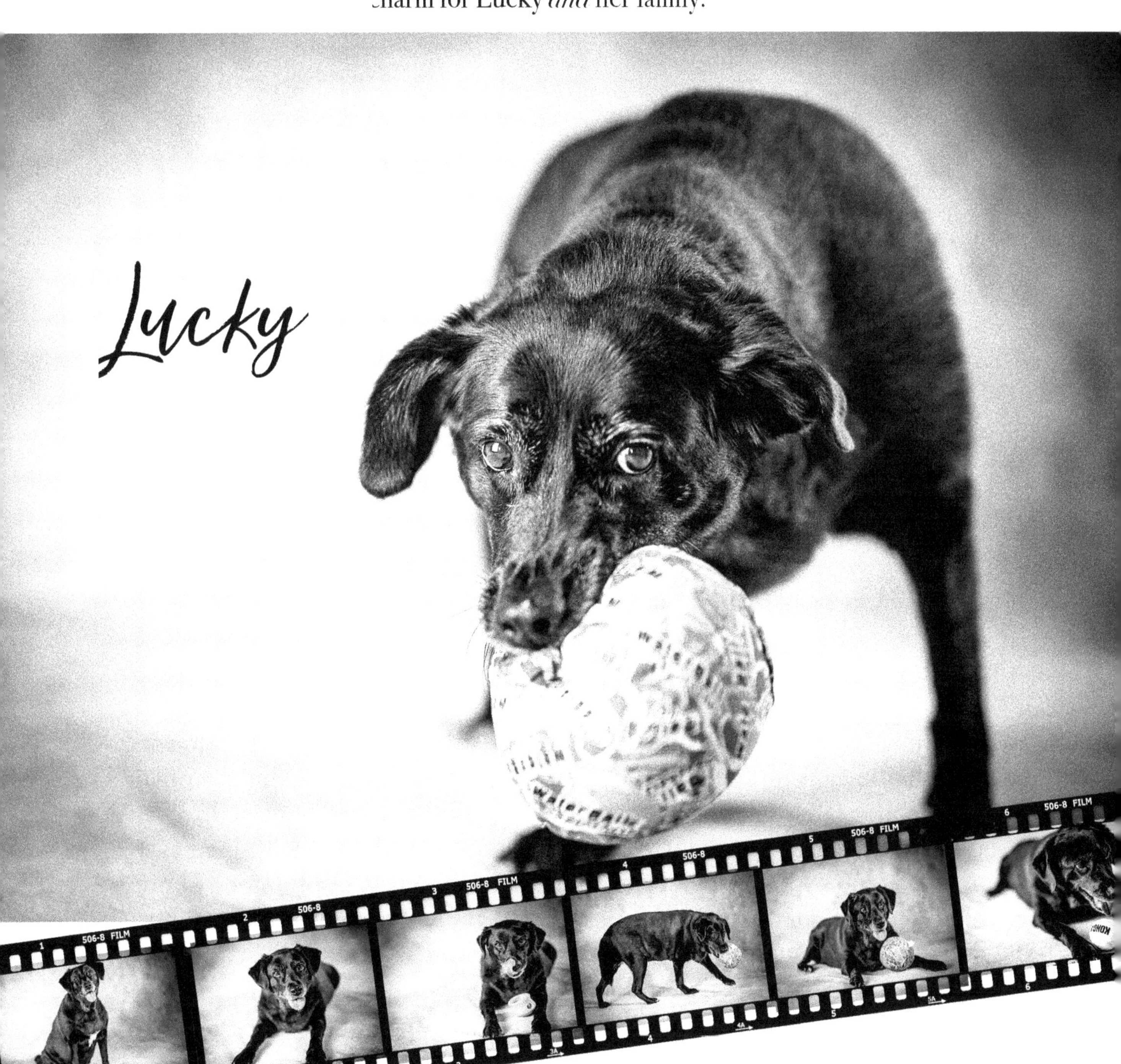

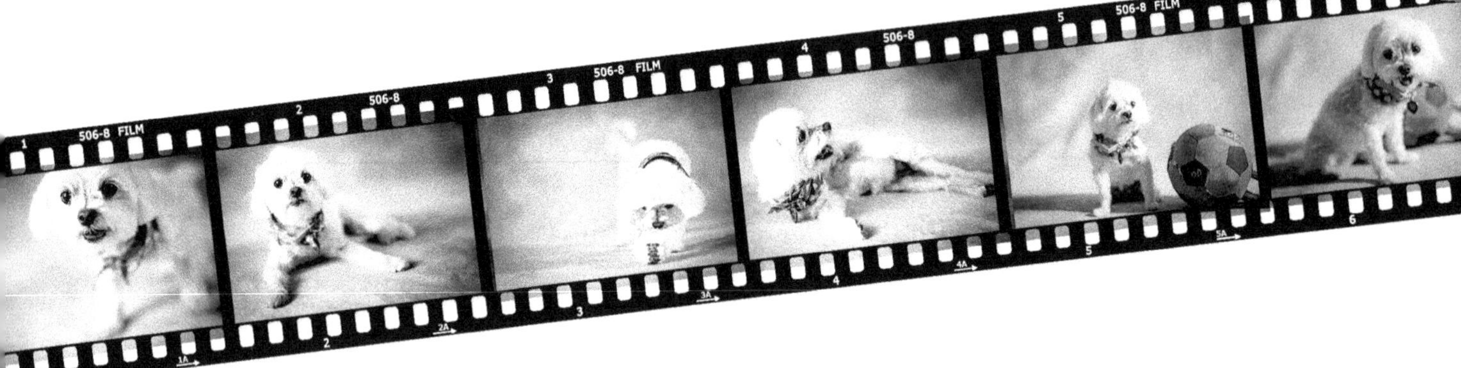

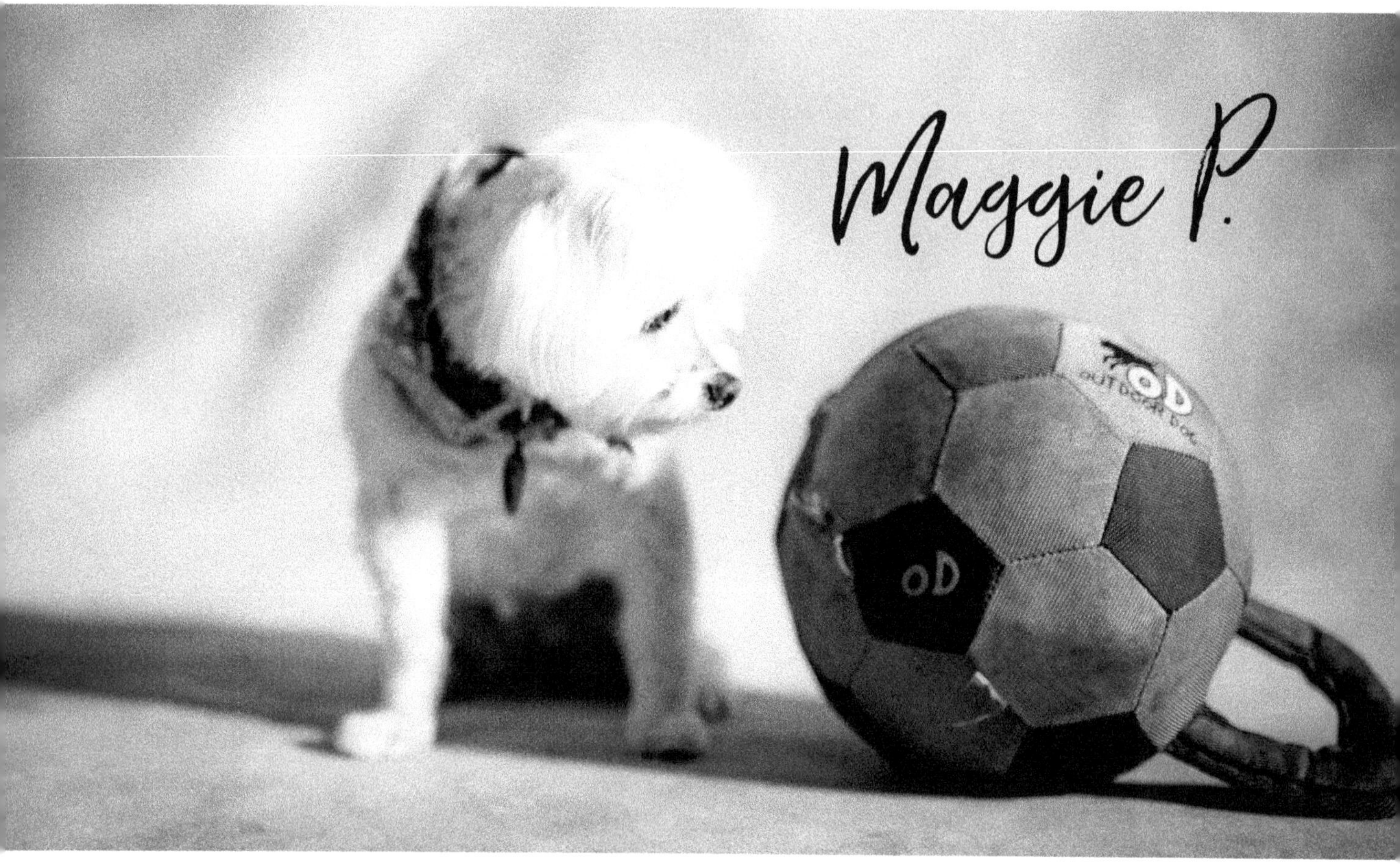

Maggie P.

We have to admit it--ten-year-old MAGGIE P isn't quite sure what to do with a ball. She has led a pampered life--first with one woman, then with the woman's grandkids when they fell in love with little Maggie. The tiny Maltese loves her blanket and she loves to sleep. She also loves belly rubs, and will shamlessly plop down and expose her belly to almost any passerby, hoping for a gentle rubdown. A giant heart resides in this little body, however--she once ran outside to chase a car, and she barks as fiercely at post office delivery people as any big dog. Her favorite treat is bacon, and the perfect day for Maggie ends with a snuggle . . . after a bellyrub and a nap, of course.

MAGGIE is a nine-year-old Australian cattle dog mix, adopted while her owner was volunteering at the SPCA. Maggie came to the shelter after being picked up with a sibling--both dogs were living in the trunk of a car, and both were in terrible condition. The sibling didn't survive, but Maggie did, though she had anxiety issues that took her a while to overcome. Maggie adores her mama and any ball that is stuffed (so she can joyfully "unstuff" it), and she sleeps and snores with her tongue out. With the love and support of her mama, Maggie has learned how to ride in a car, walk on a leash, and be loved . . .
freeing her to love as well.

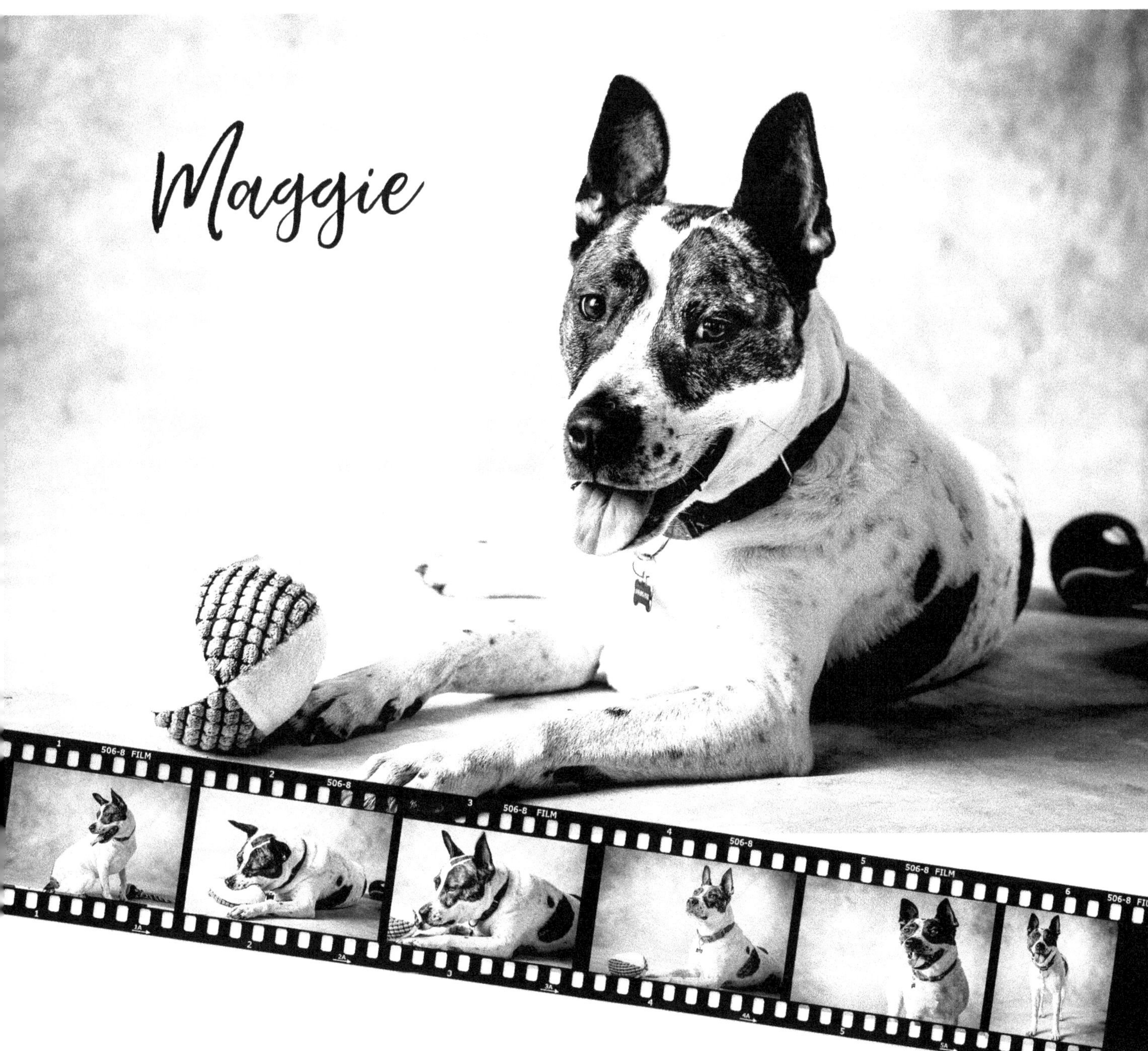

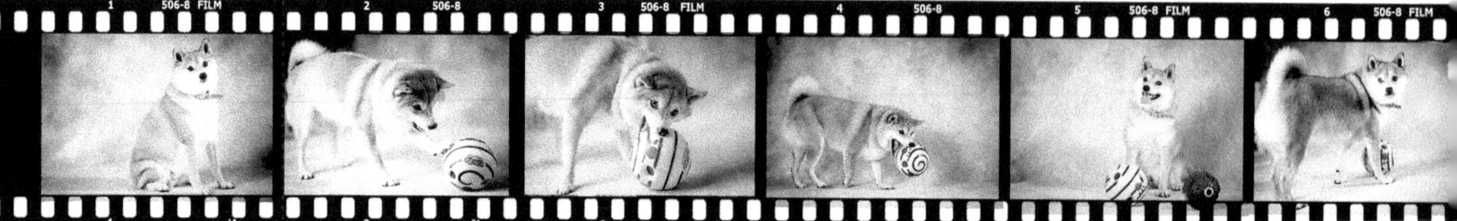

The amazing MAISY is a two-year-old Shiba Inu. Her favorite toy is anything with a squeaker, and when she plays with balls--well, the sweet, obedient Shiba turns into a ball-chasing machine. She puts on her snarly face and lets loose with a string of Shiba sounds designed to inspire terror in any ball that dares linger in her vicinity. When she's not chasing a ball, Maisy loves to give high-fives, roll over, spin in circles, and have her belly rubbed. The most terrifying thing she's ever done? When the family returned home from a trip, Maisy found a two-ounce bar of chocolate in a suitcase pocket and ate it ALL. (Chocolate is toxic to dogs). That required quick action, but Maisy survived . . . to frighten balls another day.

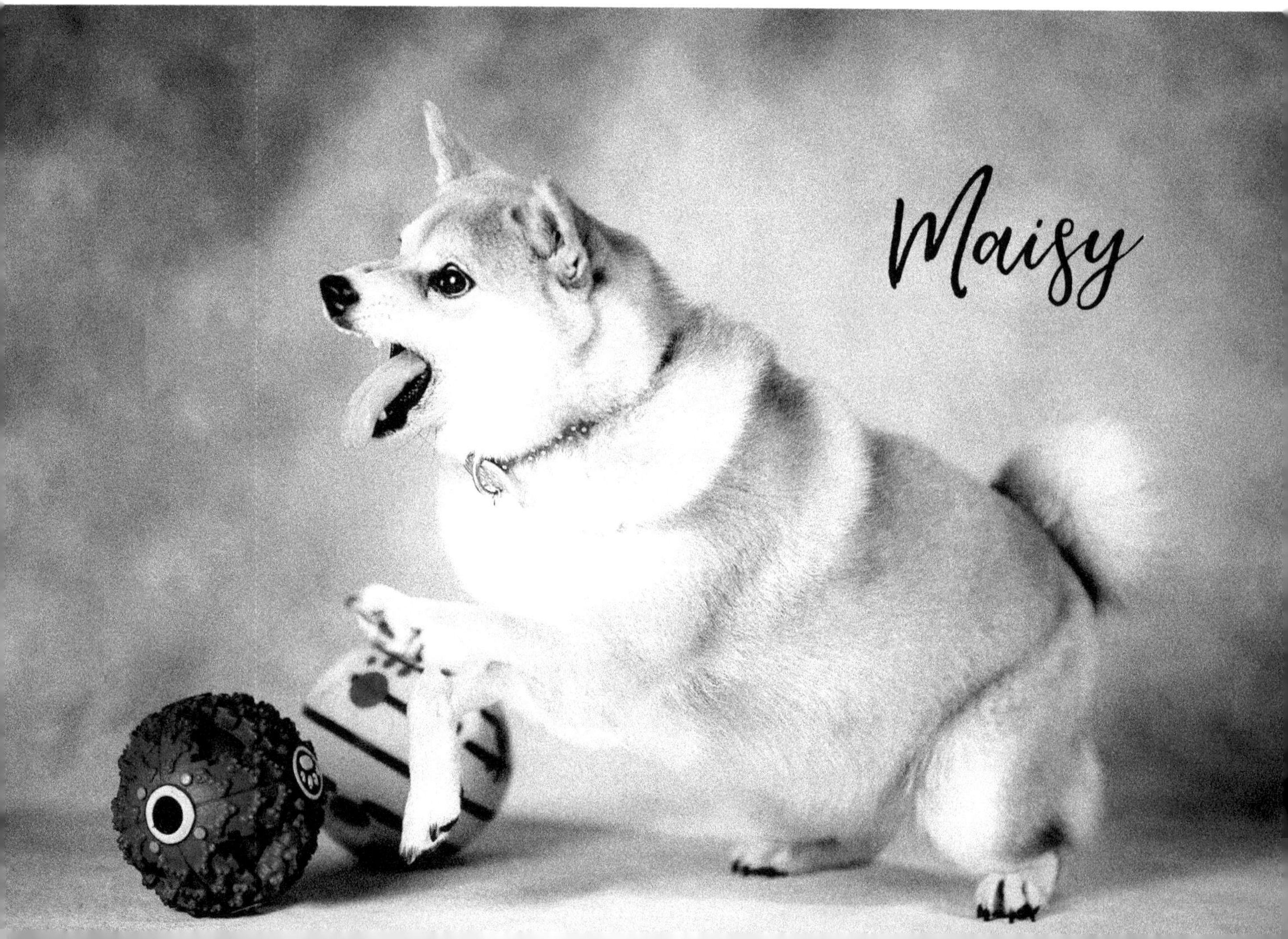

Maisy

MAX, a six-year-old Husky/Shepherd mix, joined his present family after being rescued from a not-so-good home. He now lives with his owners and three canine siblings, and he's happy have found his forever family. This enthusiastic pup loves his bone and running and playing with his canine buddies. "His favorite things on the planet," says his dad, "are treats and cuddles."

One day Max escaped from his yard and got into a skirmish with a dog down the street. He received a bad wound on his paw, and had to be rushed to the emergency vet. His owners have learned to keep a close eye on active Max . . . who not only cuddles, but gives the *best* kisses in the world.

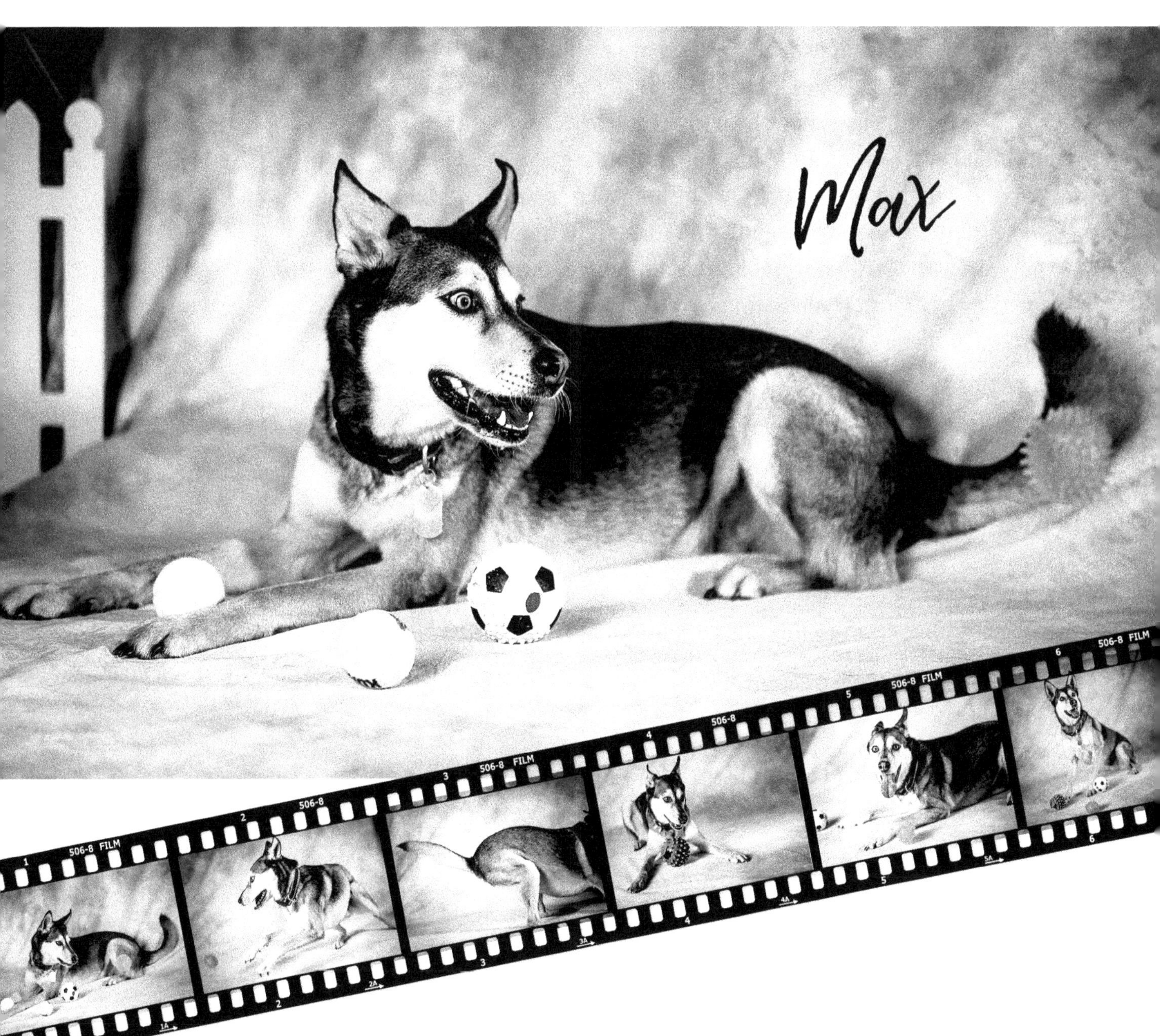

MILA is a six-year-old American Strafordshire Terrier. Her humana mama found her while she was volunteering at a county animal shelter. Her favorite toy is a tennis ball, and her favorite activity is giving kisses.

No one knows exactly what happened to Mila, but sometimes animals speak without words. When Mila was brought in, one of her front legs was shattered so badly it had to be amputated. The doctors assumed she had been hit by a car, so the amputation was done and Mila was adopted by the woman who bonded with her at the shelter. But weeks later, when her new mom reached for a broom, Mila reacted to the innocent gesture with terrified trembling. She reacted in the same way any time her mom reached for anything that resembled a stick. Mila's mom has come to believe that Mila's leg was shattered by a bat. By a human.

If that is the case, then Mila's joy and overflowing love are even more miraculous. She has learned how to trust again, and how to love, and her boundless energy is a testament to her hope and positivity.

She is a living lesson for all of us.

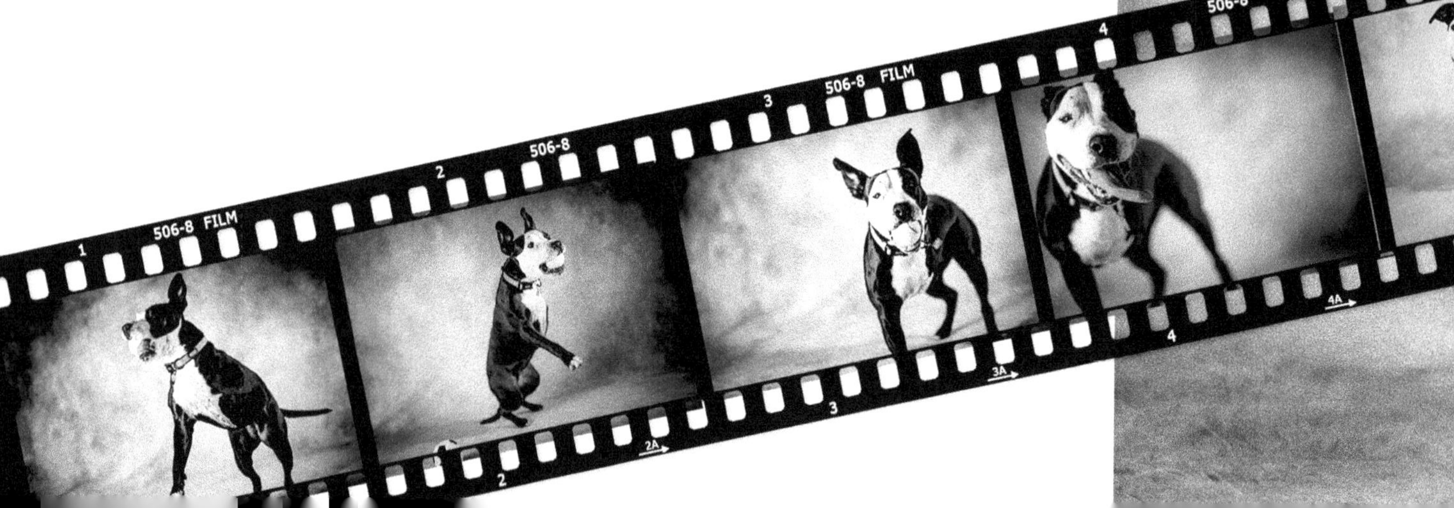

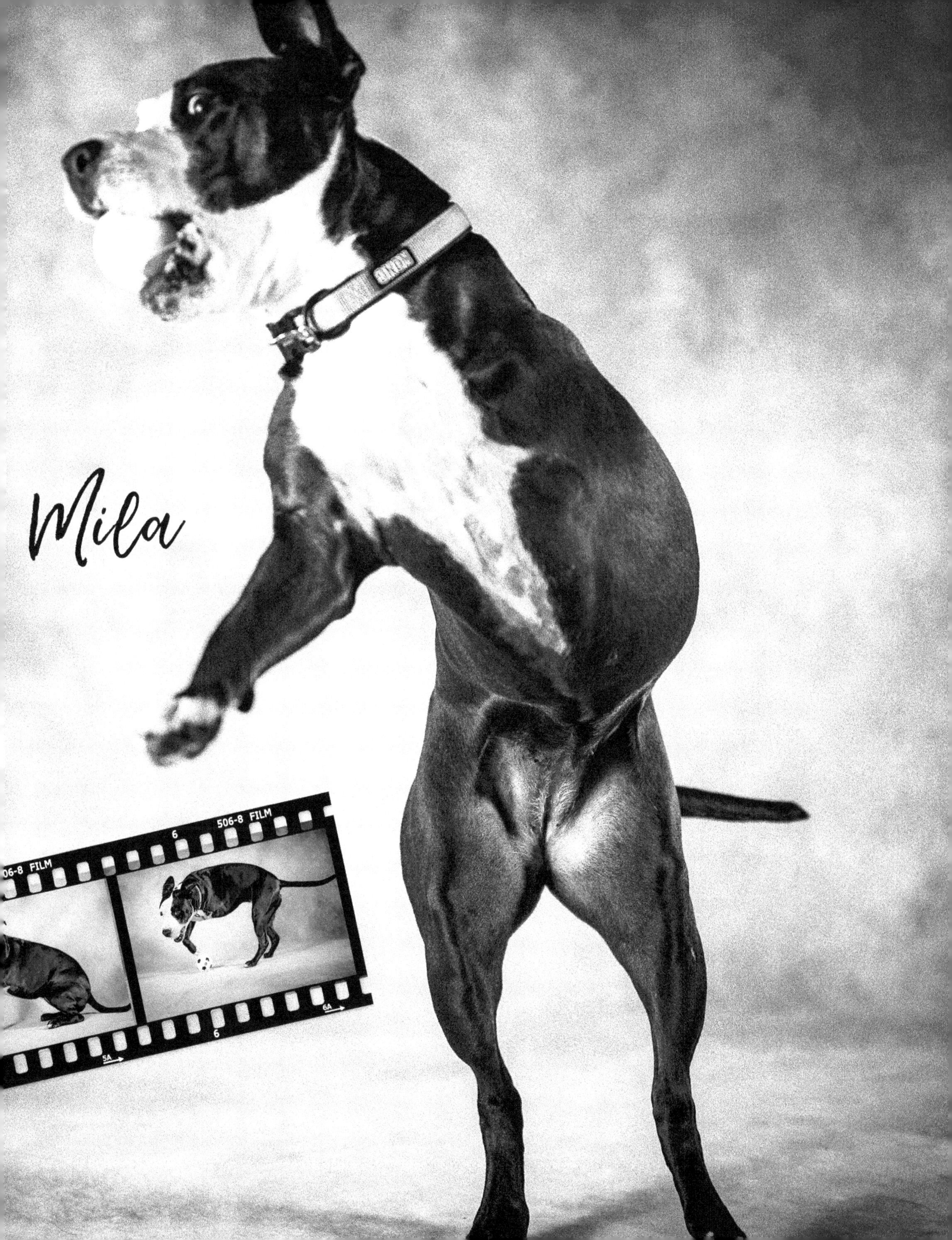
Mila
506-8 FILM
6
06-8 FILM
6A
6
5A

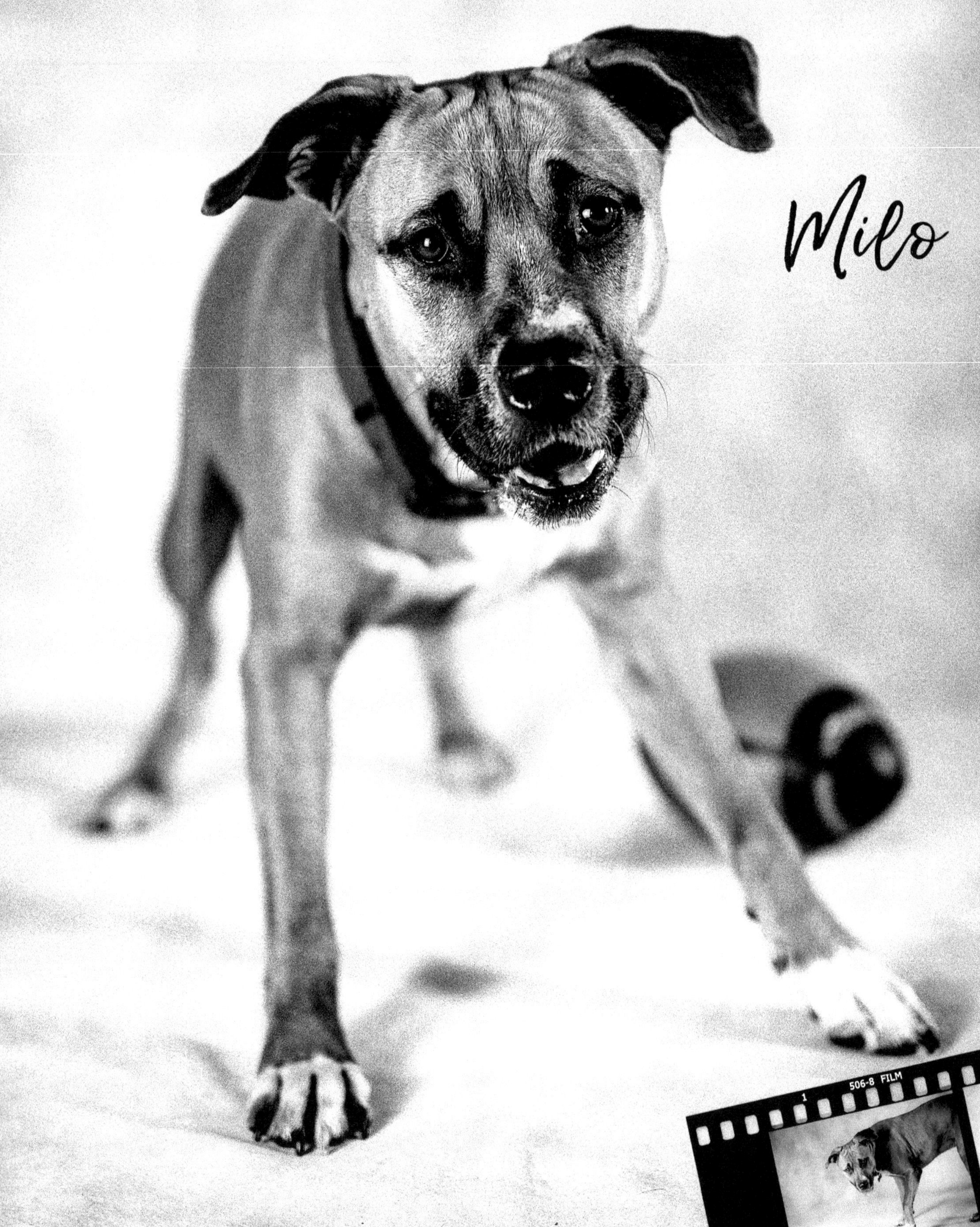
Milo
1
506-8 FILM

Four-year-old Milo, a Boxer/pit bull mix, loves his stuffed porcupine better than any of his other toys. He found his permanent home through a county animal shelter, and he has grown very protective of his human mama and grandmom. Milo can be a little guarded when first meeting new people, but he wants them to know that he's serious about taking care of his family. With those he adores, Milo is pure sweetness. He loves to lift his paw for a handshake, and he happily gives kisses when asked for them. He is closely bonded to his canine sibling, Daisy, and is never far from her side.

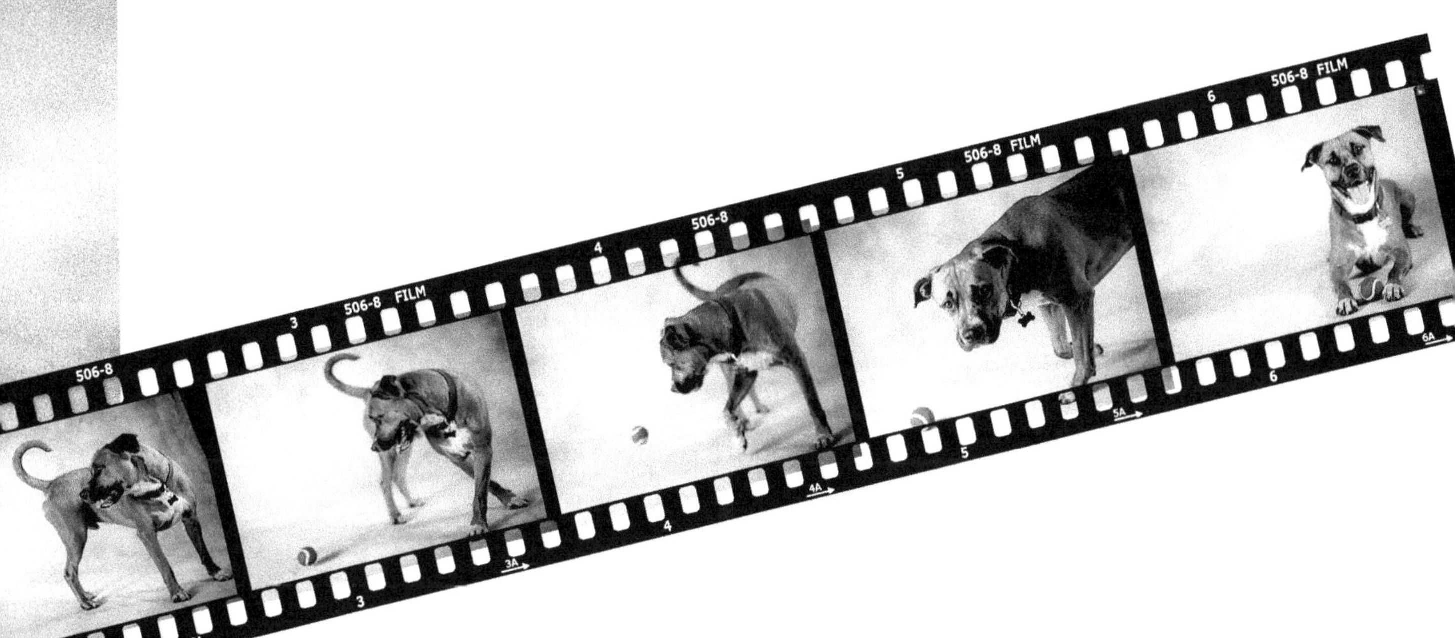

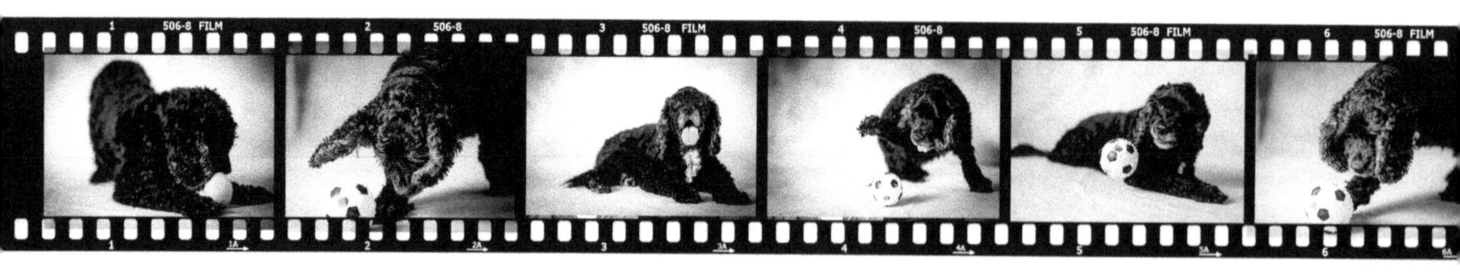

Midnight

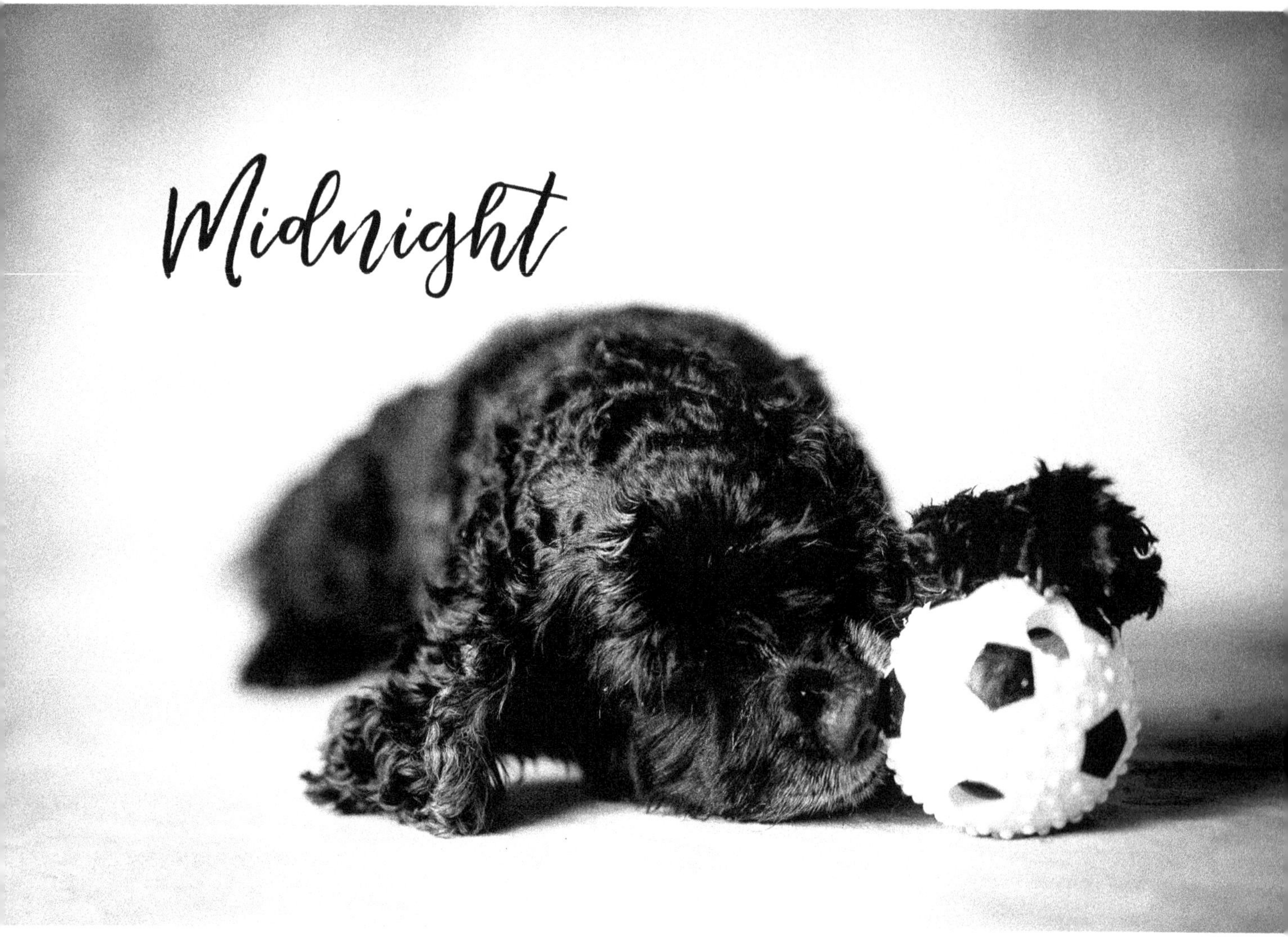

MIDNIGHT found his forever home after his first owner decided not to keep him. The eight-year-old Cocker Spaniel loves his squeaky hot dog and follows his mama everywhere. The worst thing he ever did? He has a tendency to eat tissue boxes--with the tissues still inside. Who knows why? Maybe just because they're there.

MOSES, or Mo, as he is usually called, is a three-year-old Hound/Golden Retriever mix who found his home through the SPCA website. He's a goofy, handsome guy who loves his people and his Kong fiercely--even to the point of protecting the rubber toy from other dogs. His human mama finds it endearing when he drops his Kong on her foot or in her lap when he wants to play. And playing is something he loves to do . . . whether or not his mama is in the mood. Still, who can resist a face like that?

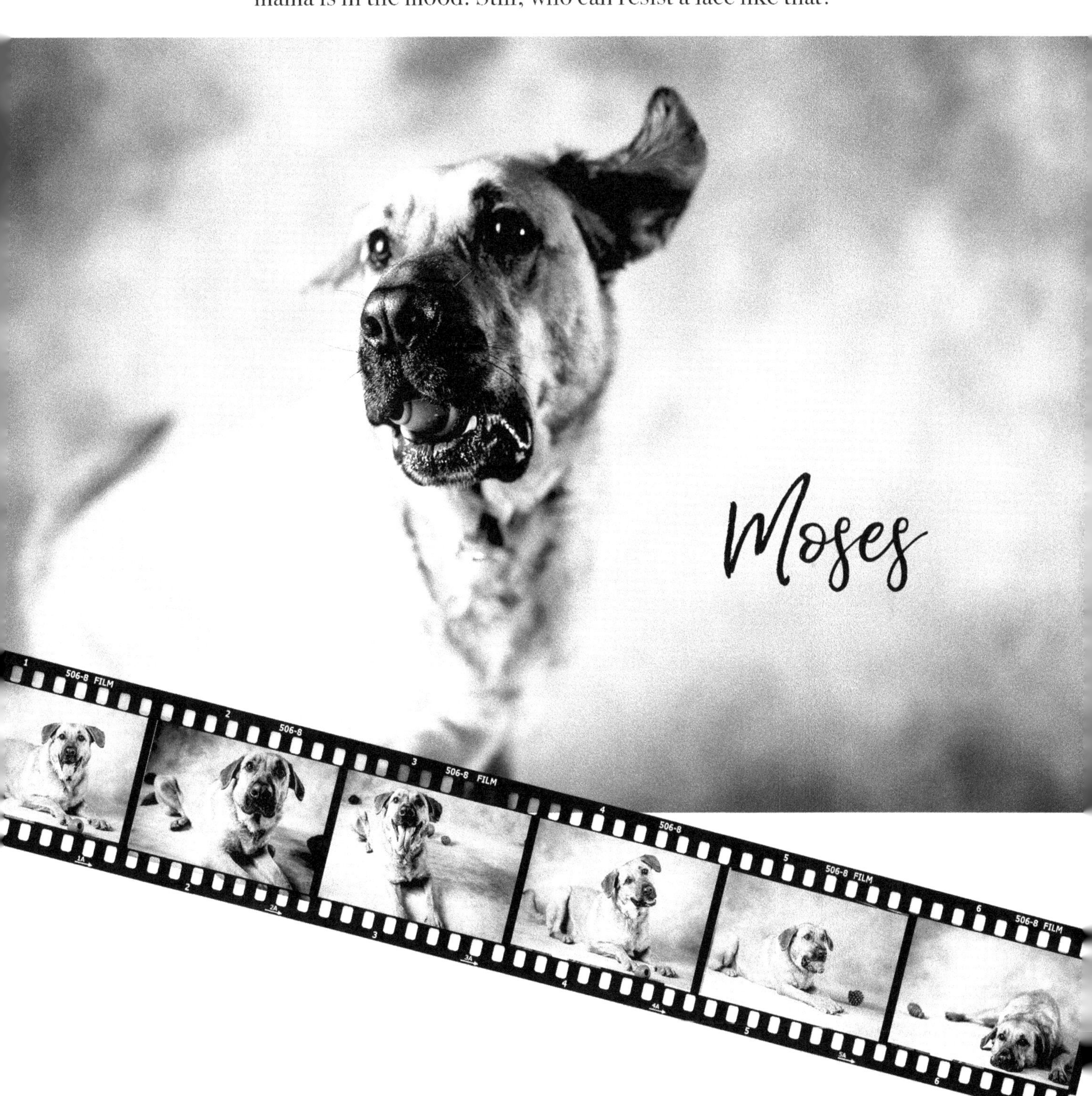

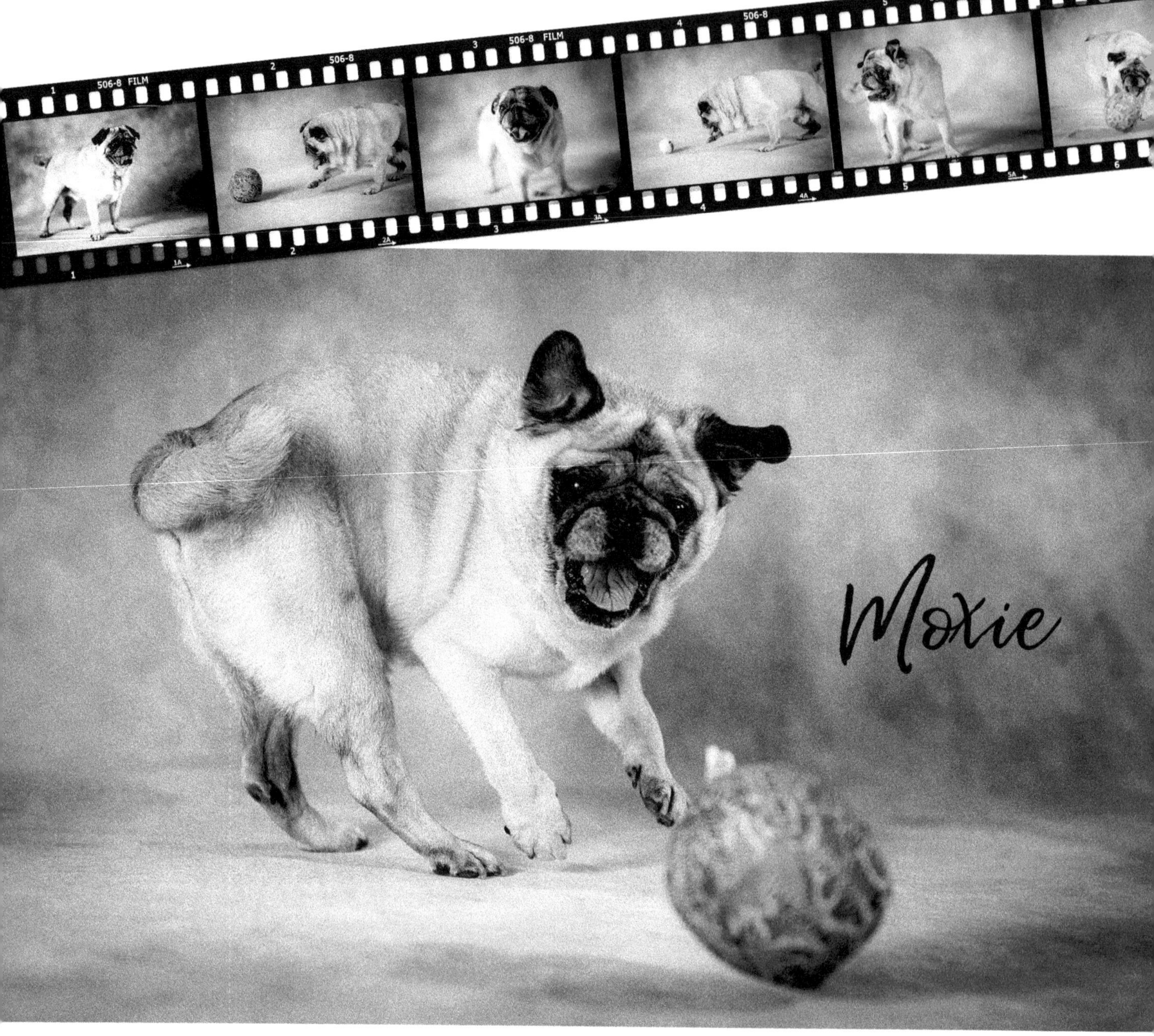

Moxie

It's not always the young, svelte dogs who love balls--meet MOXIE, a thirteen-year-old pug with the usual deep wrinkles and a distinguished white muzzle. Moxie found his forever home through the SPCA where his future mom was volunteering. Moxie's previous owner had surrendered him to the shelter wehn he was eight because they were moving. A volunteer there had just lost her nine-year-old pug to cancer, so shen she saw Moxie, she felt an instant connection. She's sure her first dog, Tortellini, sent Moxie her way, perhaps with the help of an angel or two. Moxie loves kids, and sleeps with a stuffed dog of his own. He's a senior, but he's still going strong . . . because he is cherished.

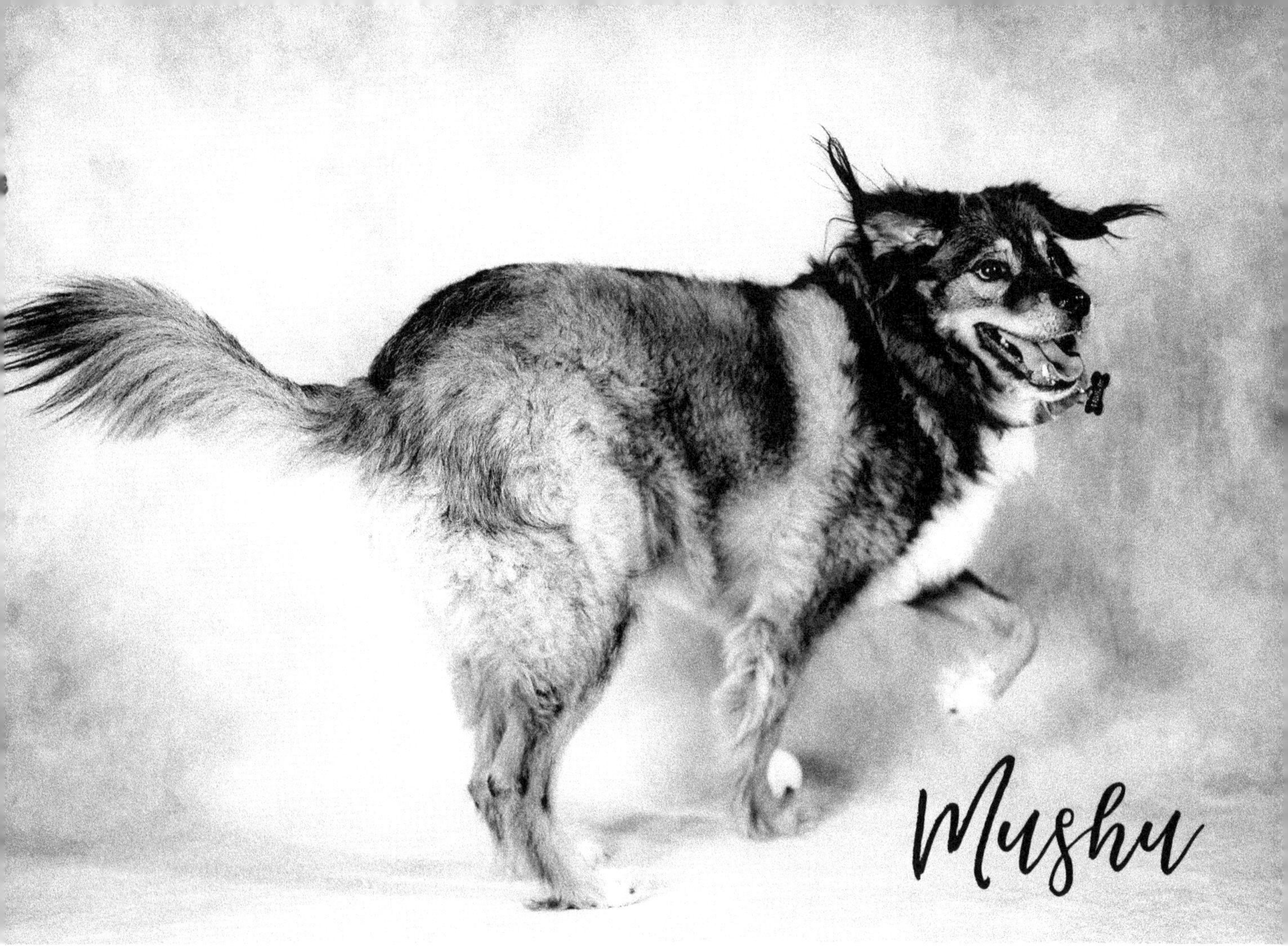

Mushu

MUSHU is a four-year-old St. Bernard mix who loves balls and squeaker toys. He found his forever home through the Humane Socity, and he loves to play and go for walks. His once vice, his mama says, is a tendency to get into the trash, but who can resist food scraps and interesting smells? This boy plays ball with all his heart--tail flagging and fur flying, even on his ears. The kind of dog you want on your team . . . forever.

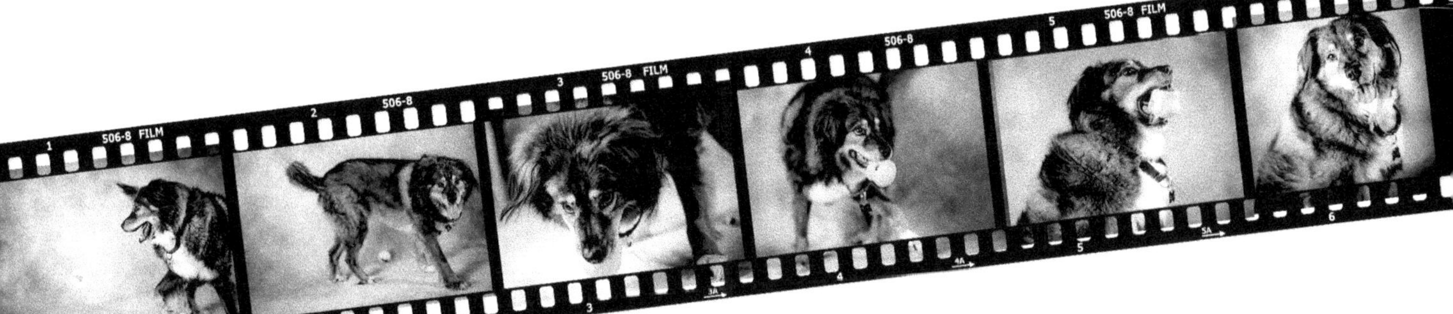

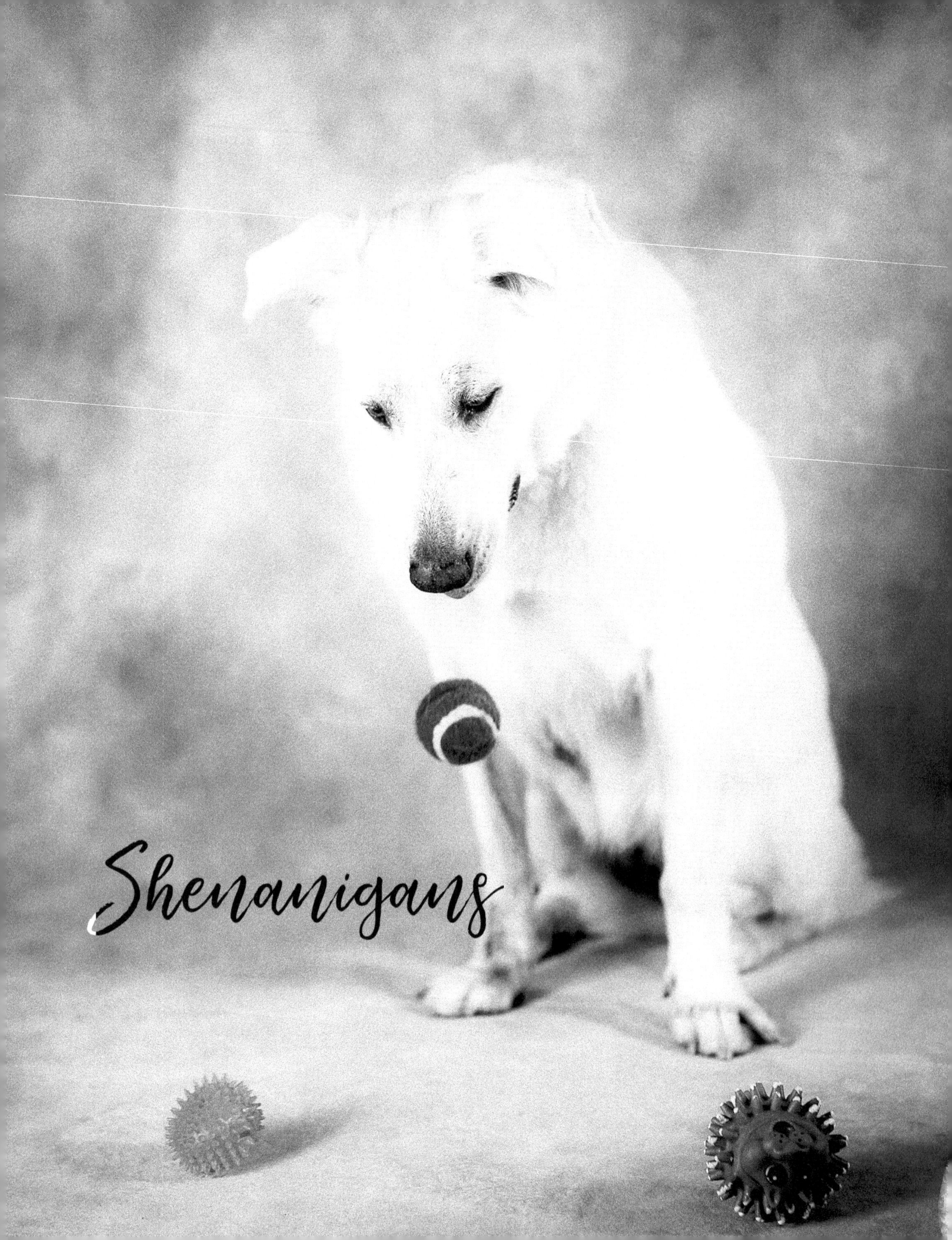

Shenanigans

SHENANIGANS (commonly known as Nan) is a seven-year old Great Pyrenees/Irish wolfhound mix. She came to her forever family through her local SPCA, and, true to her breed, she has found a job to perform at home--she patrols the yard and waits for the opossums that routinely hike along the backyard fence, then she pounds the fence to make the possums fall.

Nan's favorite toy is a squirrel, naturally, and she's very independent. But her mom can always tell when Nan is about to get into trouble--her right ear shoots straight up. Her mom calls it her "mischief meter." True to her nature, Nan is no push-over. She tends to be a little stingy with her kisses, but she does share them with her mom.

Nan wants you to know: Understanding a dog's genetic heritage is an important part of understanding your dog.

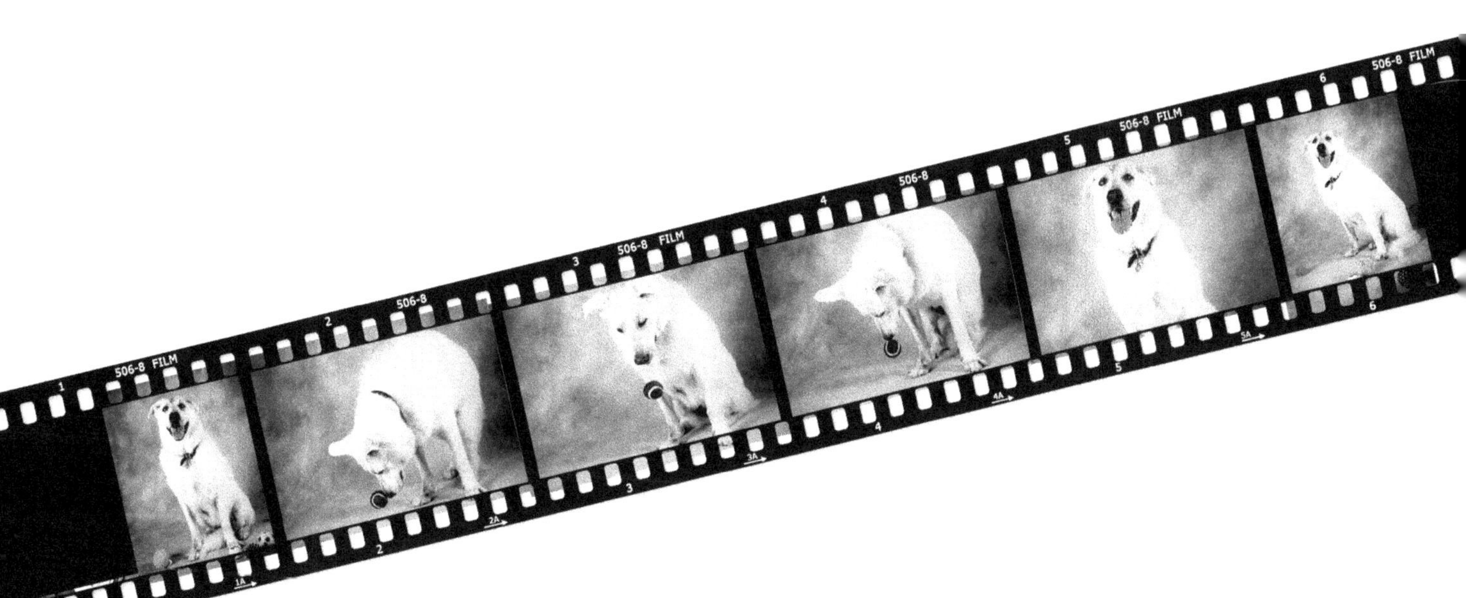

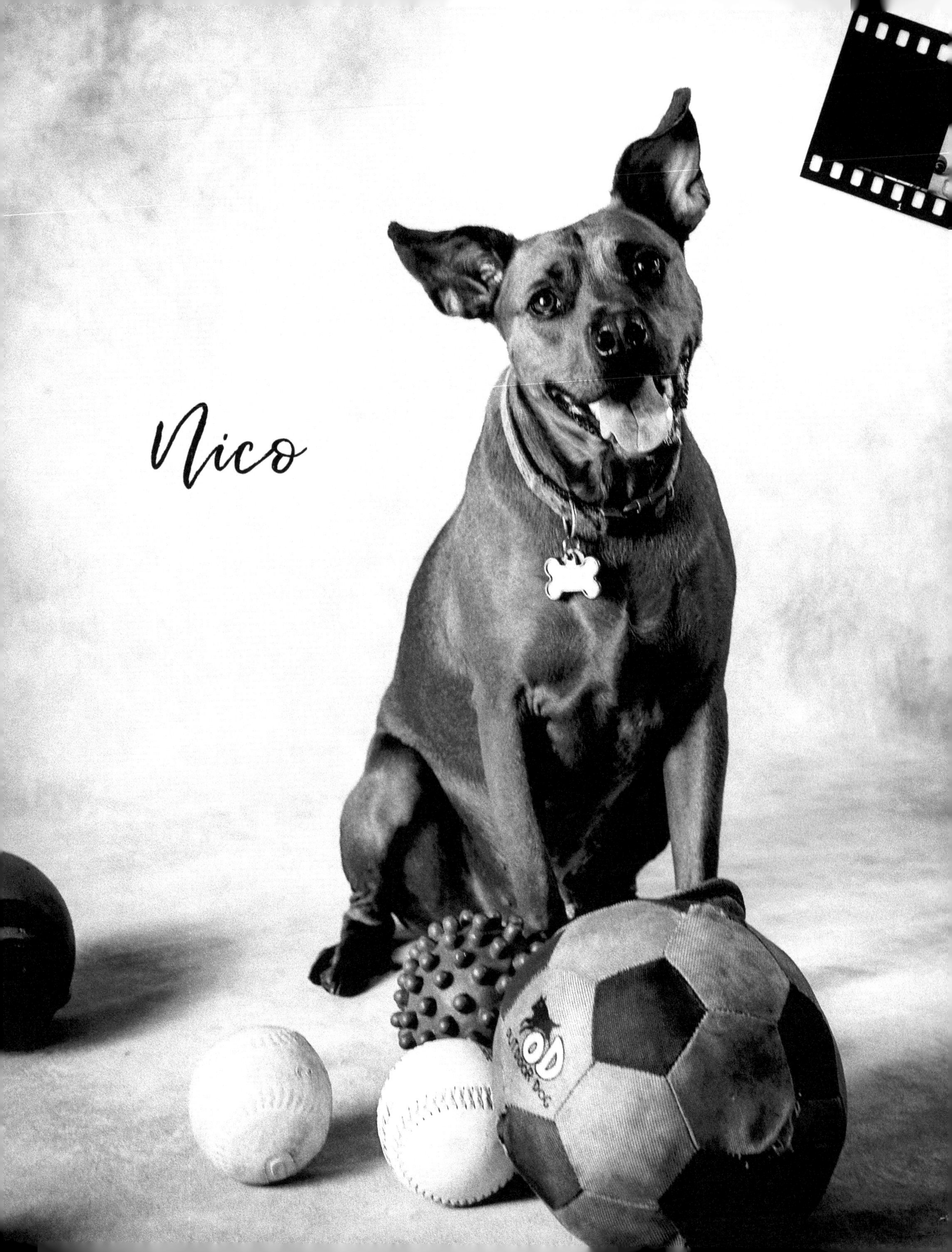
Nico

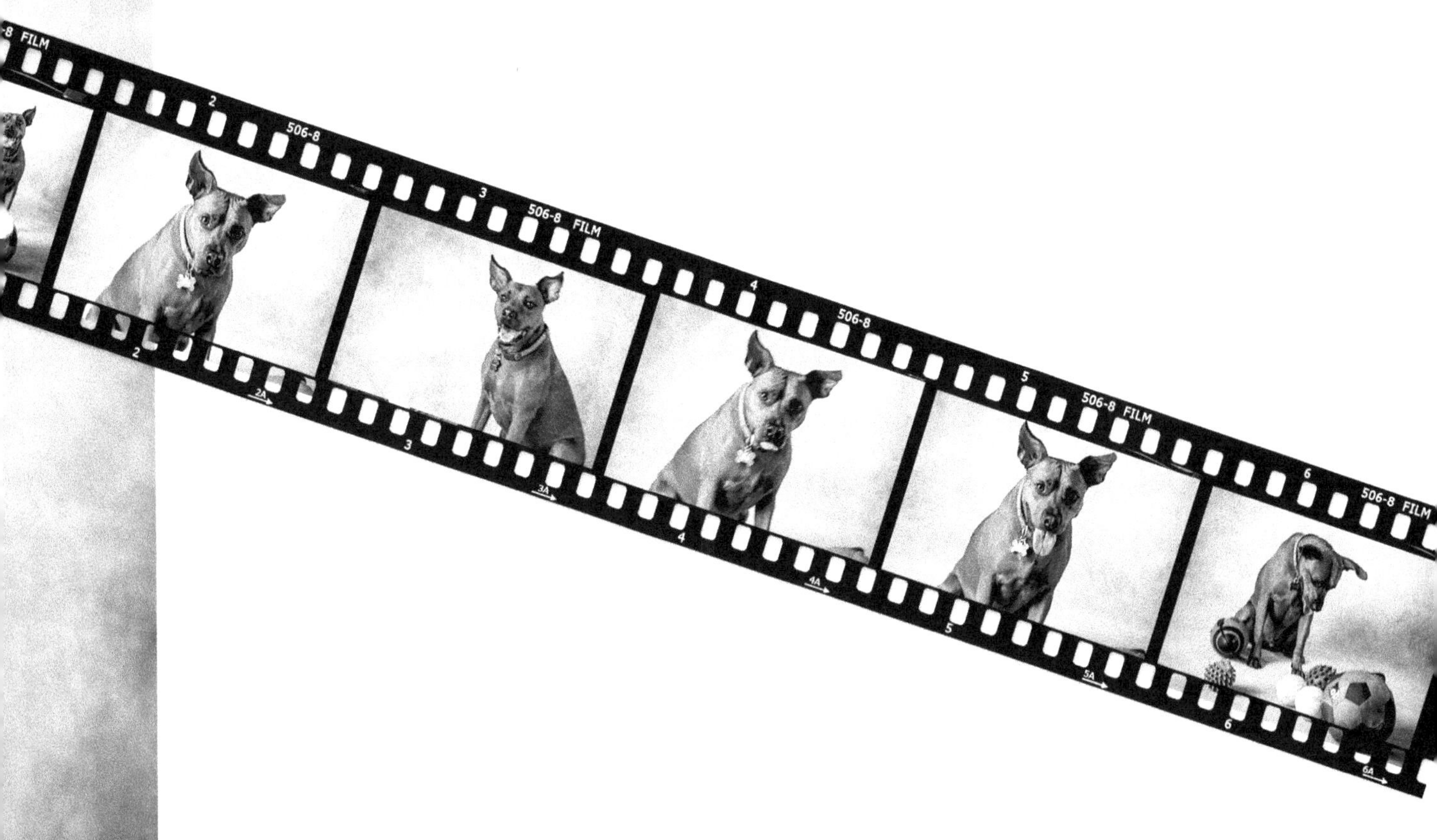

NICO's owners didn't go looking for him--Nico found them. He was a stray, trying to survive on his own, and he saw his future owners at the end of the street. He walked up to them, gave them a doggie smile, and that was that. The three-year-old Boxer mix is a cuddler, and his owner reports that Nico will "cuddle" them to sleep. "He's not big on kisses," his owner says, "but he loves to snuggle and give what we call 'face hugs.' He will shove his face up next to the side of your face, and that's how he wants to sleep."

Though he is affectionate and gentle at the end of the day, he's not without spirit. His favorite toy is "whatever his doggie siblings had first," and he once tore a hole in the new couch. But all is forgiven. Like all of us, Nico had to learn how to exercise good manners at home, but no one ever had to teach this boy how to love.

Nadine

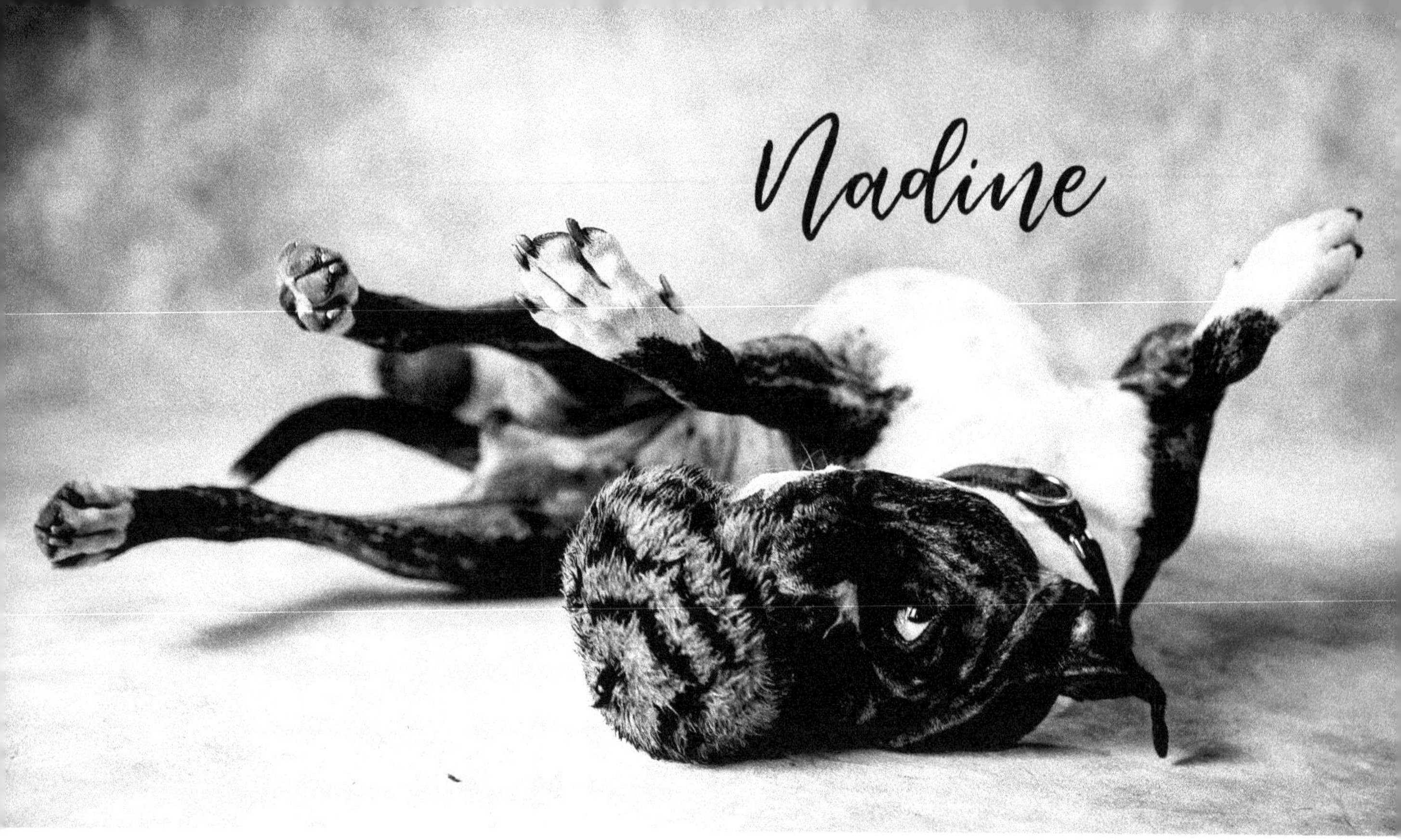

NADINE joined LUCHIA's household about a year ago. Her new dad was walking dogs at the Humane Society when he spotted her--the year-old boxer mix caught his eye because he had loved a boxer before. He hesitated before adopting her--after all, he already had a dog at home--but after sitting with her in her kennel for an hour, he decided she would be a good addition to the family. And she was. She gets along famously with her doggie sister and kisses her dad awake every morning. Once she got into the food bag, ate her fill, and upchucked four times . . . a hard lesson to learn, but now she knows she's not going to starve. She is home.

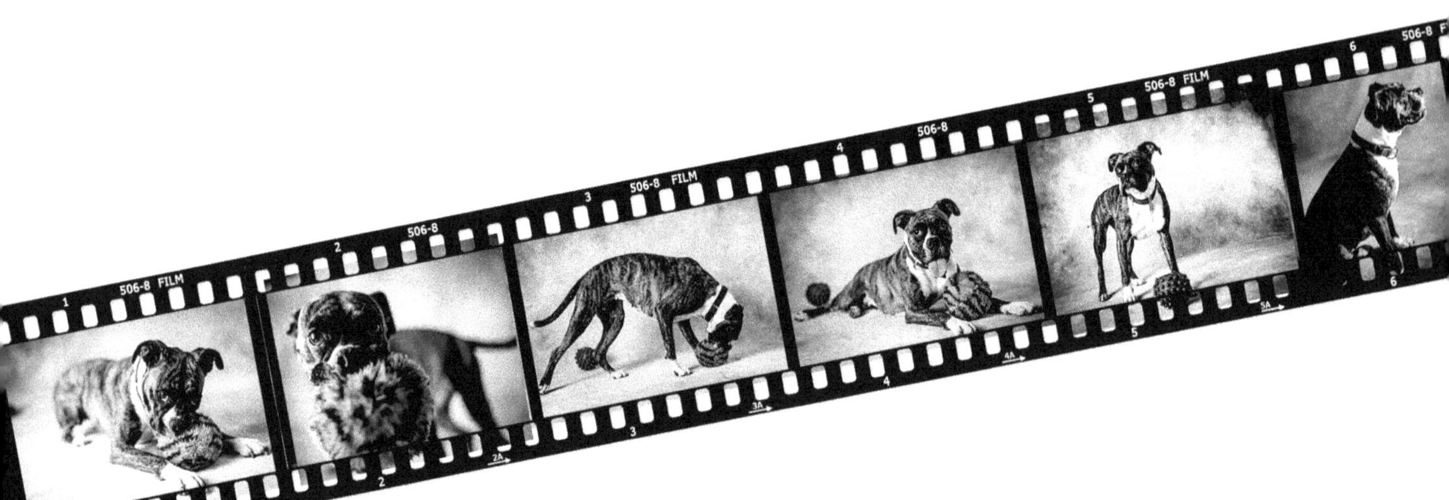

NORMAN, a four-year-old mixed breed, has a favorite toy--a red ball that can hold treats. In fact, it's fair to say that the ball is only of middling interest *until* it holds treats. Norman's human parents discovered him while browsing available animals in the small dog section--and Norman is no longer a small dog. But he's loved, and his humans say they like nothing better than when he puts his head in their laps and looks up at them with his beautiful, grateful eyes. He's the best thing they ever found online.

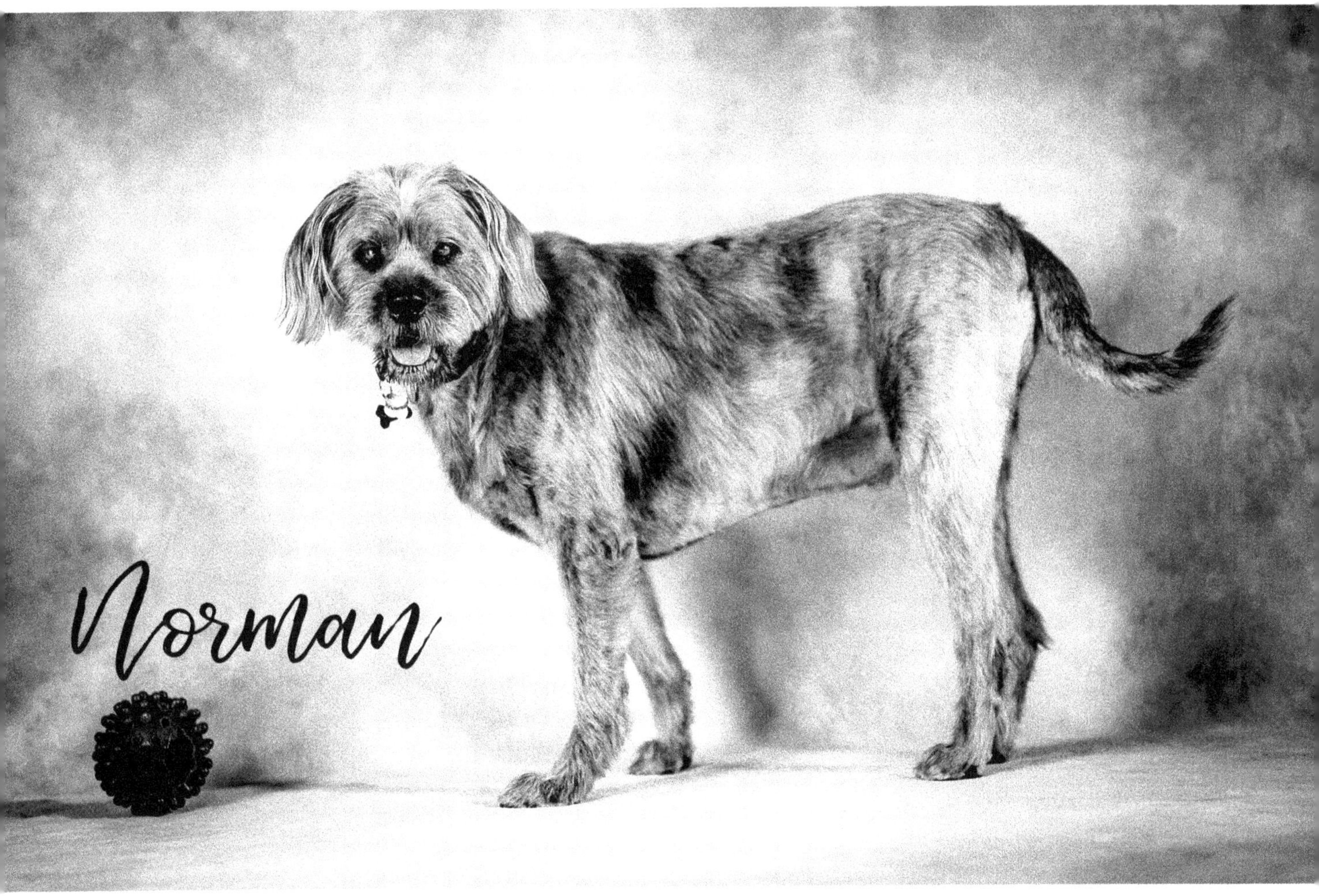

Norman

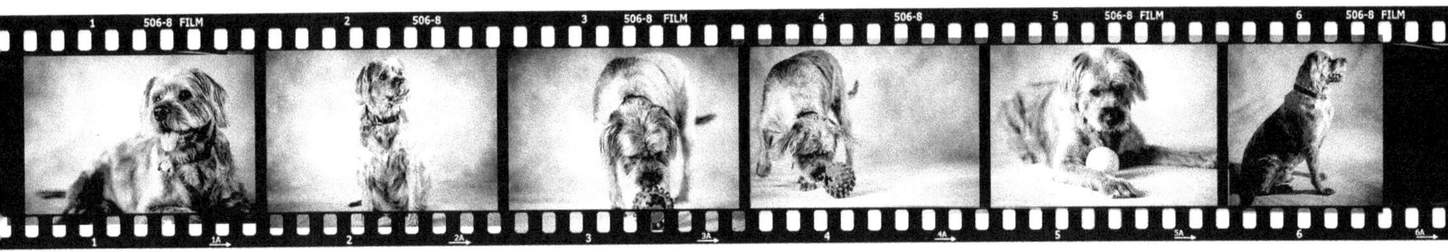

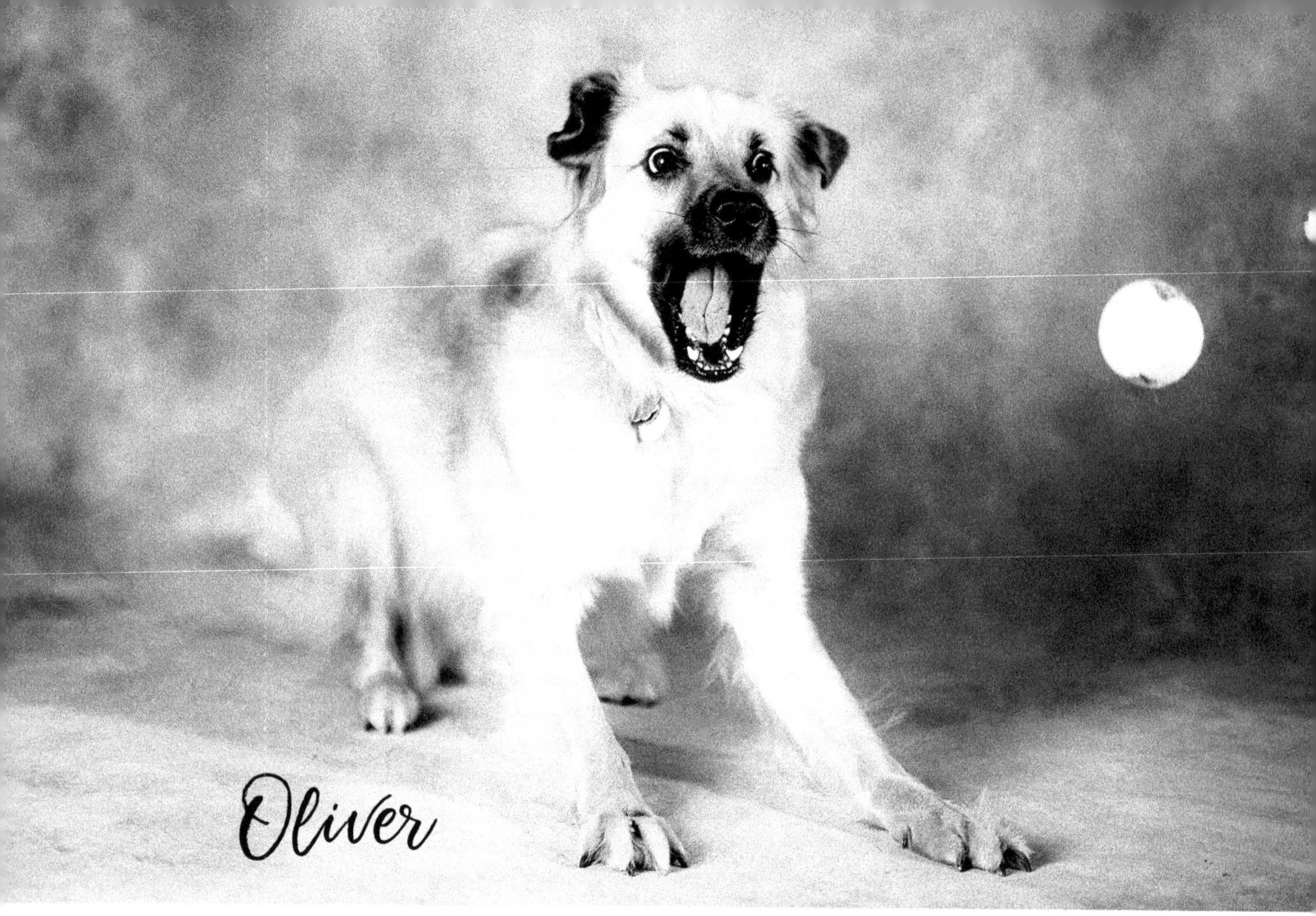

Oliver

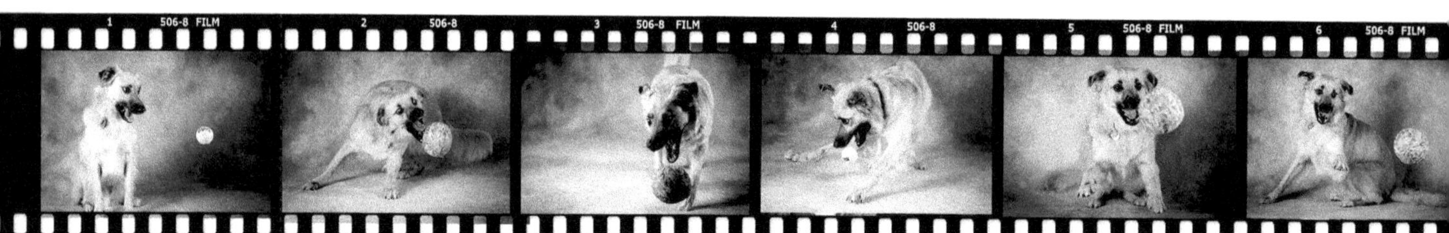

OLIVER's mom was looking through shelter dog photos on a county shelter's website and she saw Oliver. Who wouldn't fall in love with a face like his? The five or six-year-old dog is a beautiful blend of Australian Shepherd, Catahoula Leopard dog, and mutt. The most endearing thing he does is cross his front paws and "act like a dork," but he loves his stuffed animals, his humans, and his canine siblings.

And boy, can this boy play ball!

You gotta love his spirit.

Ollie

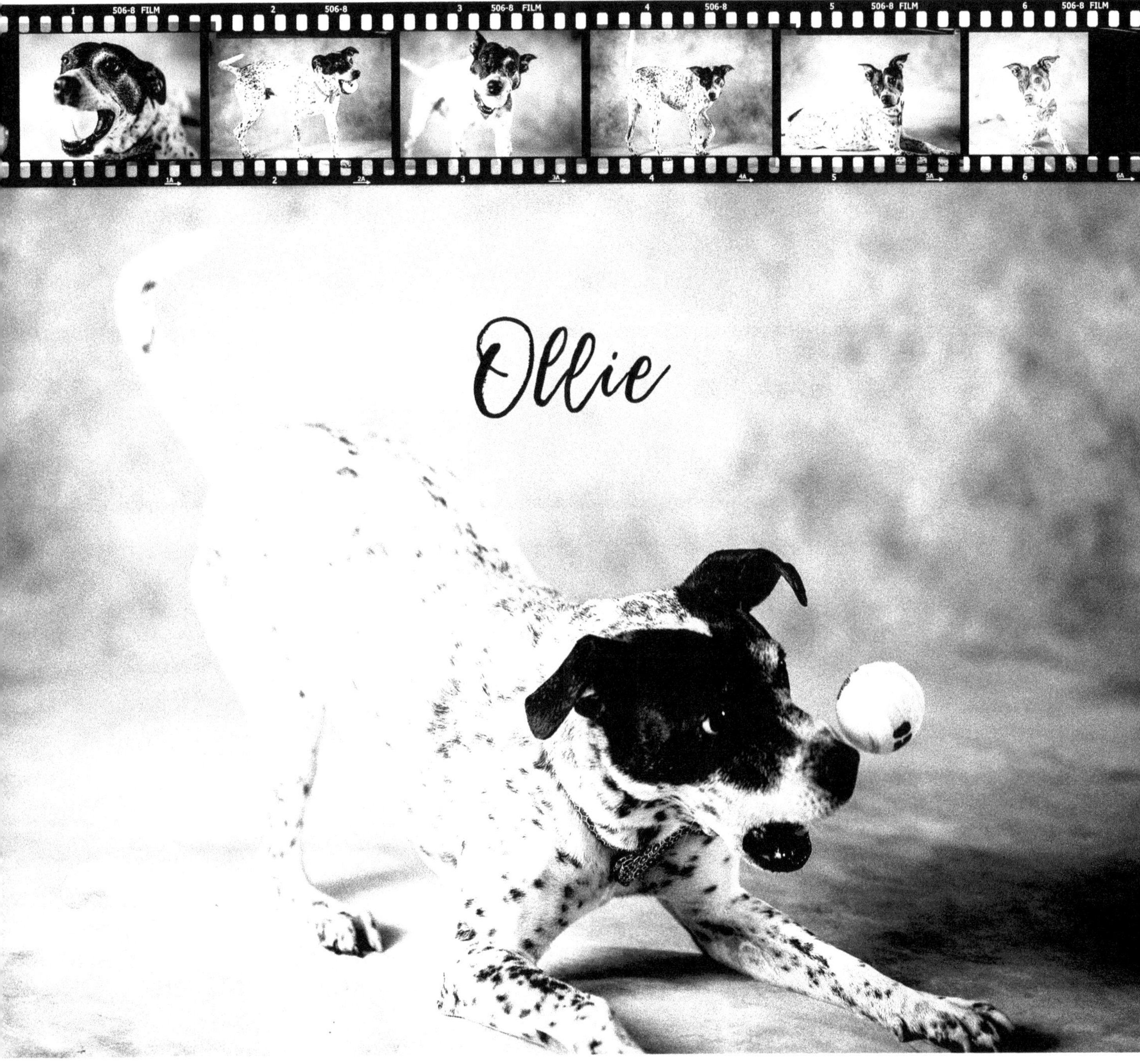

OLLIE's Mom went looking for him when she moved to a new town by herself. She wanted a companion, and through the efforts of a rescue she found Ollie, a Pointer/Pit mix. Ollie is seven years old, and is a real ball-playing dog . . . but truthfully, he likes to play with sticks just as much. He's a huge cuddler, says his mom, though he is prone to mischief. Once he climbed a pallet board to jump a six foot fence and landed in a muddy canal.

But with his good looks and a permanent superhero mask, it's good to know Ollie can leap tall fences in a single bound.

Petite PEARL, according to her mom, is a perfect princess. Her human owner found the now-five year old Chihuahua mix at a rescue, and they've been bonded ever since. Pearl loves to lick--she's always licking, but to her mama, those licks are nothing but "Pearl kisses." She can be a bit high-strung--you would be, too, if you were her size--so she is always with her bonded companion dog, Spidey Wheels.

It's nice to go through life with a friend by your side.

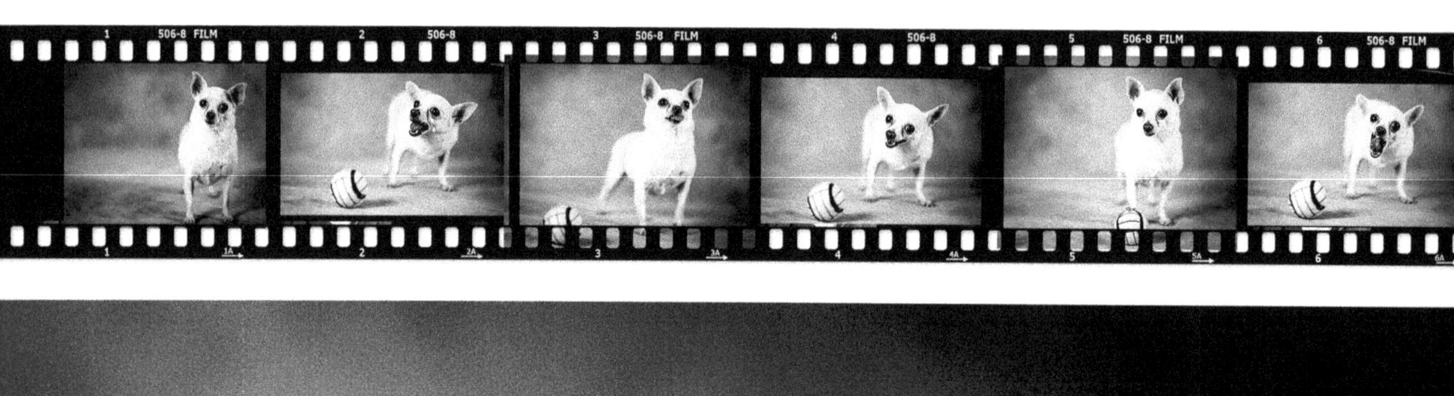

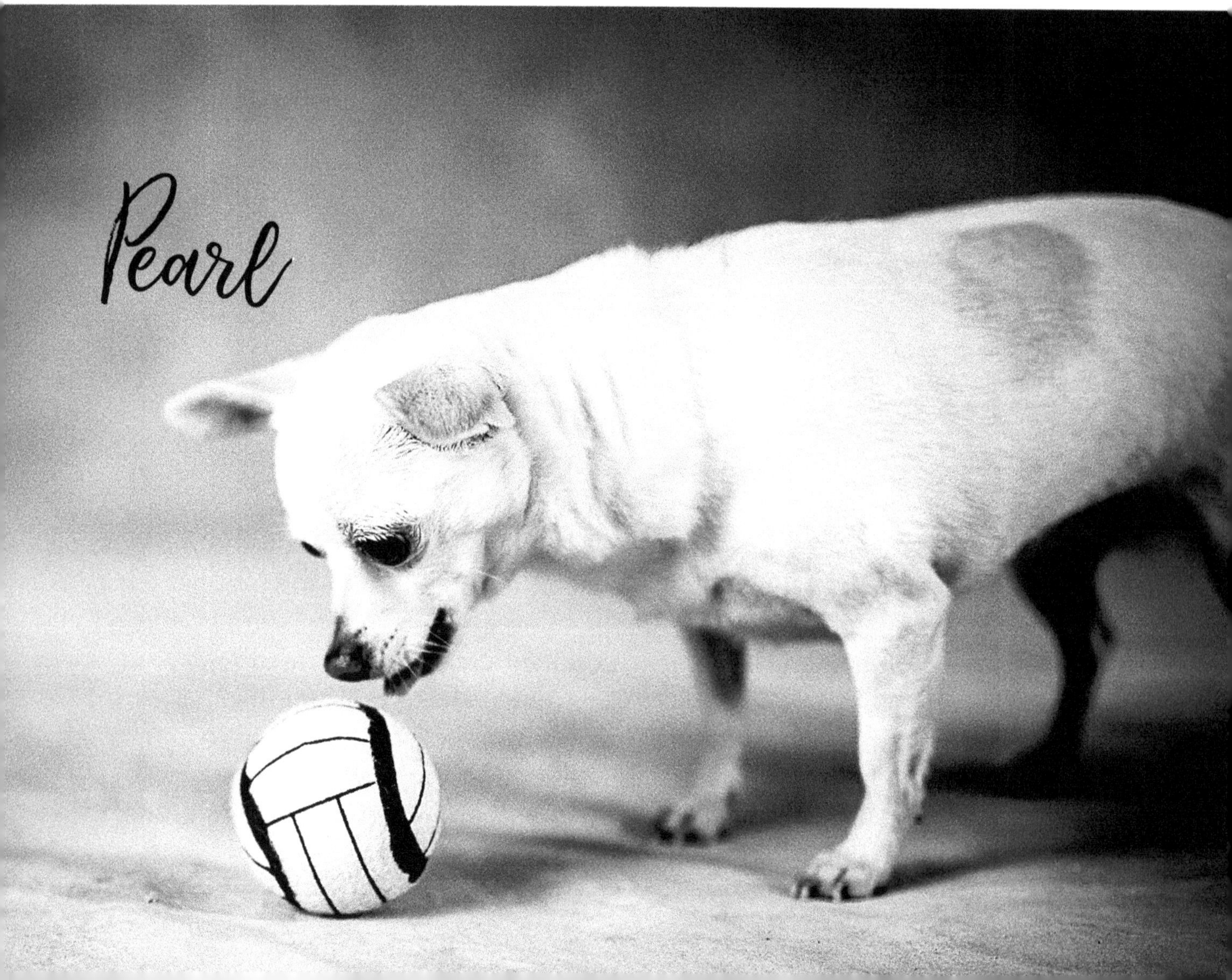

Pearl

PENNY, a two-year-old Belgian Malinois/Basset Hound mix, had a hard start in life. She was living in Miami when she was hit by a car. The Miami animal shelter was about to euthanize the injured dog when PAWS rescue stepped up. The founder of PAWS signed Penny out of the shelter, and that night the dog curled up and "spooned" her new human companion, completely trusting, completely giving her affection and loyalty. They've been together ever since.

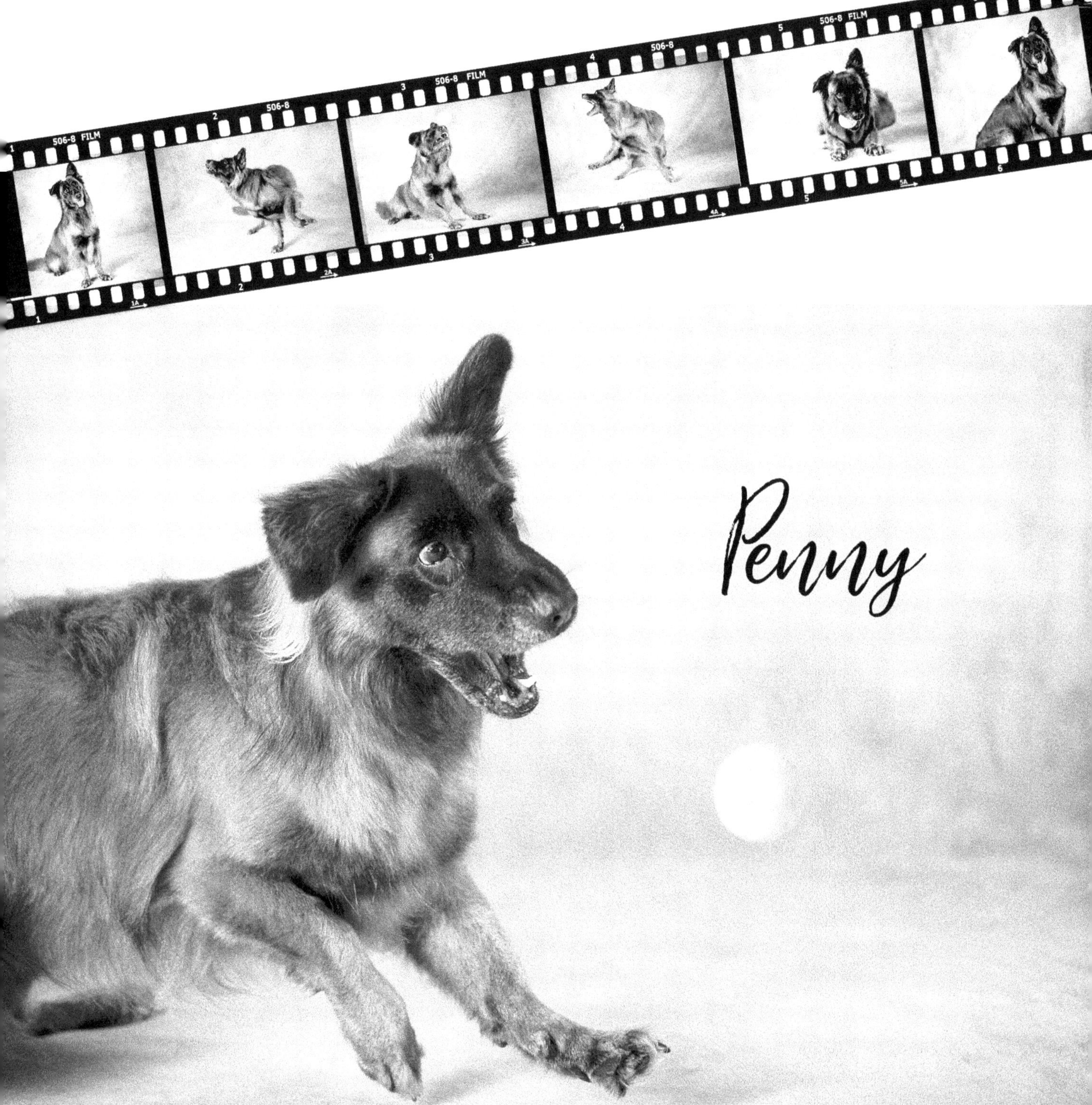

POOH and ROO are fourteen-week-old miniature Poodles--and brothers. They love to play with balls, though they seem to think that playing keep-away-from-your-brother is the *real* name of the game. These puppies love rawhide chew toys and Roo loves to fall asleep in his human mama's arms. Pooh loves to nuzzle and give kisses. The worst thing they do? Pooh Bear is the overbearing pup, and can bite his brother to the point of real pain. Roo's only fault is that he is too shy.

Neither pup could be any cuter.

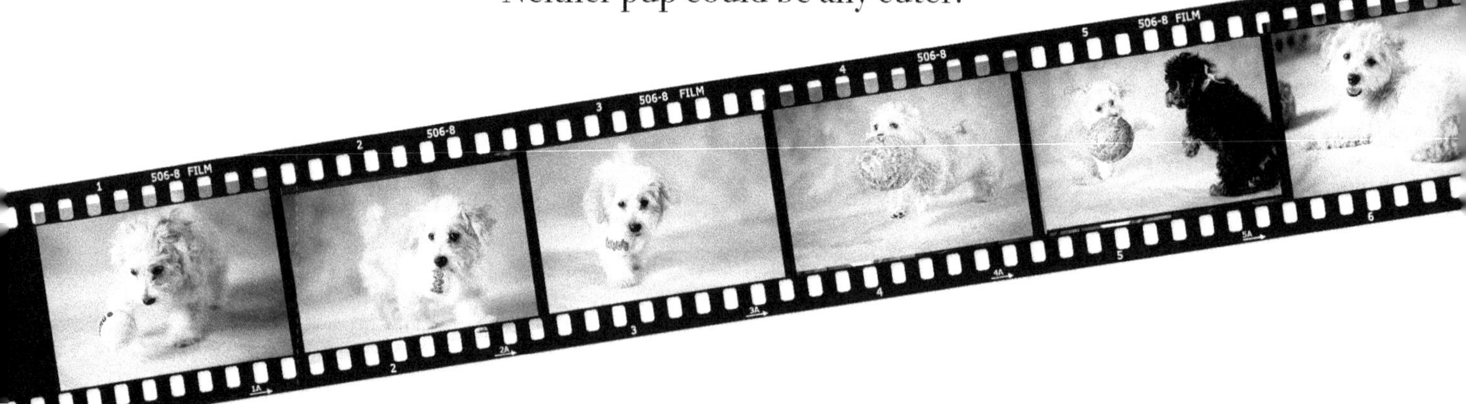

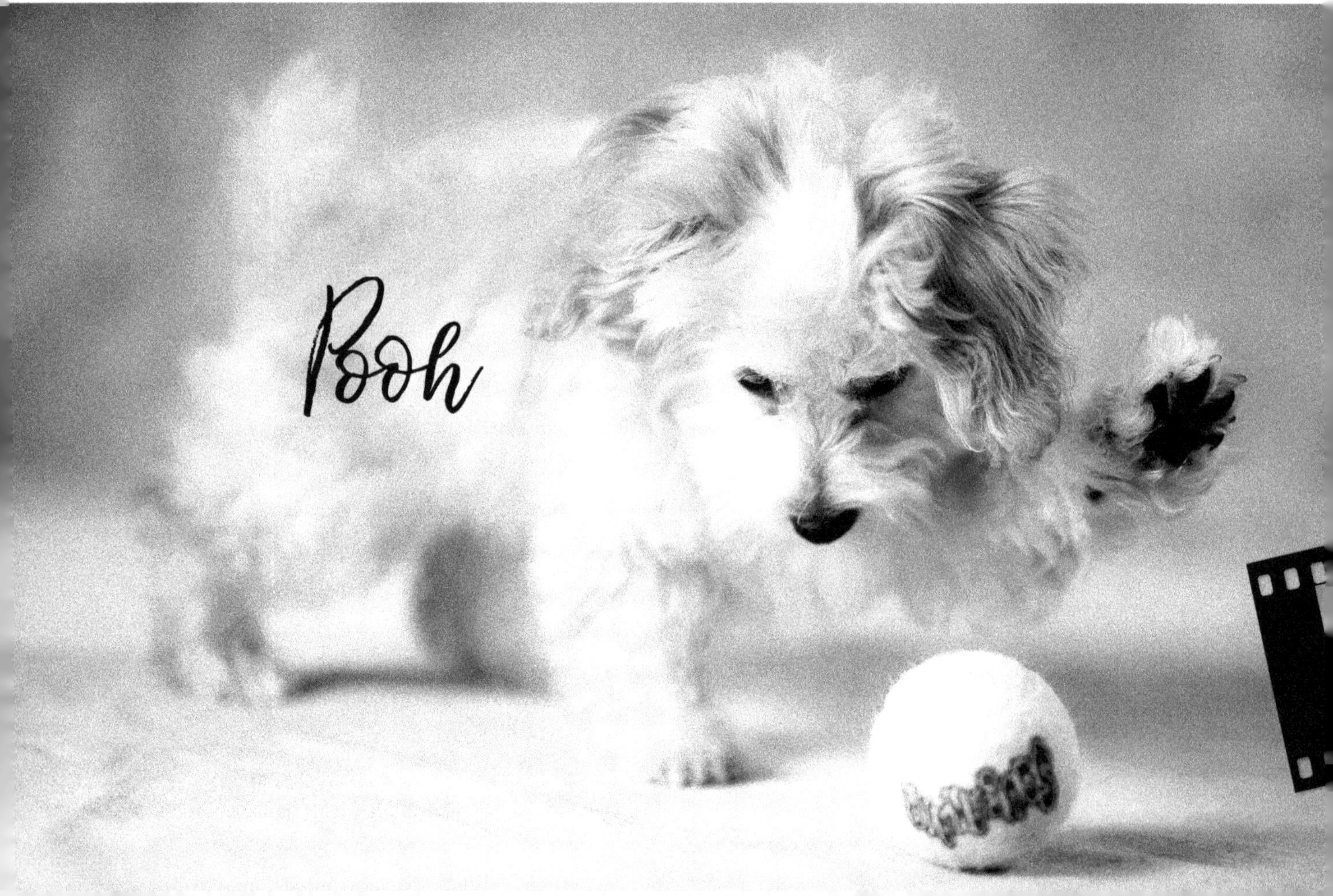

Pooh

Roo

506-8 FILM
1
1A
2
506-8
2A
3
506-8 FILM
3A
4
506-8
4A
5
506-8 FILM
5A
6
506-8 FILM

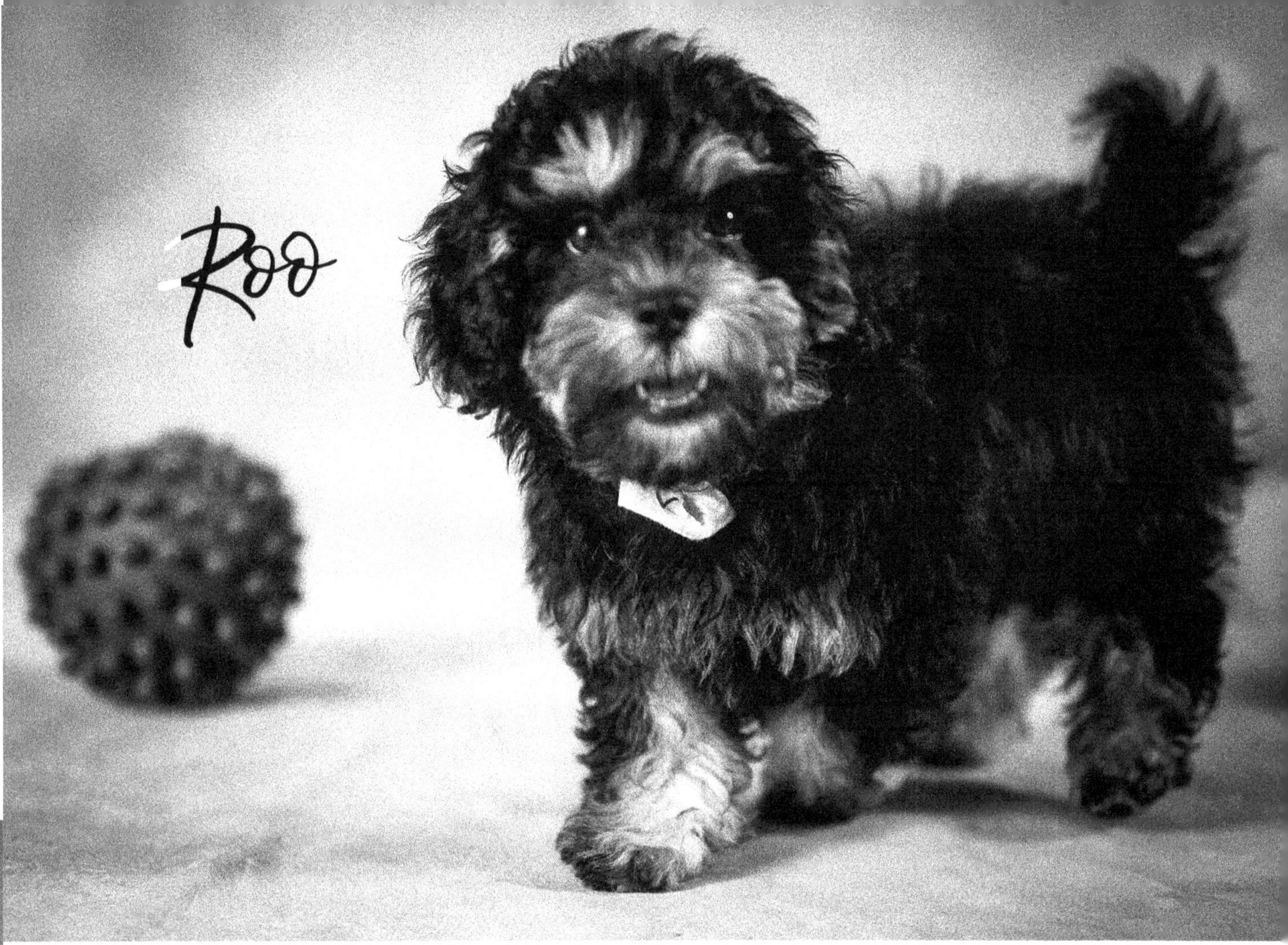

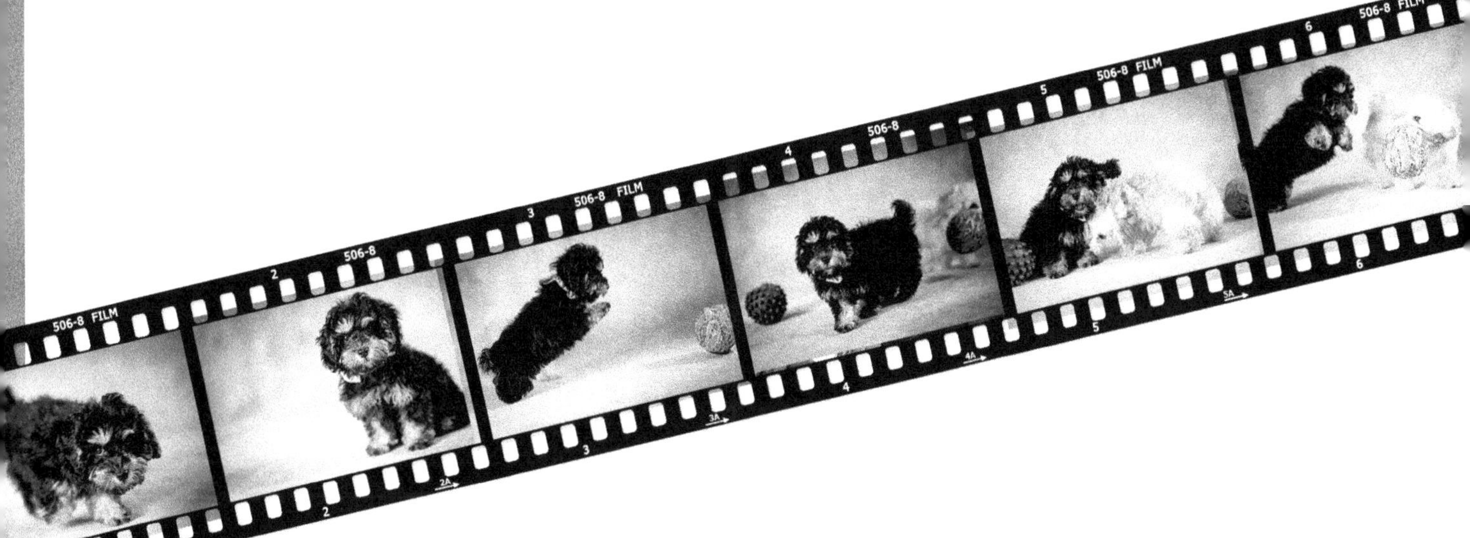

If POOLAK has a unique, exotic air, it's because she's not the usual dog you meet in downtown USA. Poolak is a four year old Saluki/Shepherd mix who was found as a puppy in Tehran, Iran, so she has come a long way since puppyhood. Her favorite toy is bones, and her favorite attitude is "princess." The worst thing she's ever done, says her mom, "is take breakable dishes off the counter, break them, and then eat the contents." Maybe the princess has a thing for fine china.

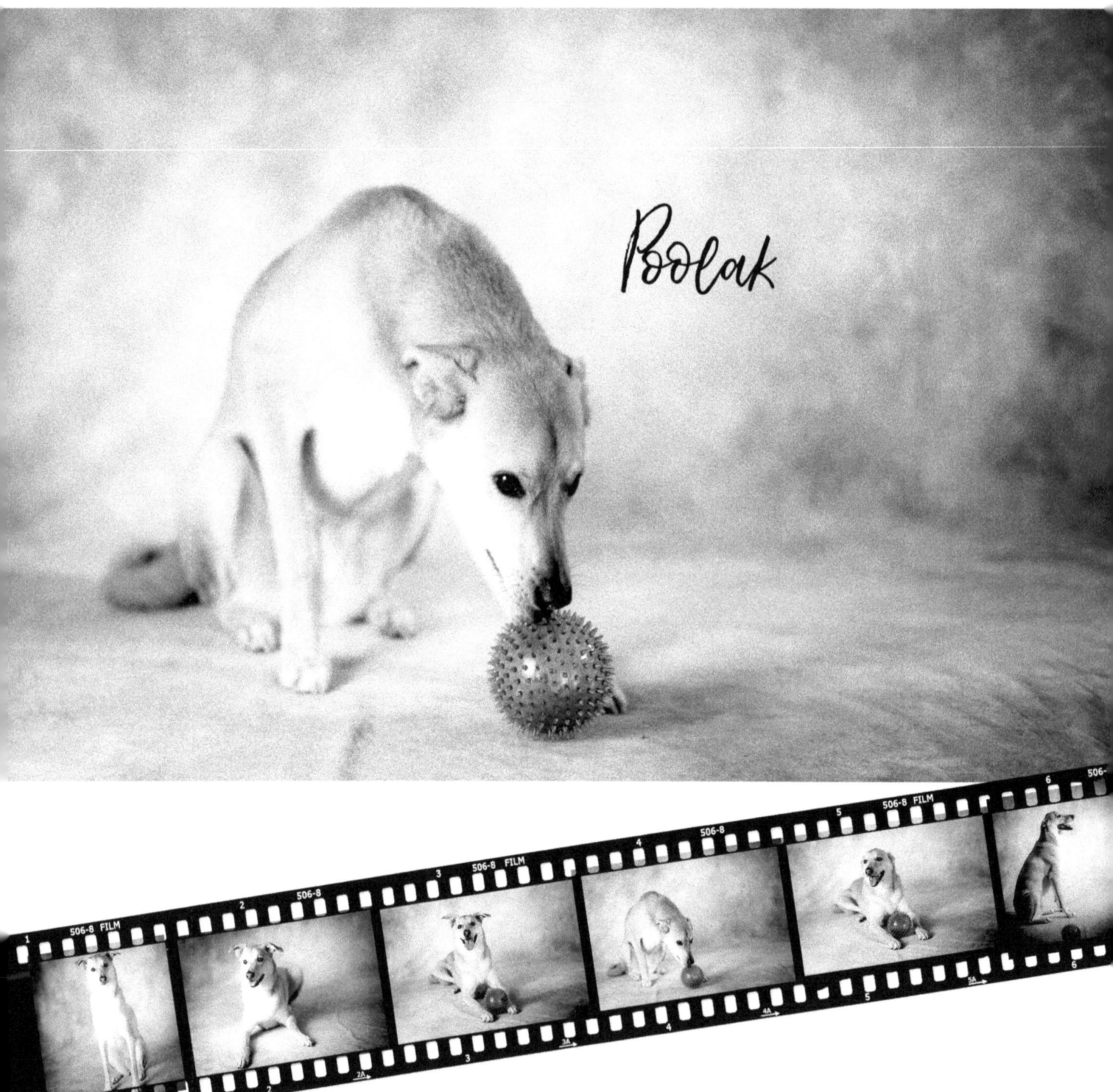

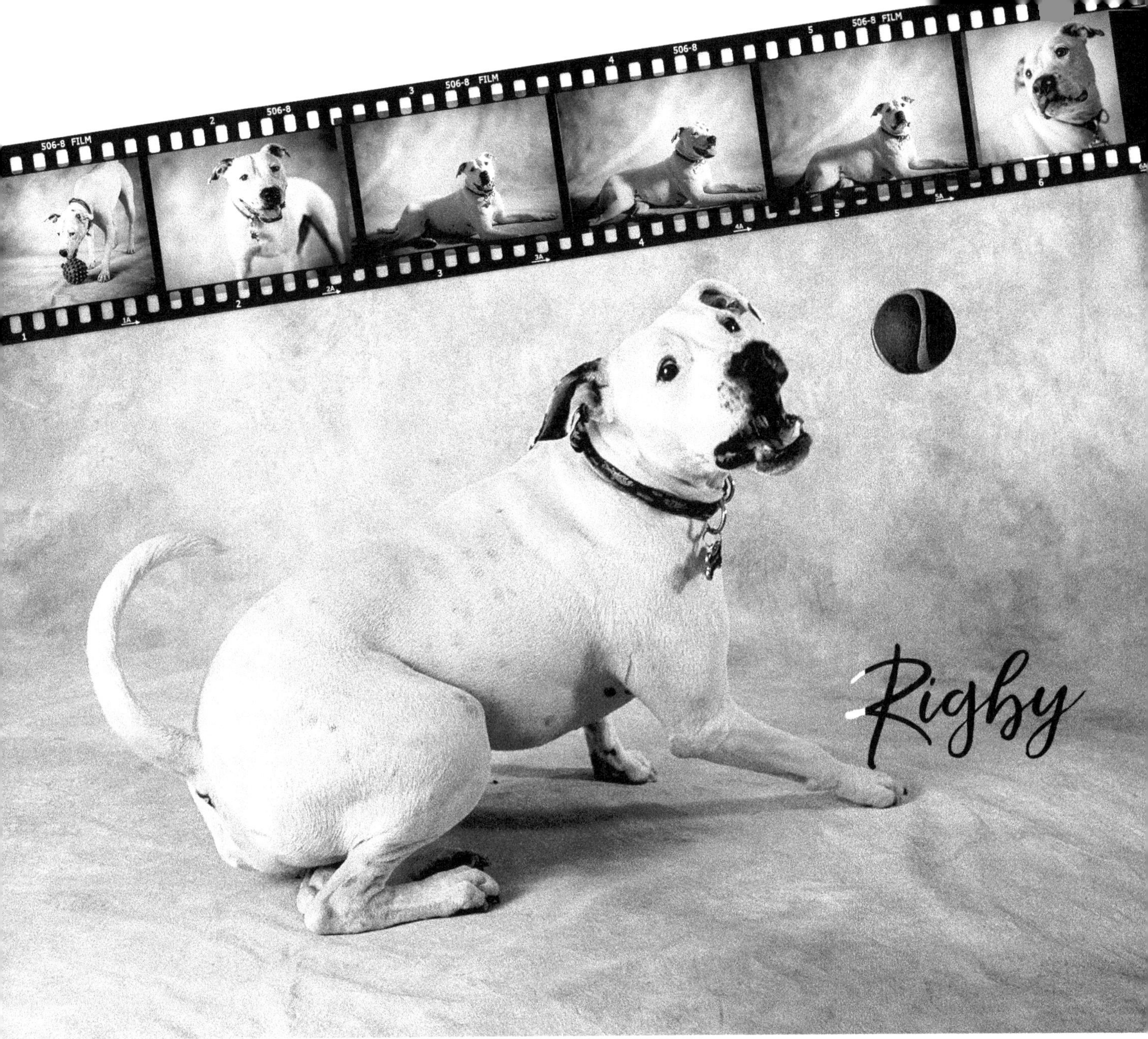

RIGBY is an 18-month-old Bully mix who came to his family through PAWS rescue. His settling-in period was memorable--in three days, he ate three TV remotes, an ottoman, and the couch. After that, he seemed to realize that chewing was better applied to dog food and treats. His favorite toy is his bed, and his favorite friend is his doggie sibling, Cardi. And balls, of course. Rigby loves to play ball . . .
when he's not sniffing around for the TV remote.

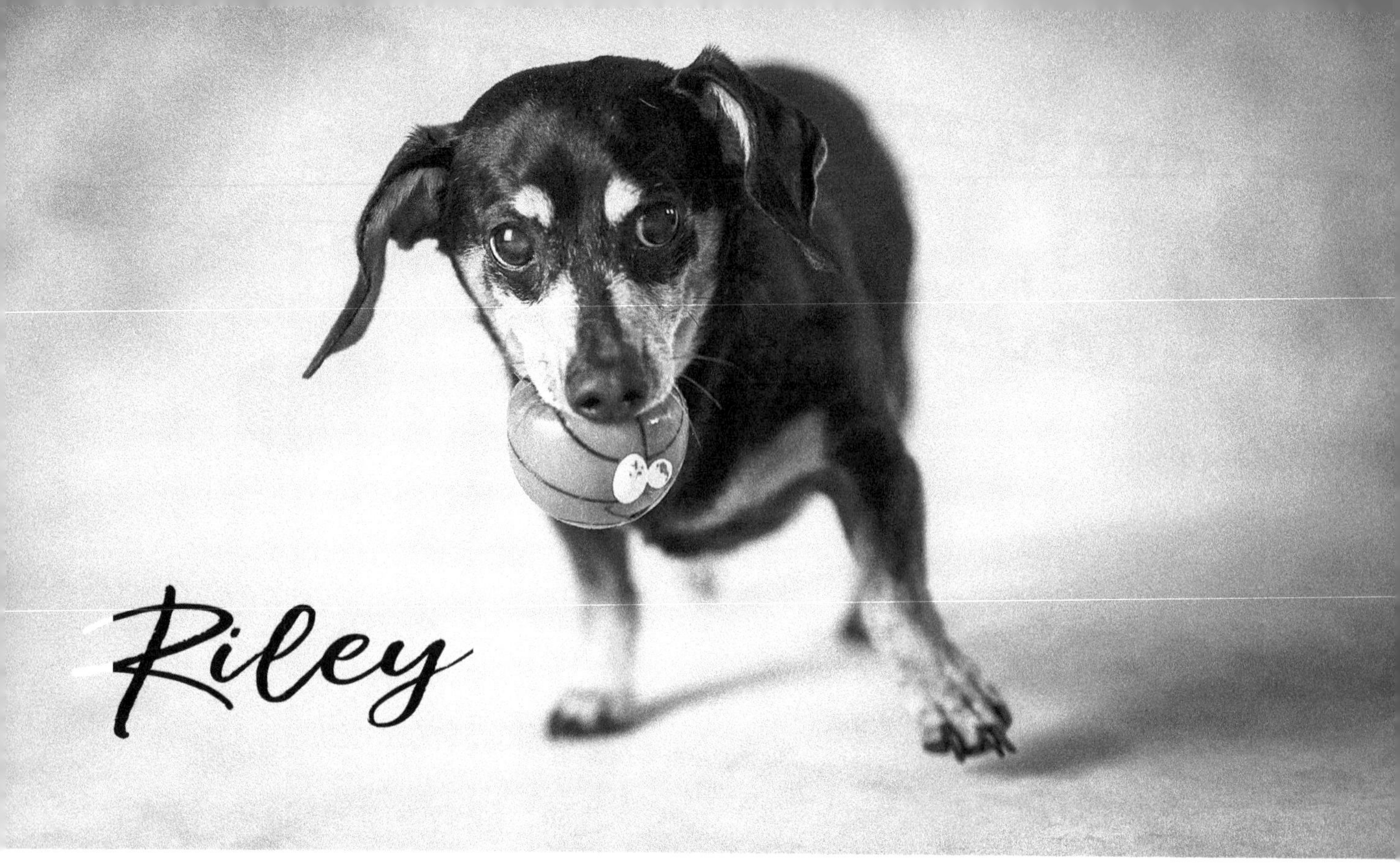

Riley

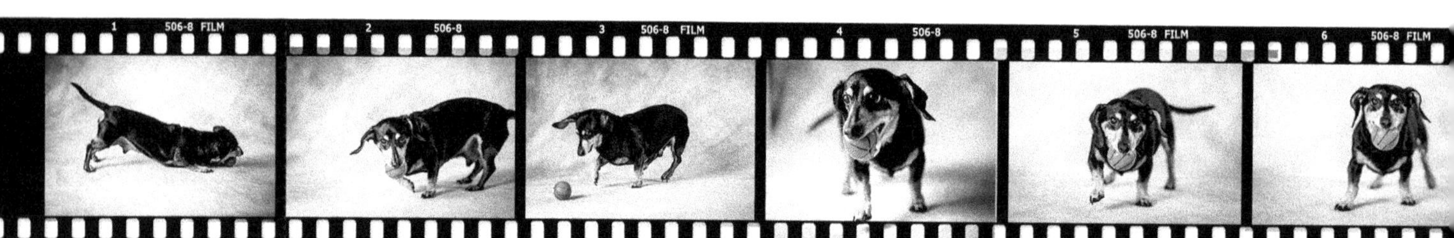

RILEY is a sixteen-year-old Dachshund who came with his own ball. A red ball, well-suited for his size, and his favorite possession in all the world. His human parents took great care of his little red ball, but one day it disappeared. They looked everywhere--under beds, chairs, in corners, outside--and finally gave up and bought Riley a new little red ball. Then one day his mom checked a basket of tomatoes in the fridge--and there, beautifully camouflaged, was Riley's red ball!

Riley is a smart little guy--when he wants to play and his humans are busy, he will hide his red ball under furniture and then bark continuously until they get it out for him--and once it's out, he reasons, why not play fetch? This little guy never tires of chasing his ball and bringing it right back, scooting it forward with his nose until it's within reach for his playmate. Gotta love this guy!

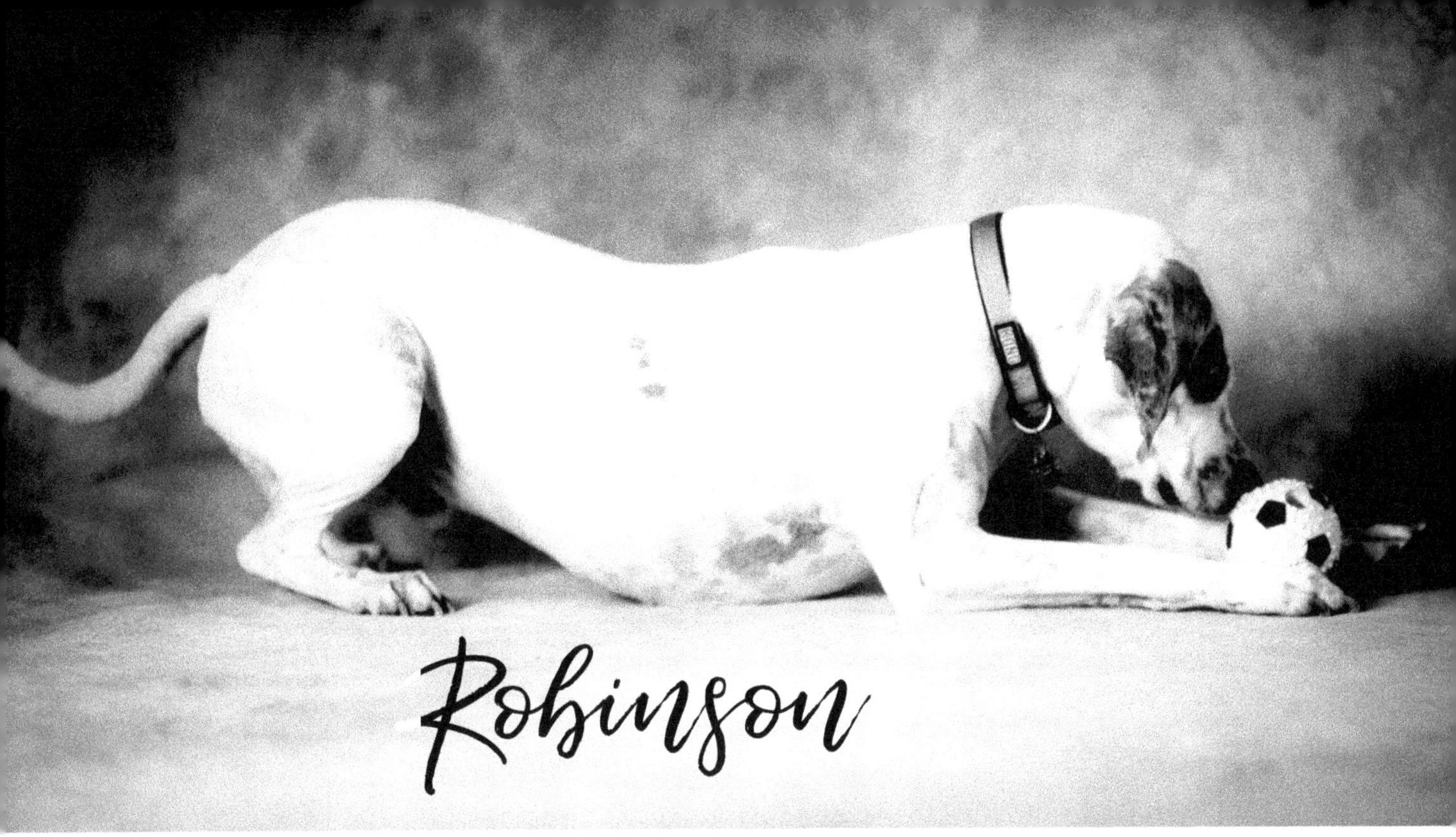

Robinson

ROBINSON, now known as ROB, was about to be euthanized when PAWS Rescue pulled him from a county shelter. The Treeing Walker Coonhound was discovered in horrible condition--extremely emaciated, covered with fleas and tics, with two broken front legs, and buckshot in his hindquarters. PAWS supporters raised money for his medical treatment, and his foster mom, who was also mom to Mila, thought the two dogs would be good for each other. She adopted him on Christmas Eve.

Rob has come a long way since being adopted. Though still a bit fearful during storms, he loves his new family and loves earning treats--especially when they are tucked inside a ball. While his sister, Mila, loves to give kisses, Rob is one of those rare dogs who loves to give hugs. The sweet boy feels secure, not threatened, when he's encircled by loving arms.

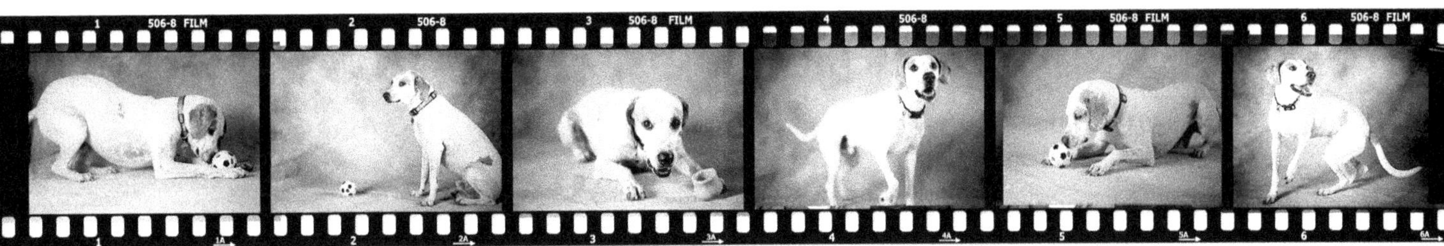

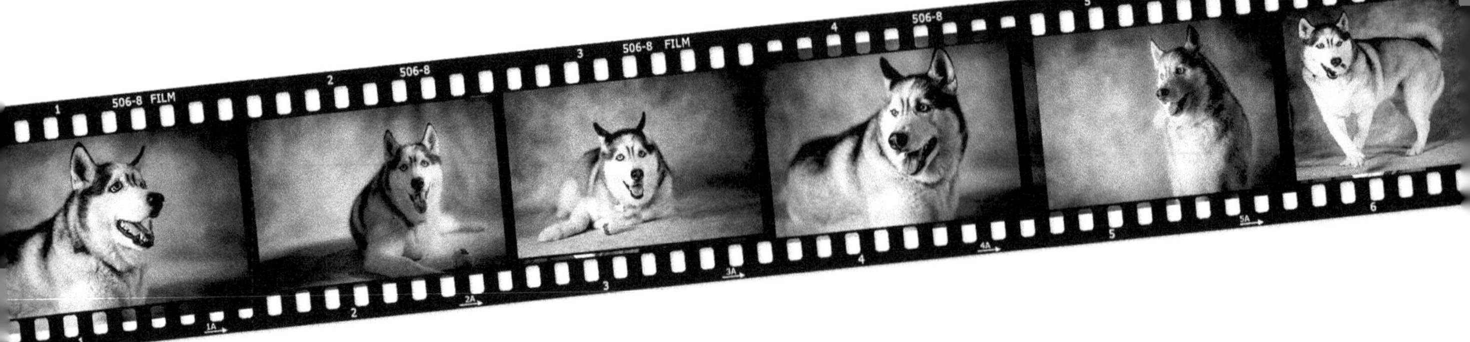

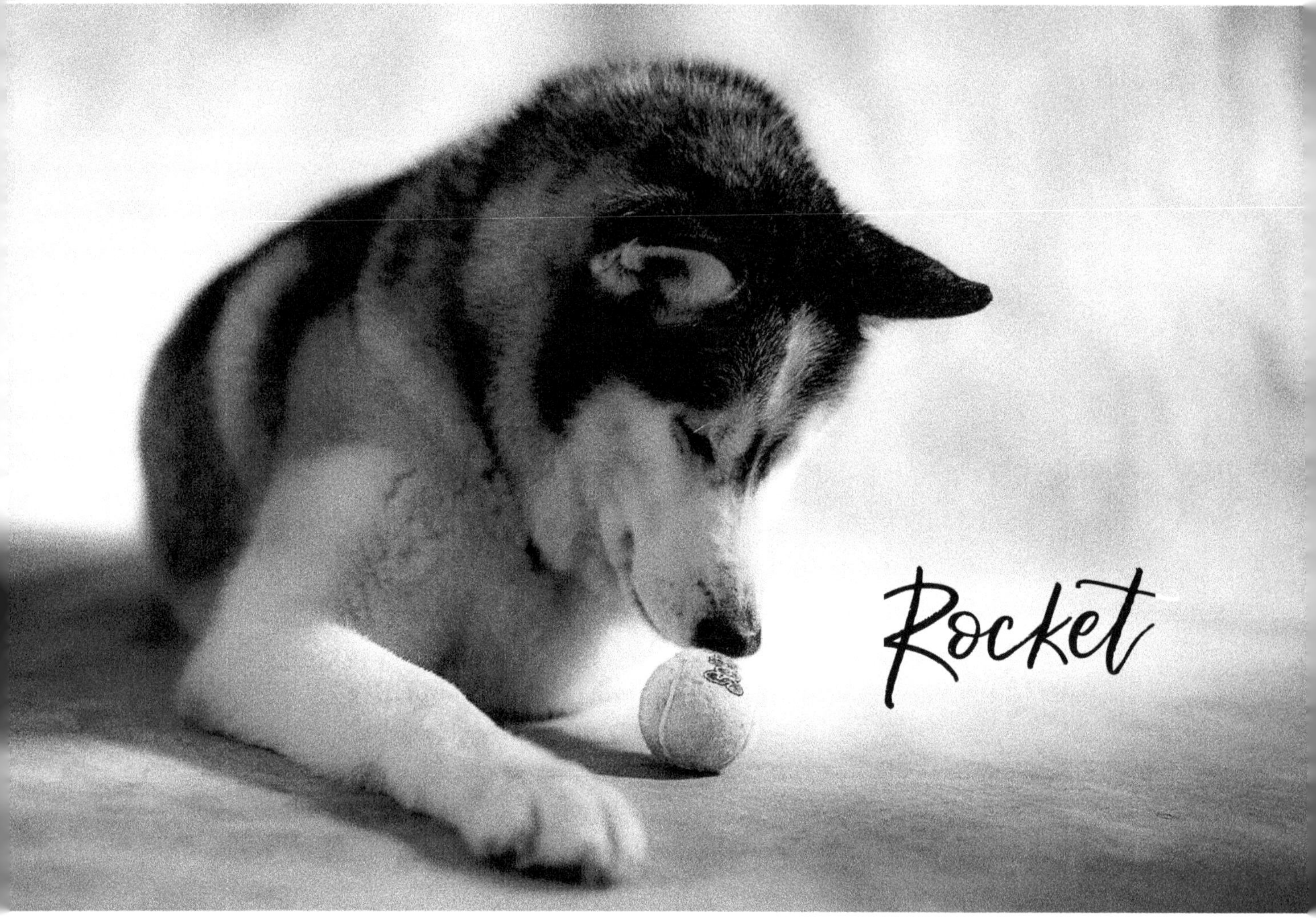

Rocket

ROCKET is a ninety-pound, six-year-old Siberian Husky who loves playing with balls. He was rehomed to his current family when another family realized they weren't prepared to deal with a big boy like Rocket. Now he lives with a Husky sister, Fleur, and the two are inseparable. He also loves his human parents. At the dog park, says his dad, he "guards" them, sitting in front of them and not allowing anyone else near. The worst thing he's ever done is eat a towel . . . and had trouble passing it. We hope he's learned to stick to dog food.

ROMIE, a six-year-old American Pitbull Terrier, is a wonderful representative for her breed. She has earned her Canine Good Citizen award, and she is every bit the lady. Adopted from a county animal shelter where her human mama volunteers, Romie has also earned the nickname "Princess Diva" because she loves to be the center of attention. She is her mama's shadow, following her everywhere--a habit her mom finds endearing. The worst thing she does? She sees squirrels as mortal enemies and chases them every chance she gets. So squirrels, be forewarned--this diva is not above chasing you out of her yard and up the nearest tree!

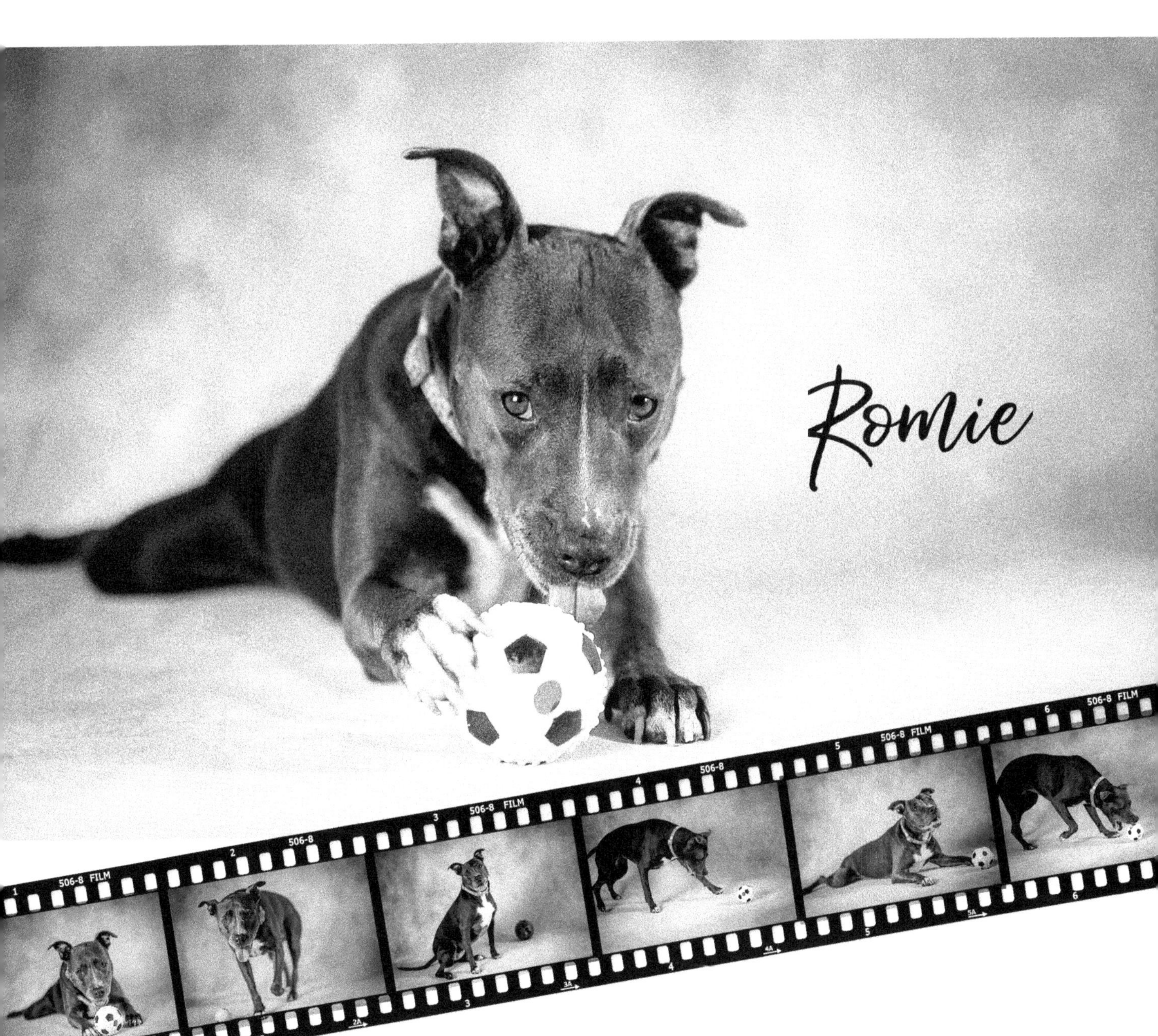

Beautiful ROSE traveled from Alabama to Florida to find her forever home. She's a Golden mix, about seven years old, and her favorite toy is a squeaky ball. No one--dog or human--is perfect, but Rose comes pretty close. She likes to hide by the front gate and jump up to scare whoever comes by, but she wouldn't hurt a flea. Rose has learned many tricks, and her family says they don't know how they did without her. A recent surgery has slowed her down a bit, but she never wants to be left behind when the family takes a road trip. She is beautiful in every way.

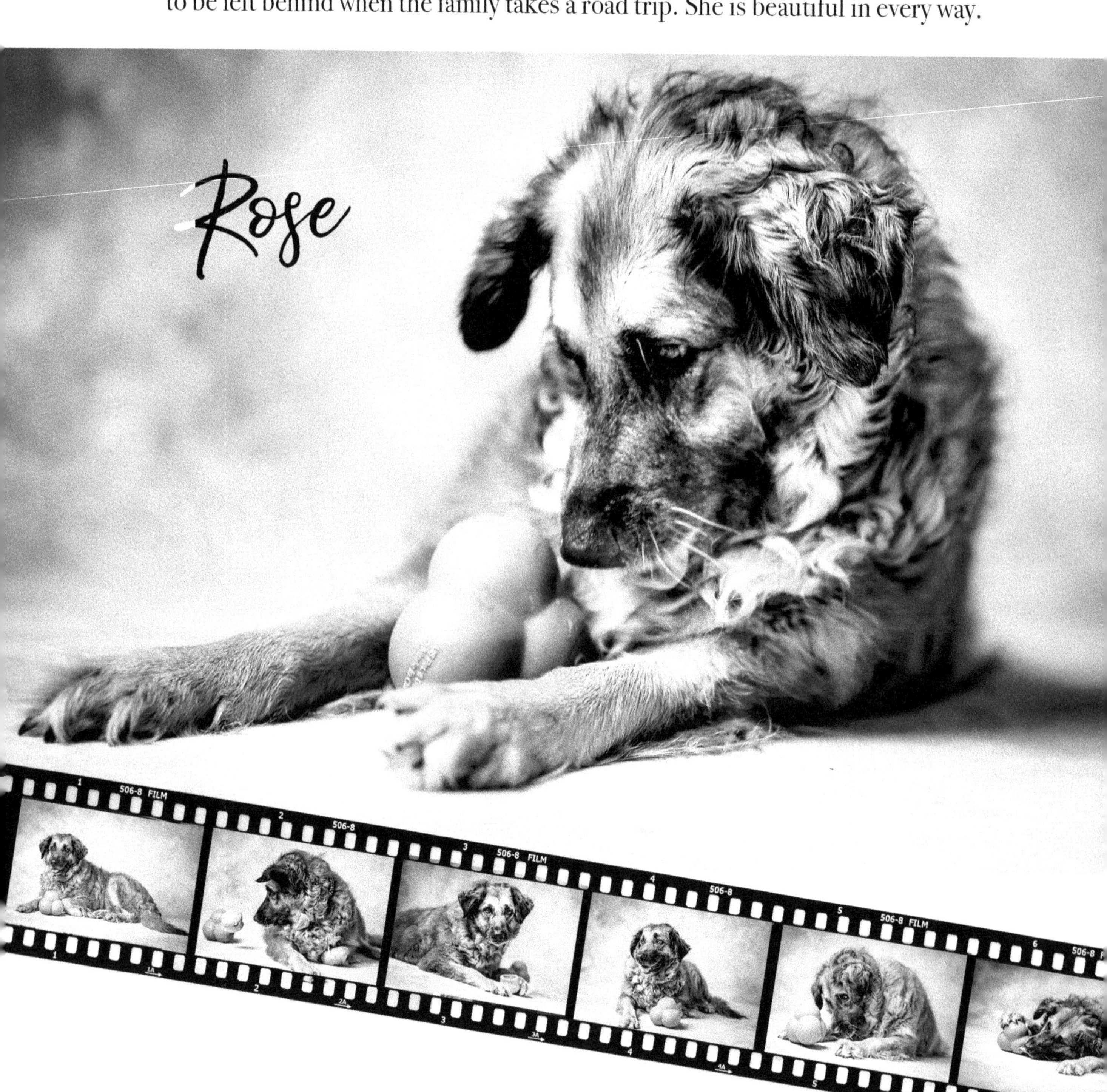

ROSIE H found her forever home through the SPCA's annual Pet Walk. The now-eight-year-old Dachshund went home with her new mama and Sam, another dog adopted at the same event, only to find that her human dad wasn't wild about the idea of two new family members. Mom took the dogs *back* to the SPCA, but when Dad came home the next day, he found himself missing the dogs--so Mom went down and paid the adoption fees a second time to bring the dogs home. That's devotion.

Rosie loves anything that moves or squeaks, and she loves affection from anyone. She adores her canine sibling Sam, and will share her toys only with him.

Rosie was worth every penny of those double adoption fees.

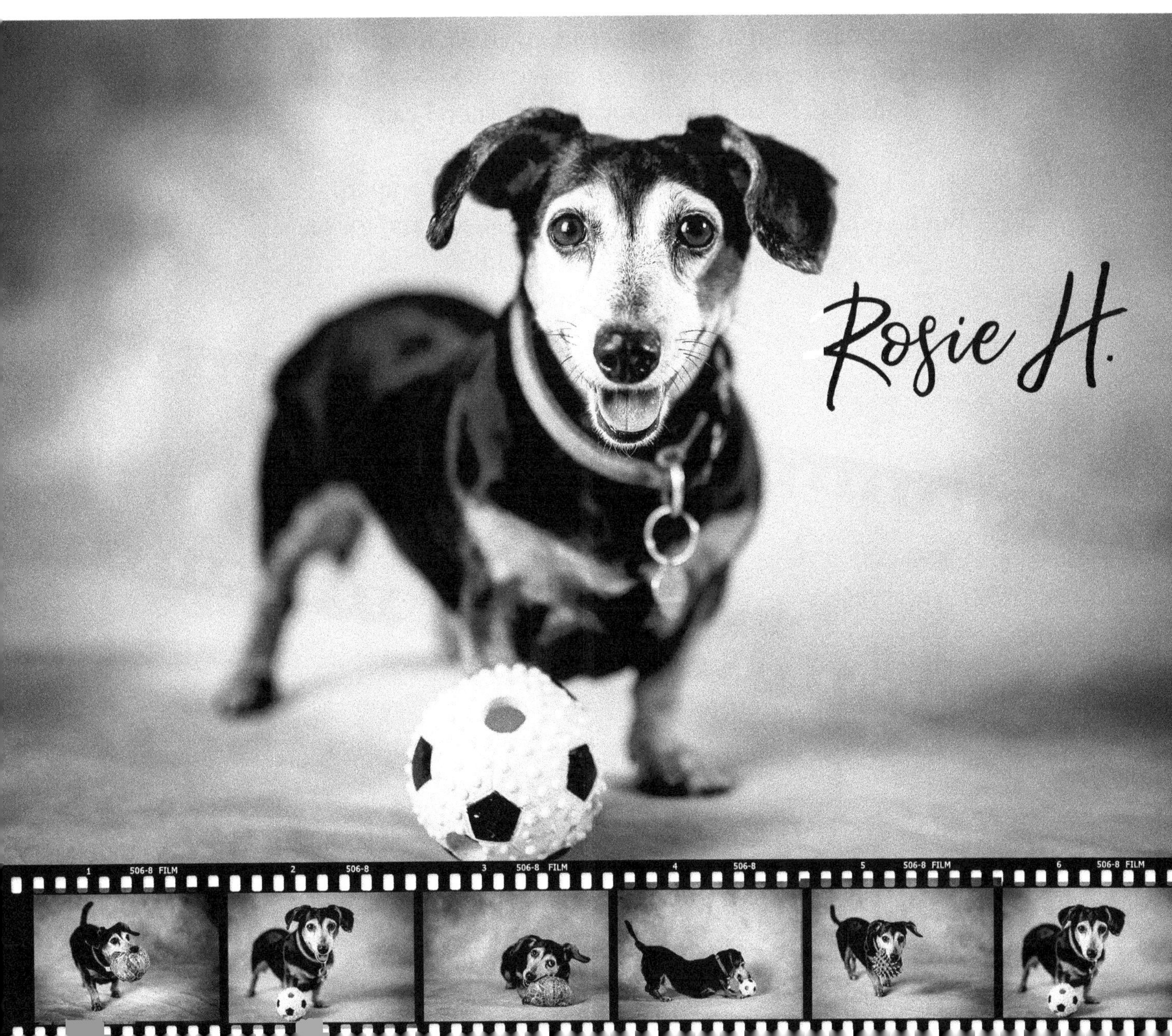

SAM H. was adopted from an SPCA Pet Walk along with his sibling sister, Rosie. Sam is a Norfolk Terrier mix who is between eight and nine years old. When he came home, his human mom reports that he did not know how to play--perhaps the result of a play-deprived childhood? He doesn't really know what to do with a ball, except look for treats in it, but this boy has earned an A+ in snuggling. "He has to have Mom snuggle with him all the time," says his human mother. "And I'm happy to do it when I can."

The worst thing this boy has ever done? Escaped! But he is home with his humans and his sister, and for Sam, all is right with the world.

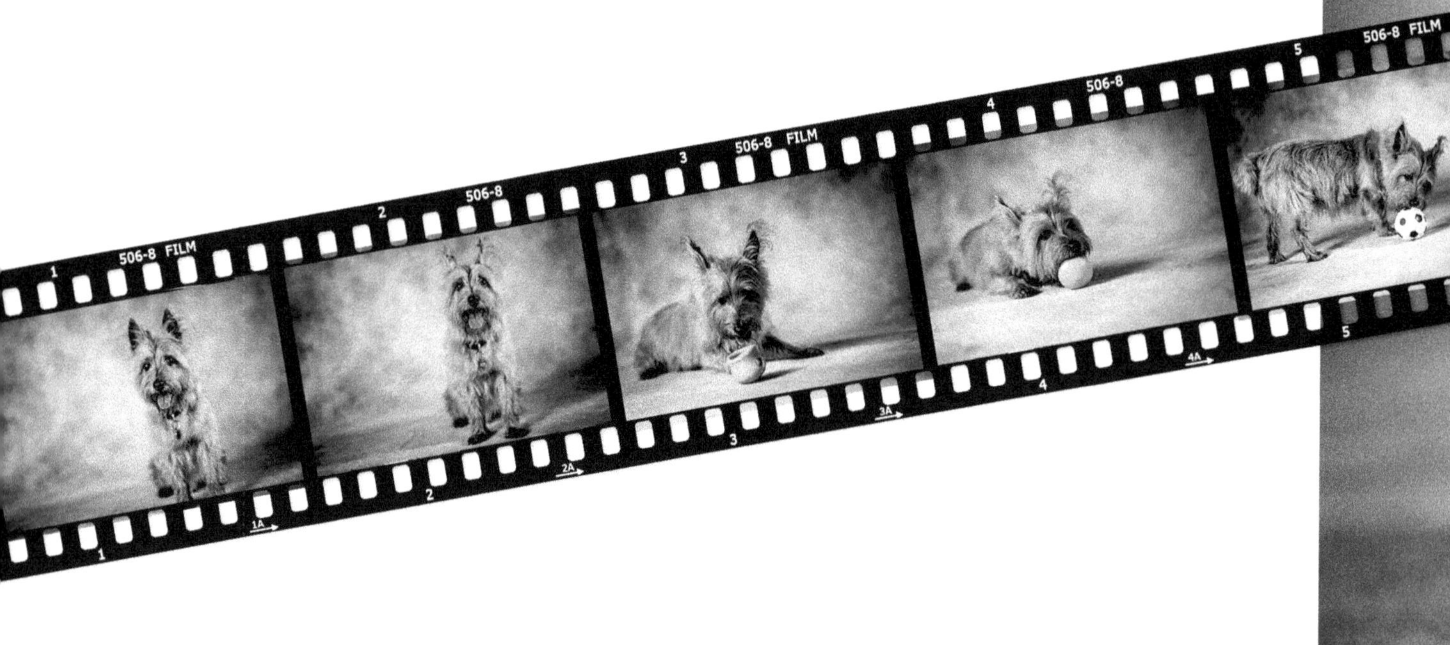

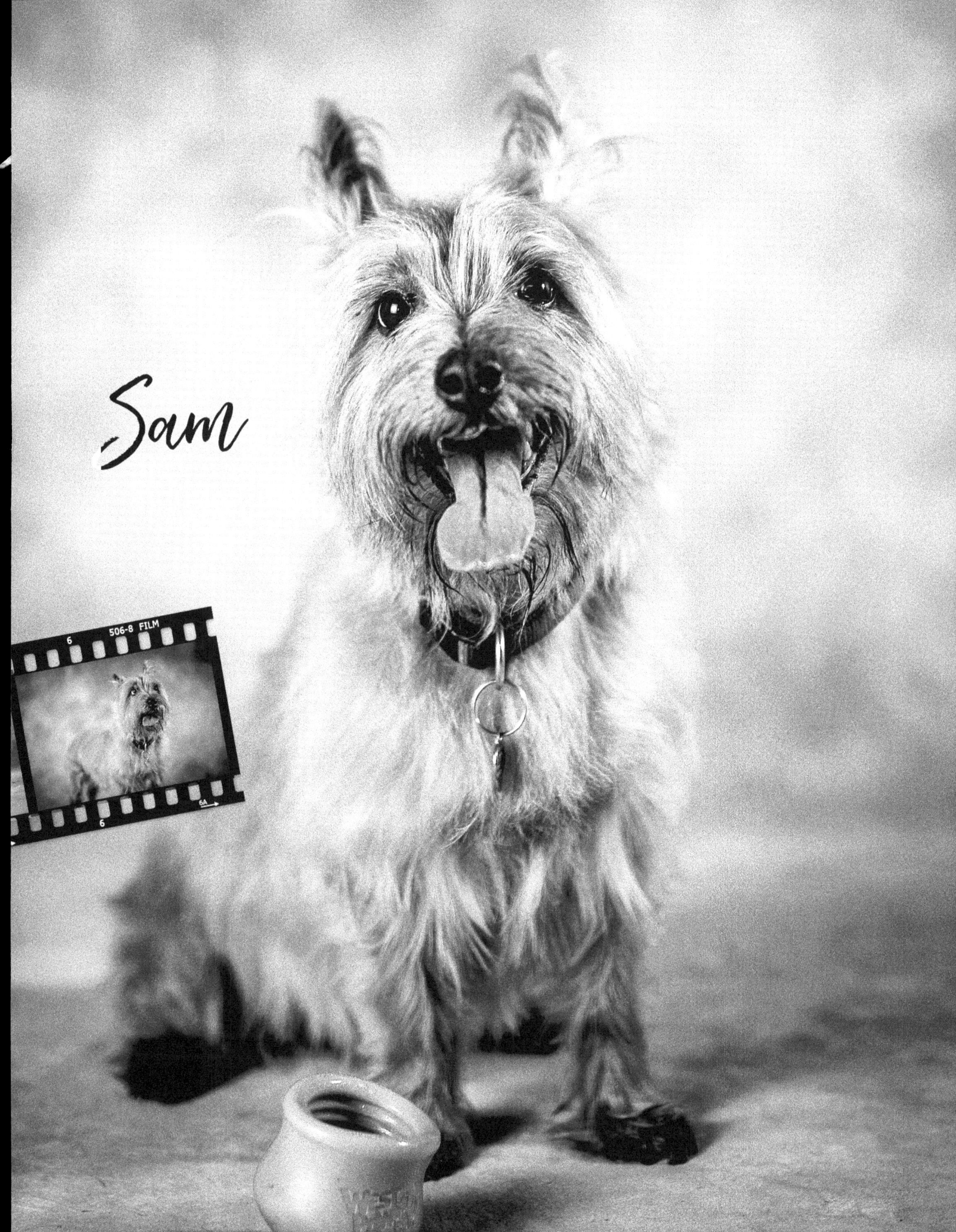
Sam
6
506-8 FILM
6A
6

ROSIE is a seven-year-old boxer mix who loves everybody and everything. She began life with her human mom as a foster who decided that "sit/stay" meant forever. She's not exactly the cute and fluffy type; she's lean and athletic. So you can imagine how startled some people working at the Dunkin' Donuts drive-thru window were when Rosie and her mama pulled up . . . and Rosie jumped out of the car to greet them. At least she didn't eat all the donuts.

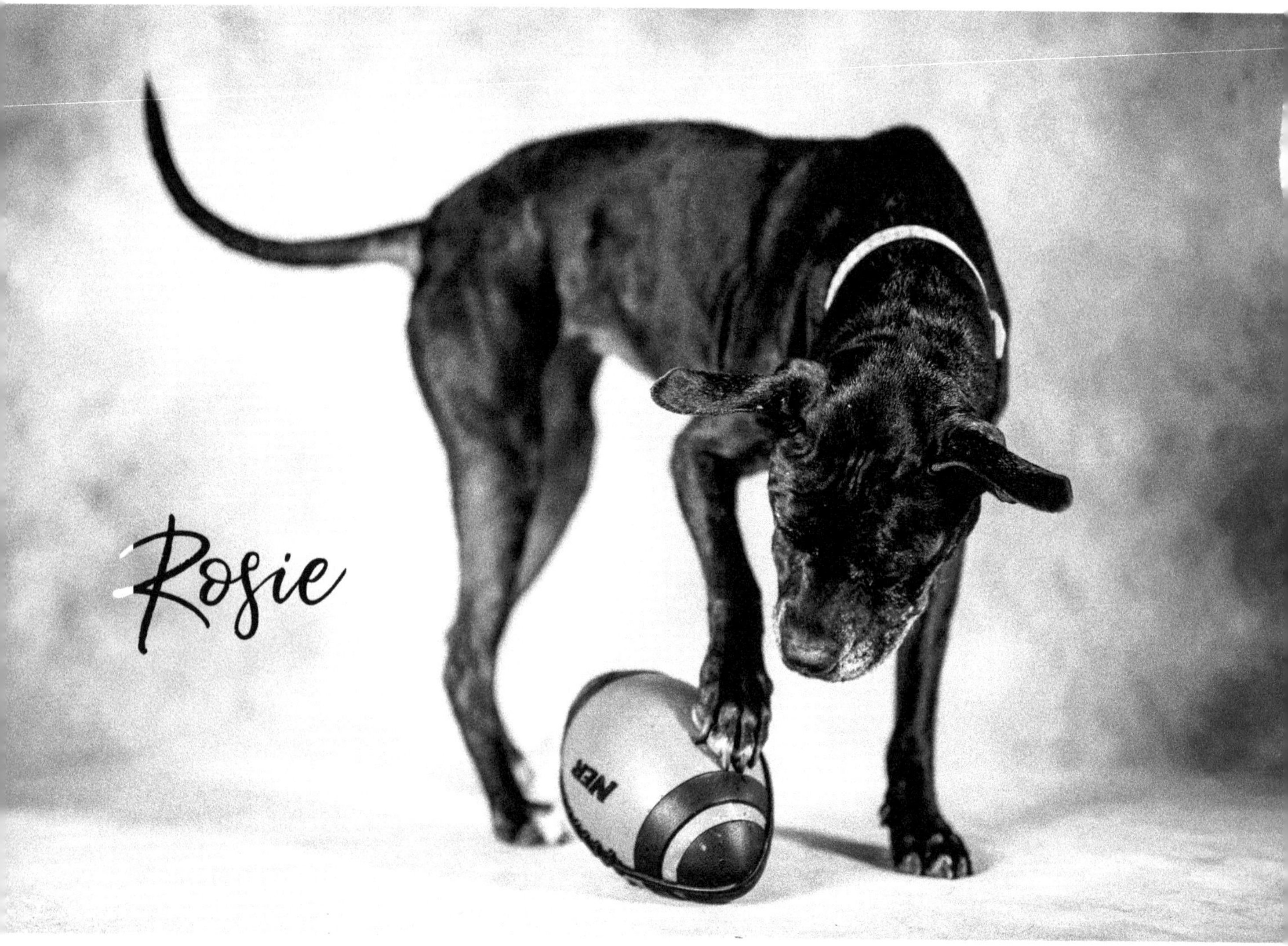

Rosie

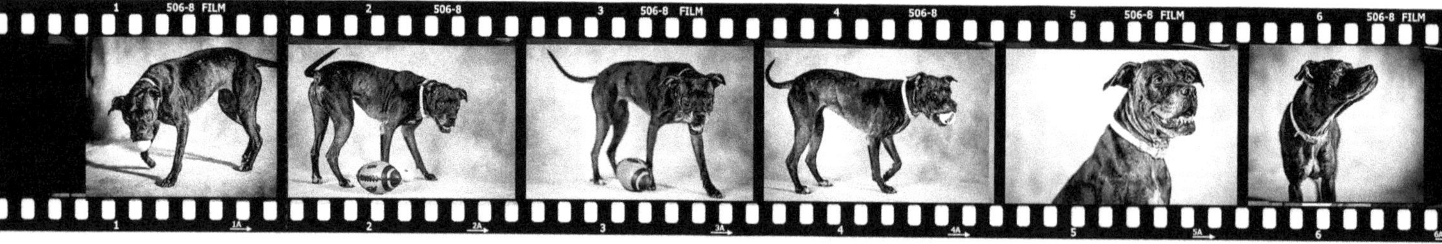

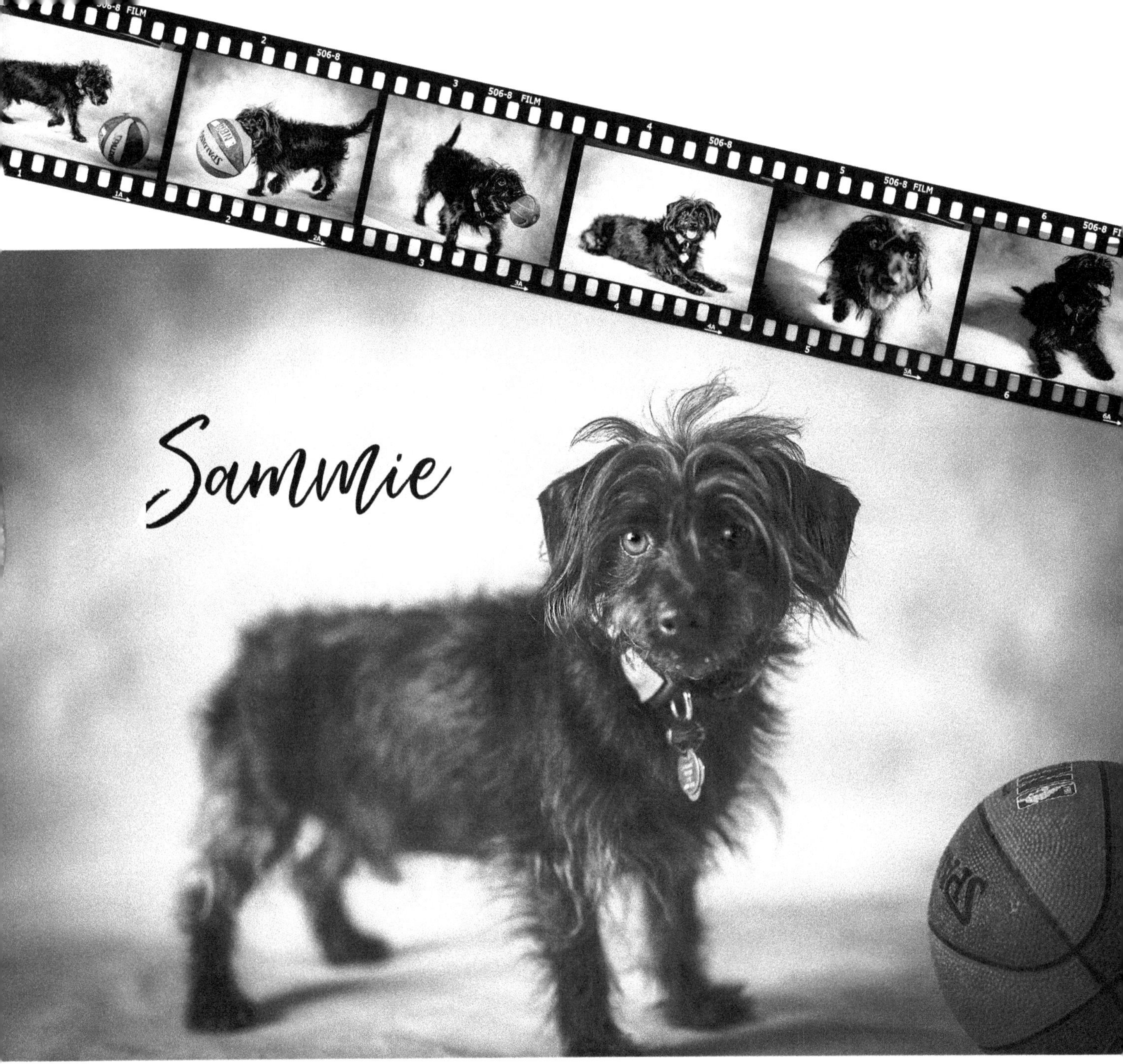

Sammie

SAMMIE only weighs fourteen pounds, but you'd never know it by the way he goes after a basketball. Sammie, a four-year-old wire-haired Dachshund mix, was adopted from the SPCA. He has been to obedience class, where he learned to dance on command, and now he dances all the time. The worst thing he has ever done, says his mama, is do what Dachshunds do--he caught two moles and brought them up from their underground tunnel with one hanging out of each side of his mouth. He was showing off for his new family . . . a gesture they had to learn to appreciate. But they love this smart little guy, and we hope he keeps dancing for a long time to come.

You would never know it, but SHEENA is a fourteen-year-old Westie who loves chasing balls . . . when she's in the mood. Mostly she loves lounging in the hammock with her mama, watching the squirrels and butterflies as they dance by. At 14 (about 98 in dog years), who can blame her? Sheena was purchased from a pet store, a practice her owner does not recommend, as many of those dogs come from puppy mills. The puppy was sick and nearly died when a case of kennel cough turned into pneumonia. The pet store offered a refund, but who can return a puppy as if it were only merchandise? Fortunately, Sheena recovered to live long and propser.

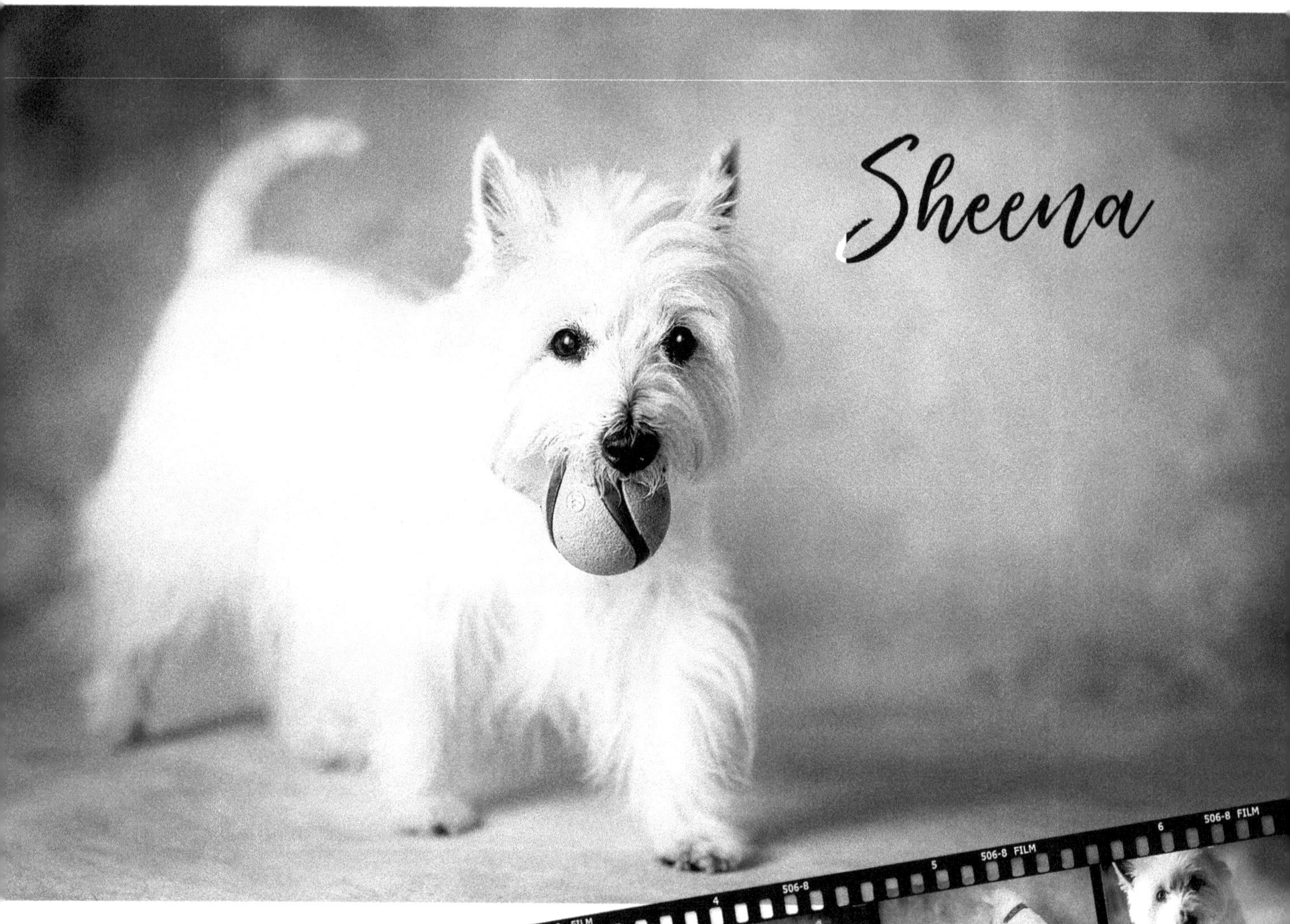

Sheena

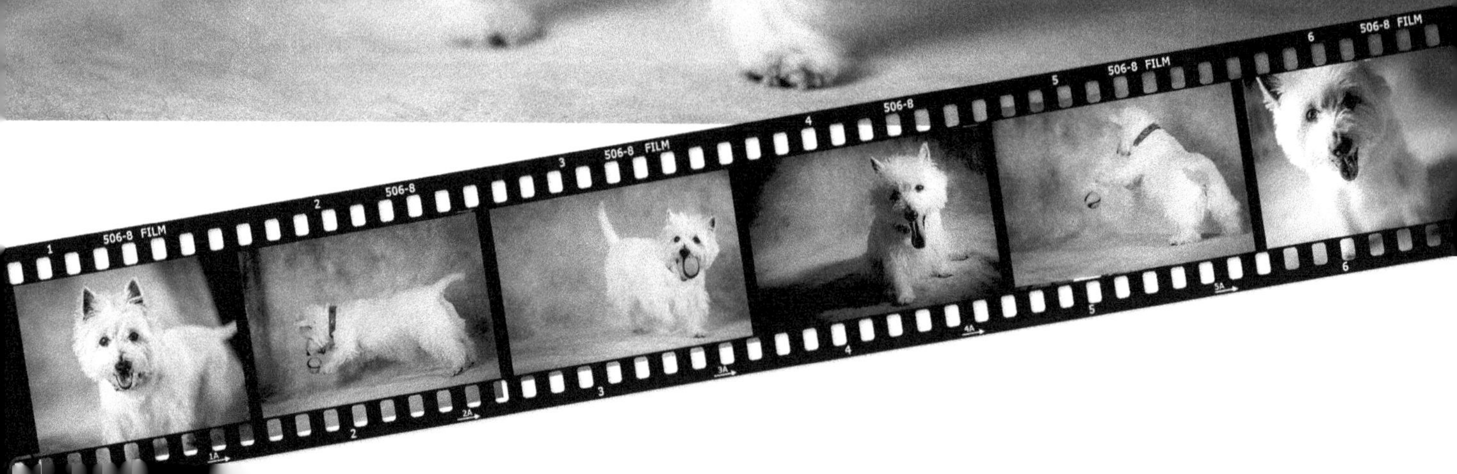

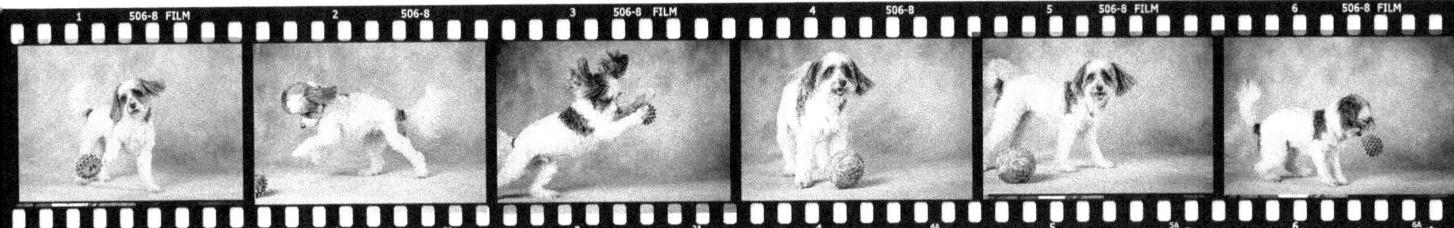

SKIPPER found his way home via an ad in the paper. His human mom called the people who'd placed the ad, and there was Skipper, a Havanese/Malti-poo mix, with his sister, Bindi. Both puppies went home together, and they've been together ever since. They are now eight years old, and Skipper's favorite toy is his frisbee--and he's very good with a ball, as you can see. He says "hi" (while yawning) when Mom comes home every day, but this boy is not 100 percent angel--he once disemboweled his dog bed while he was staying at a kennel.

Angel or not, he is loved, and he is home.

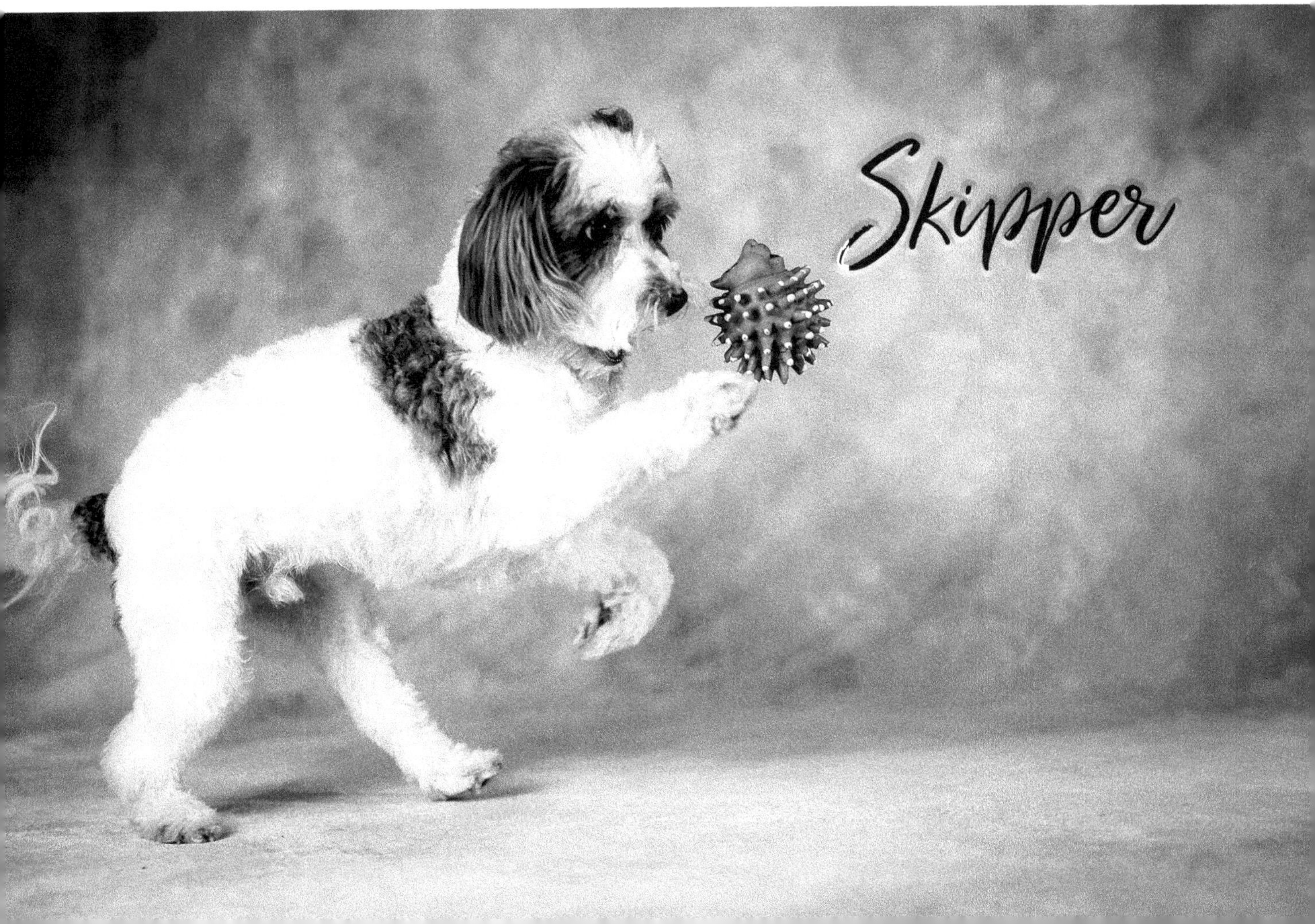

Skipper

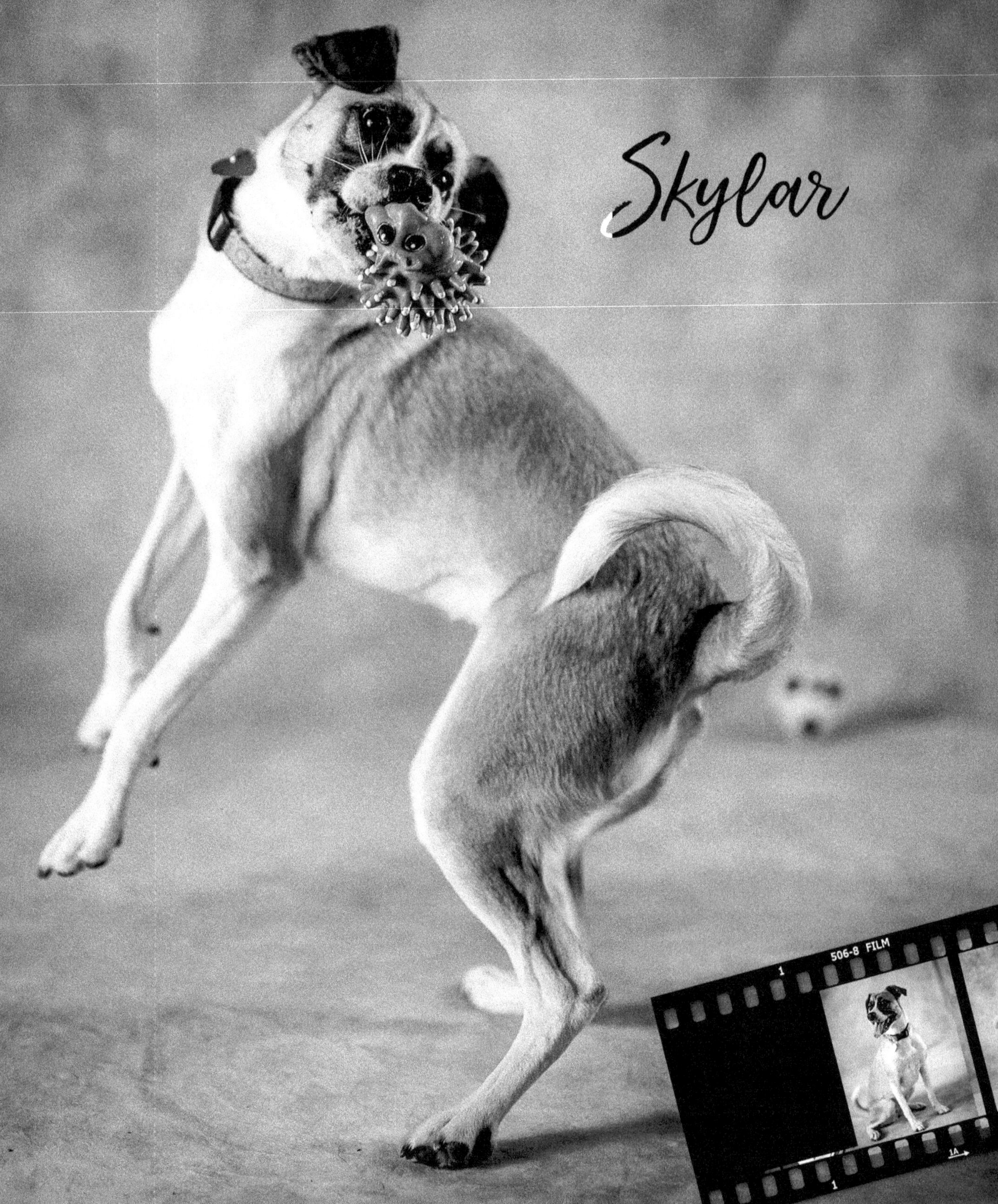
Skylar
506-8 FILM
1
1A
1

Two-year-old SKYLAR, a Terrier mix, is happily adjusting to a new home. Her new human mom volunteers with a Florida rescue, and that's where she met Skylar. The dog had recently lost her home when her family moved and couldn't take her with them. Skylar was bounced from place to place until she was taken in by a private rescue organization.

She was so frightened and broken when she first arrived that the volunteers had to wear protective gloves when they removed her from the dog carrier. When she first met her new mom at a Petsmart adoption event, however, she met a woman who was willing to sit on the tile floor to get down on her level . . . and then lie down by the dog's side, where woman and dog ignored the shoppers and "spooned" on the floor. A bond was formed in that moment, and Skylar--and her mom--knew they'd be together for a long, long time.

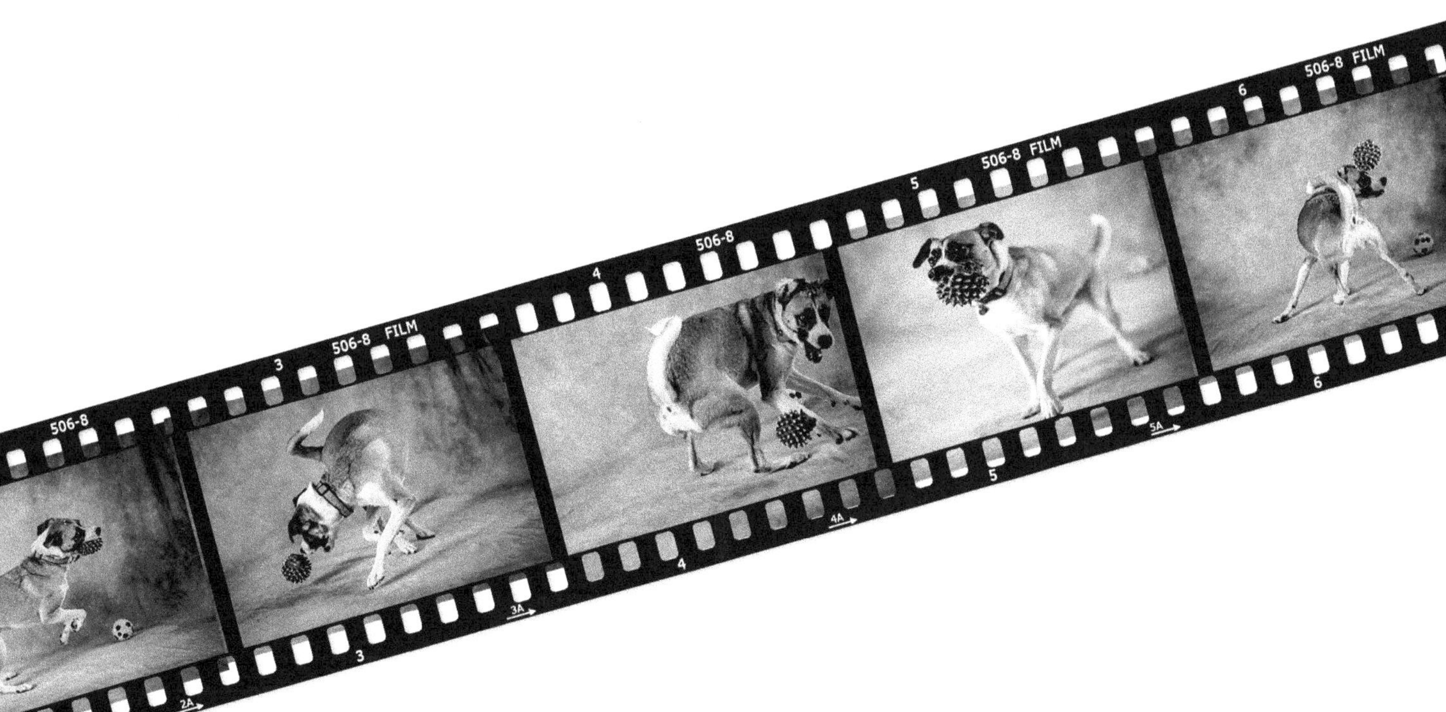

SMOOCH is a six-year-old Anatolian Shepherd who came to his forever family via the Humane Society. He loves to play with balls, but he would rather give kisses. Smooch lives with his human mom and her 93-year-old Pop. He plays hide-and-seek with Pop (by hiding in the shower), and when Pop falls asleep in his chair, Smooch frequently goes over and simply touches his arm to make sure he's okay. When it's time for bed, Smooch doesn't go off with Mom until he's given Pop a good-night kiss. Smooch also visits the kids at a domestic abuse center, where he sits nicely and lets the kids pet and adore him.

A gentle giant . . . with a big, big heart. That's Smooch!

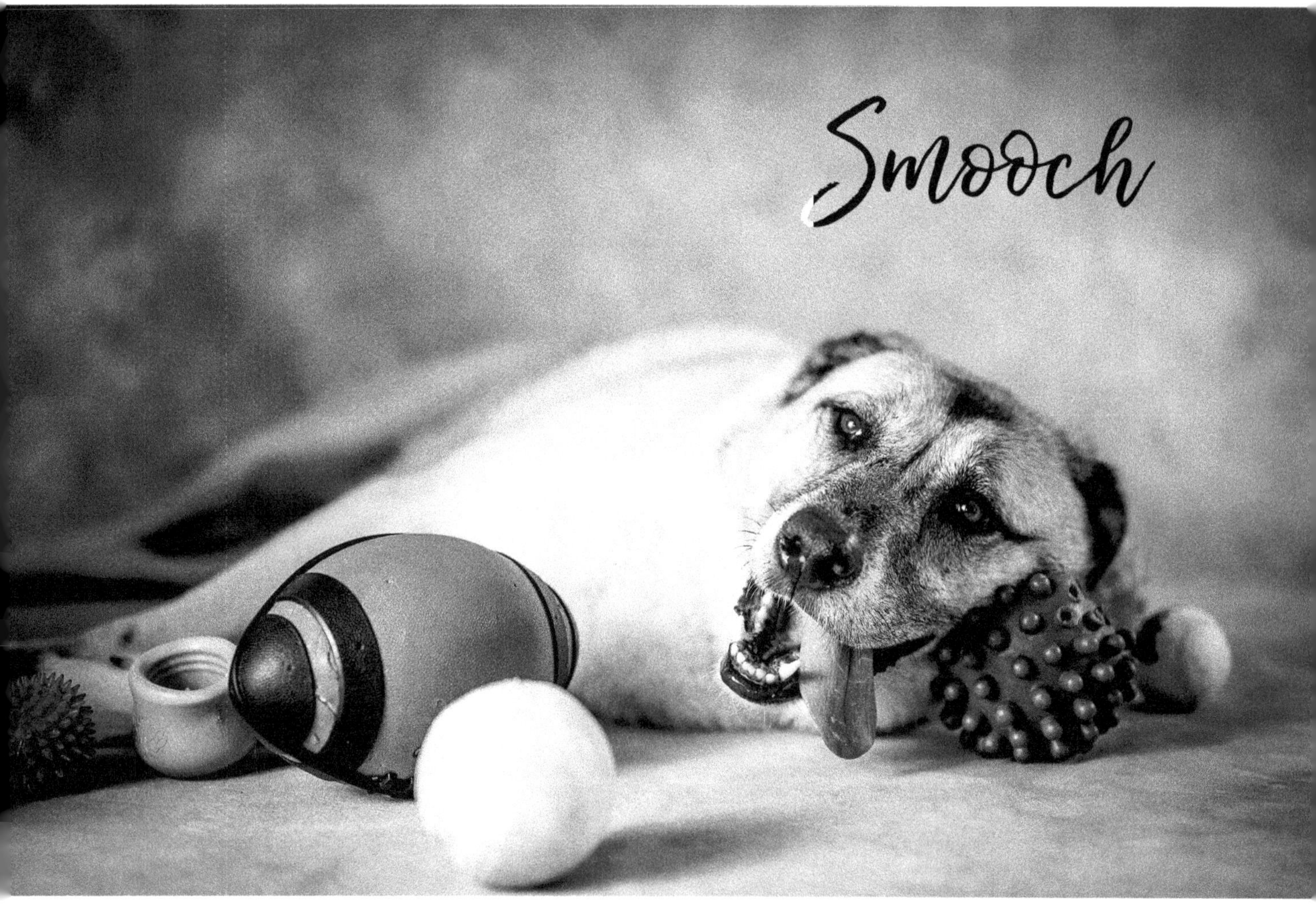

Smooch

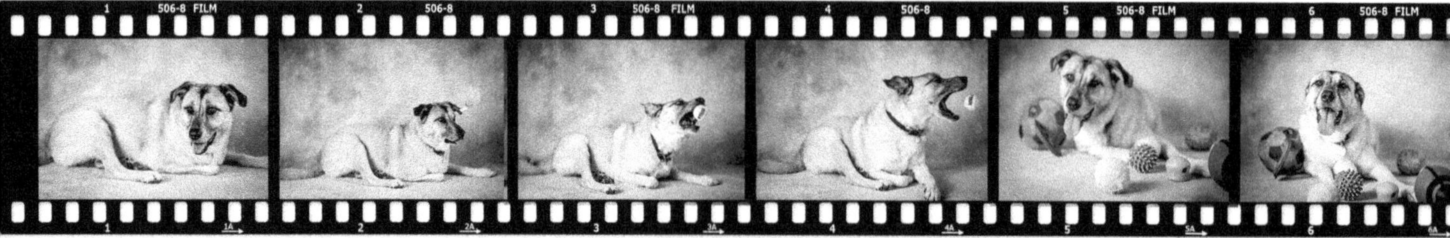

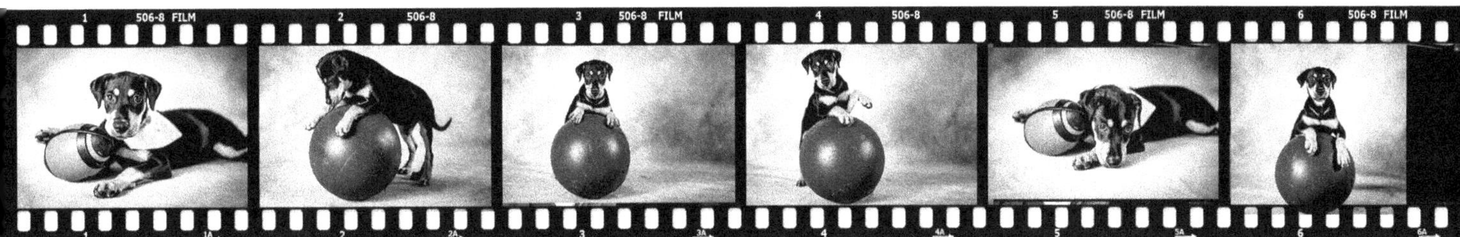

SNICKERS is up for adoption! Not all dogs in this book have found their forever homes yet, and we hope Snickers will find his way home before this book goes to press. This adorable Lab/Rottie mix is three-months old and a real sweetheart. He is one of five puppy siblings who were turned into a shelter in north Florida. His favorite toy is a shoe, and he loves to give kisses and wag his tail. If your heart is moved by this little guy, know this--there are others like him at your local shelters and rescue groups.

One of them may be perfect for your family!

Update: Snickers was adopted not long after his photo session!

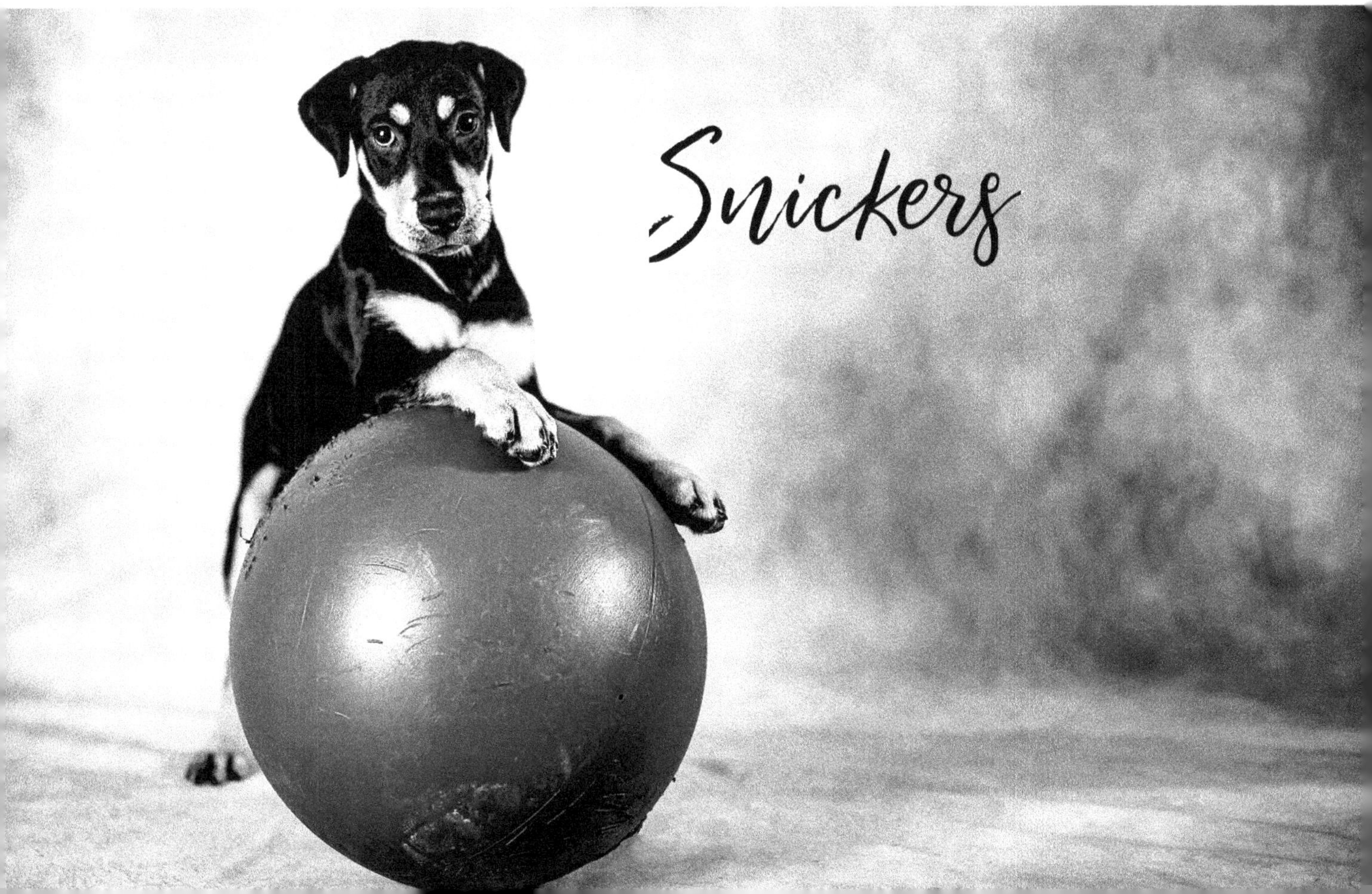

Snickers

SOTHEBY the Labrador isn't supposed to play with balls. Why ? Because if Sotheby, a five-year-old seeing eye dog, was distracted by a ball while he was working, the result could be disastrous. But Sotheby's human mom allowed this special dispensation because Sotheby loves balls and she loves Sotheby. "He is so devoted to guiding me," she says. "And he thinks everyone is his friend." When he's wearing his harness, he's 100 percent working dog, but when he's not working, this boy can be a counter surfer. Mom says: "He would eat all the bread in the house, if we let him."

That's okay, Sotheby. You're pretty close to perfect.

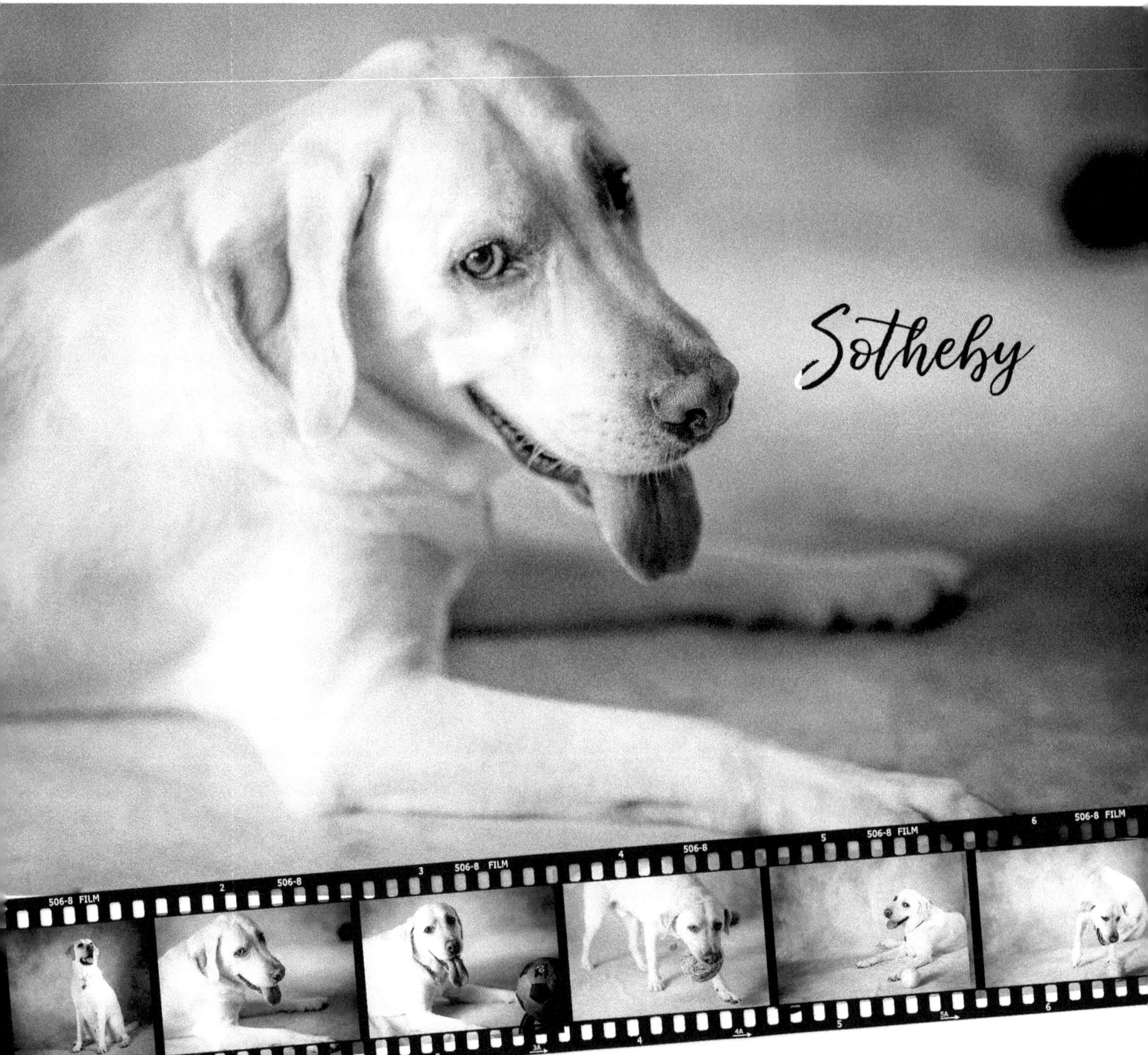

Eight-year-old SPIDEY WHEELS loves three things--her human mom, her companion Pearl, and being held. The chihuahua came to her family from a county shelter, where she had been returned twice. And you know what a twice-returned dog is --it's a dog who hasn't found the perfect home yet. The third time was the charm for Spidey, and her mom thinks she's absolutely perfect. She will stand on her back legs and paw her mom's leg until she's picked up, and that's okay. Because her mom loves carrying this little dog close to her heart.

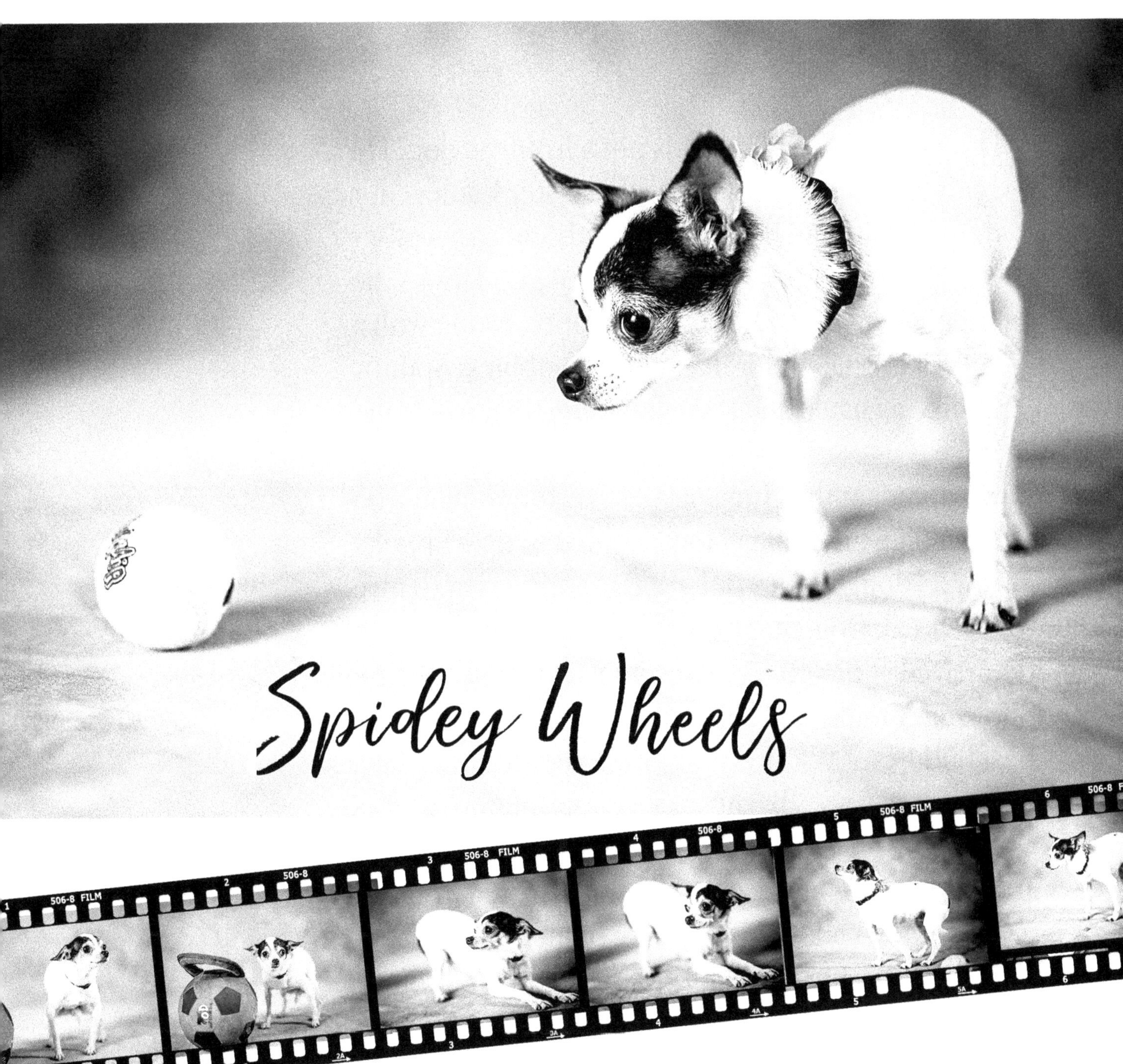

Spidey Wheels

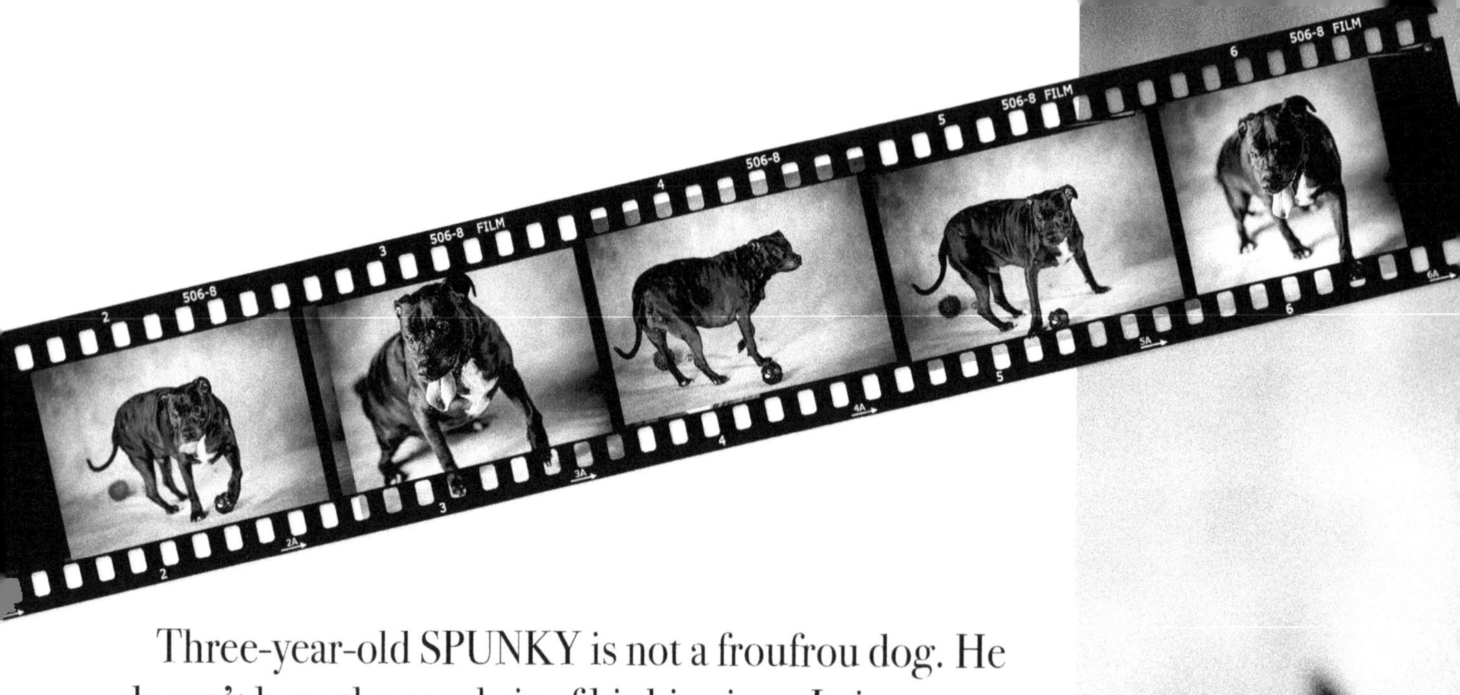

Three-year-old SPUNKY is not a froufrou dog. He doesn't have the regal air of his big sister Lainey, nor does he have the beautiful striped coat of his other sibling Zola. But what Spunky lacks in good looks, he more than makes up for in personality. Along with a remarkable talent for making spit bubbles, Spunky snuggles like a champ and kisses anything that will stand still.

As a volunteer at the Humane Society, the woman who would become his human mom decided to take Spunky home for a "doggie's day out"--a temporary visit to give the dog a break from the noisy shelter kennels. Once he arrived at her house, Zola immediately loved him, following Spunky and playing with him as if they were best buddies. "We always say Zola adopted him," his mom says. "Because even now they are always together."

Spunky arrived at the shelter as a stray covered in scars. No one knows about his past life, but it couldn't have been good. Now life is great. Love made the difference.

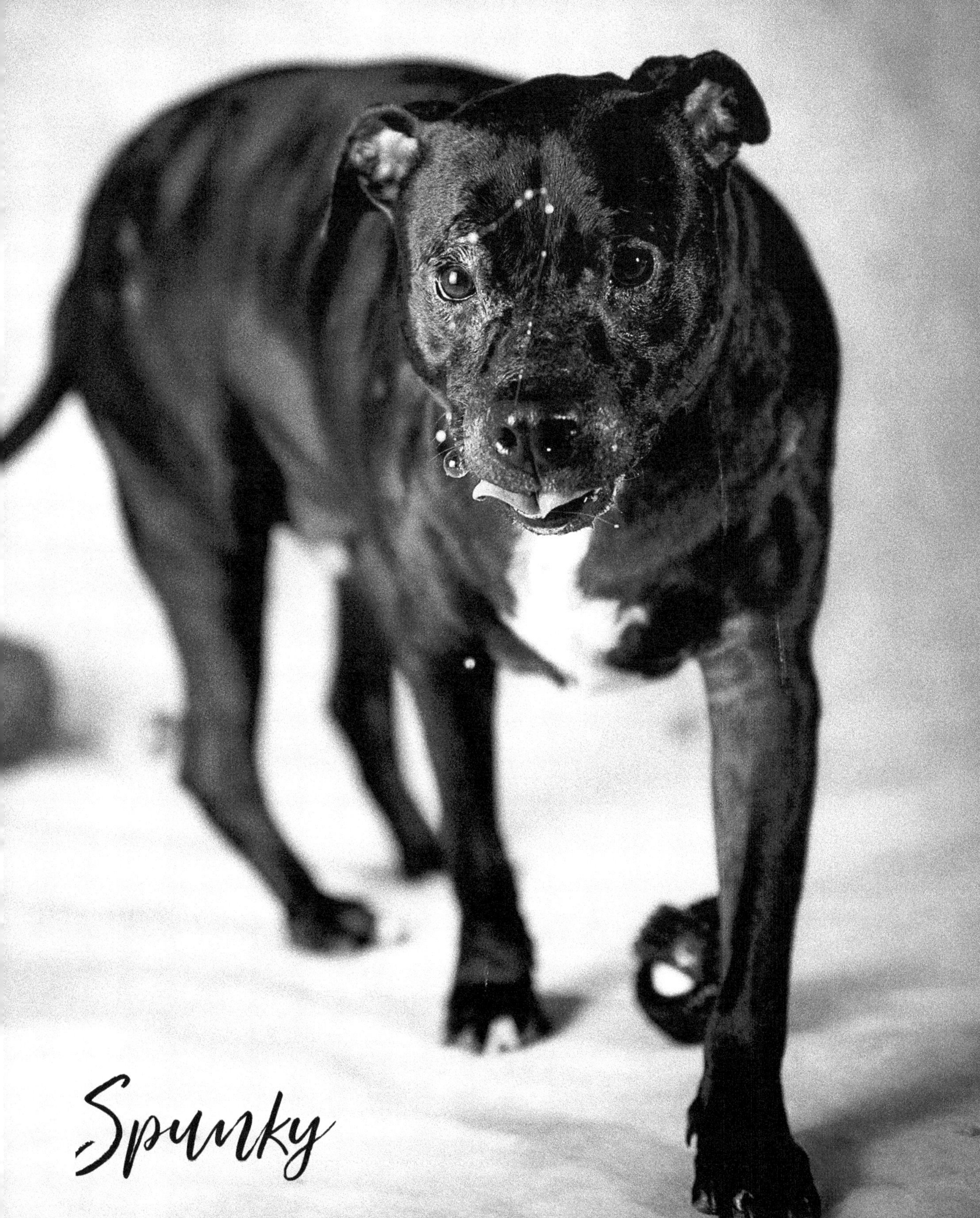
Spunky

Who doesn't love a pair of puppies? Meet TURNER AND TUCKER, two puppies who were in foster care with the Suncoast Animal Leage at the time of their photo shoot. These littermates love cuddling, playing, and chewing things, including any available ball. They are Lab mixes and super smart.
Best wishes to this adorable pair!
Epilogue: they were adopted!

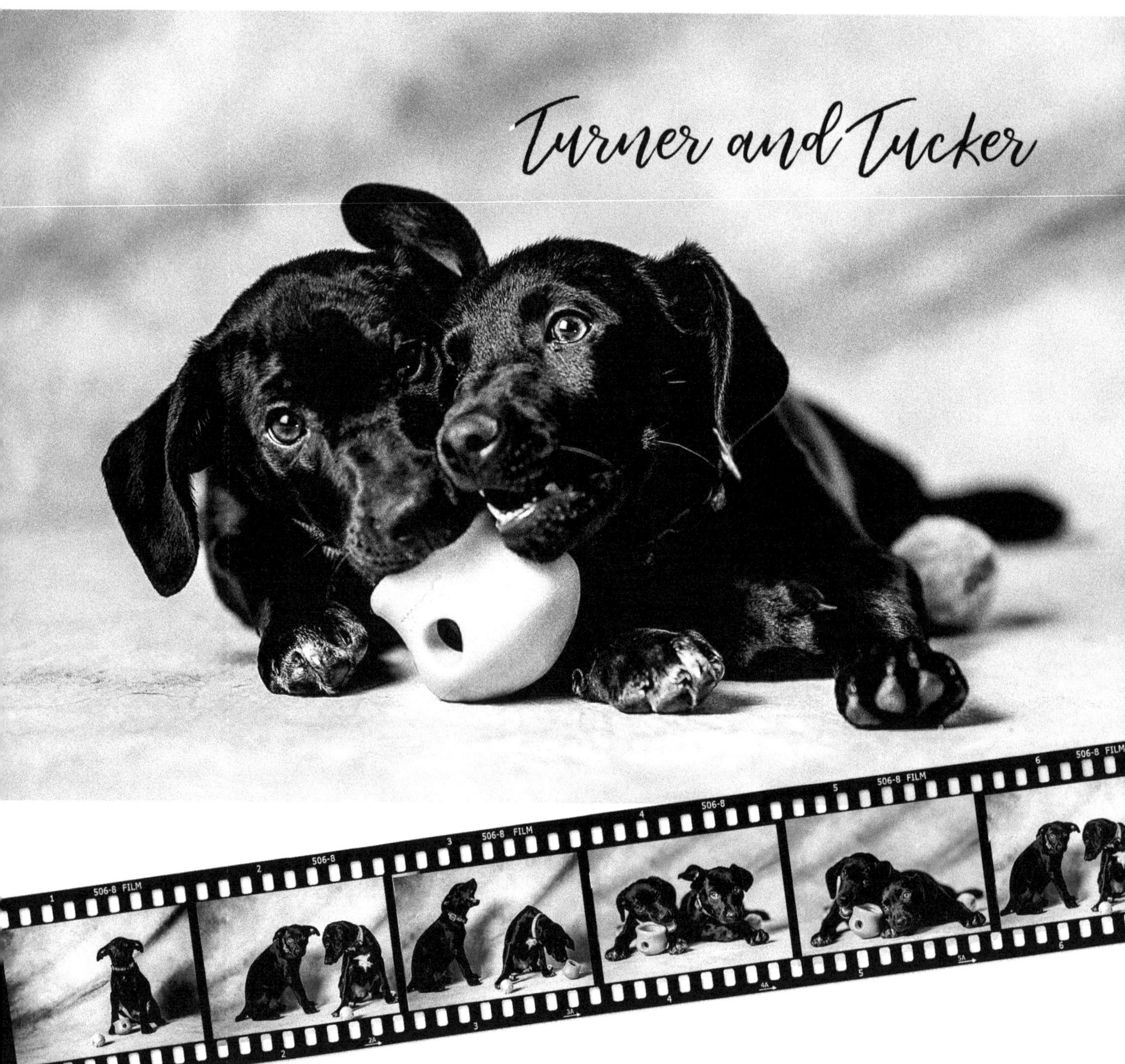

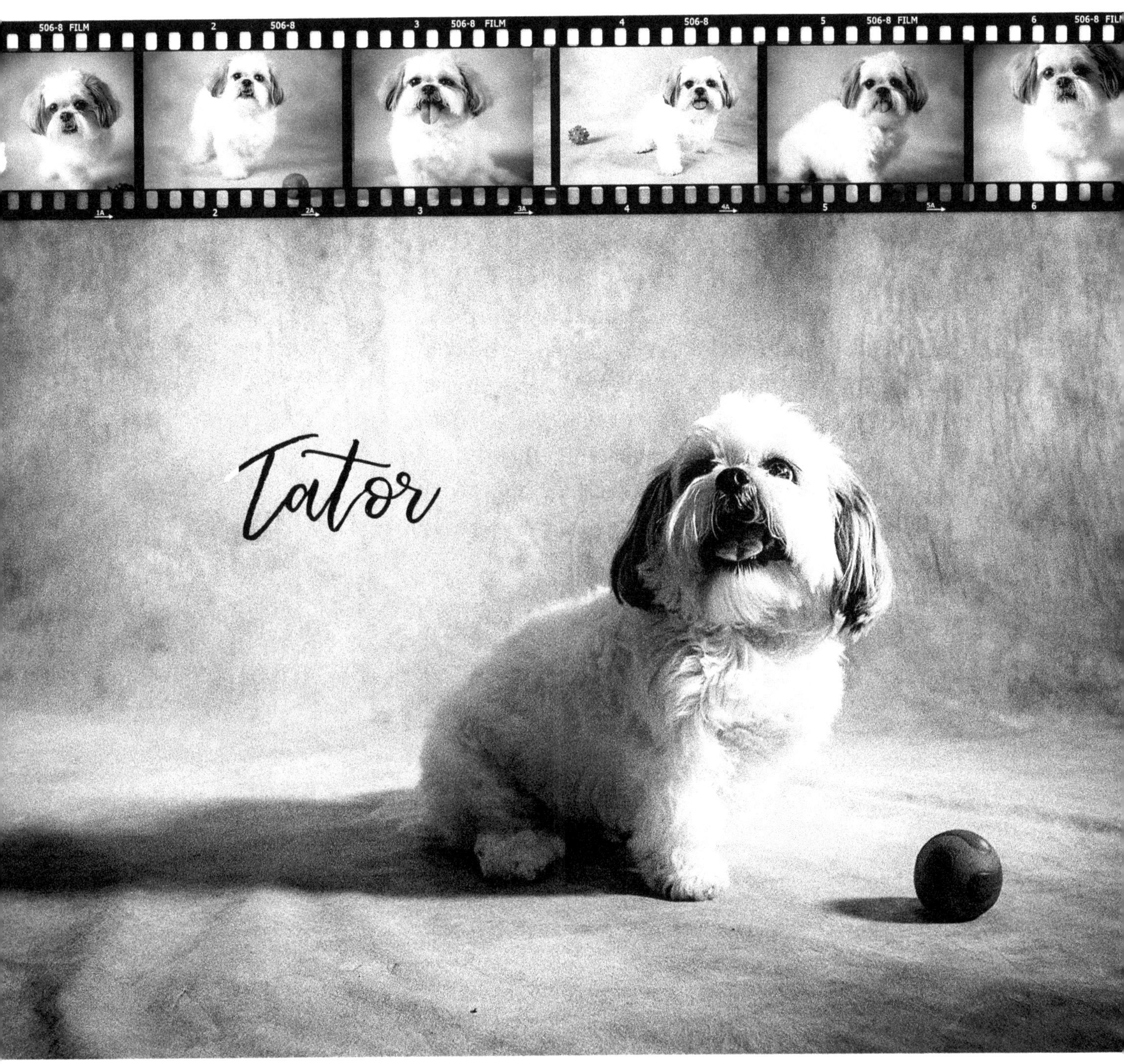

With eighty other dogs, four-year-old TATOR was rescued from a hoarding/puppy mill situation. The vet who evaluated the Shih Tzu puppy discovered an injured leg that had to be amputated. Little Tator was fostered until his incision healed, then he was adopted by his forever family. His new mom was hesitant at first--she was still getting over the loss of another dog--but the dad insisted. They adopted Tator, and not many months later, Tator's human dad passed away. Tator has been a comfort to his mom. He loves to sit and snuggle in her lap, reminding her she is not alone.

Like his sister Daisy Mae, TEDDY is a well-trained Chesapeake Bay Retriever with a hidden talent: this boy is a great dock-diving dog, and even participates in dock-diving events. (Who knew there was such a thing?) Teddy is seven years old, and came to his forever home through a county animal shelter. Though he has never worked the dog show circuit, Teddy is well-trained and can catch a ball like an outfielder. He loves affection from humans, and will do anything for pets and scratches, especially on his lower back. The worst thing he's ever done? "That's easy," says his mom. "He pooped in the photography studio!"

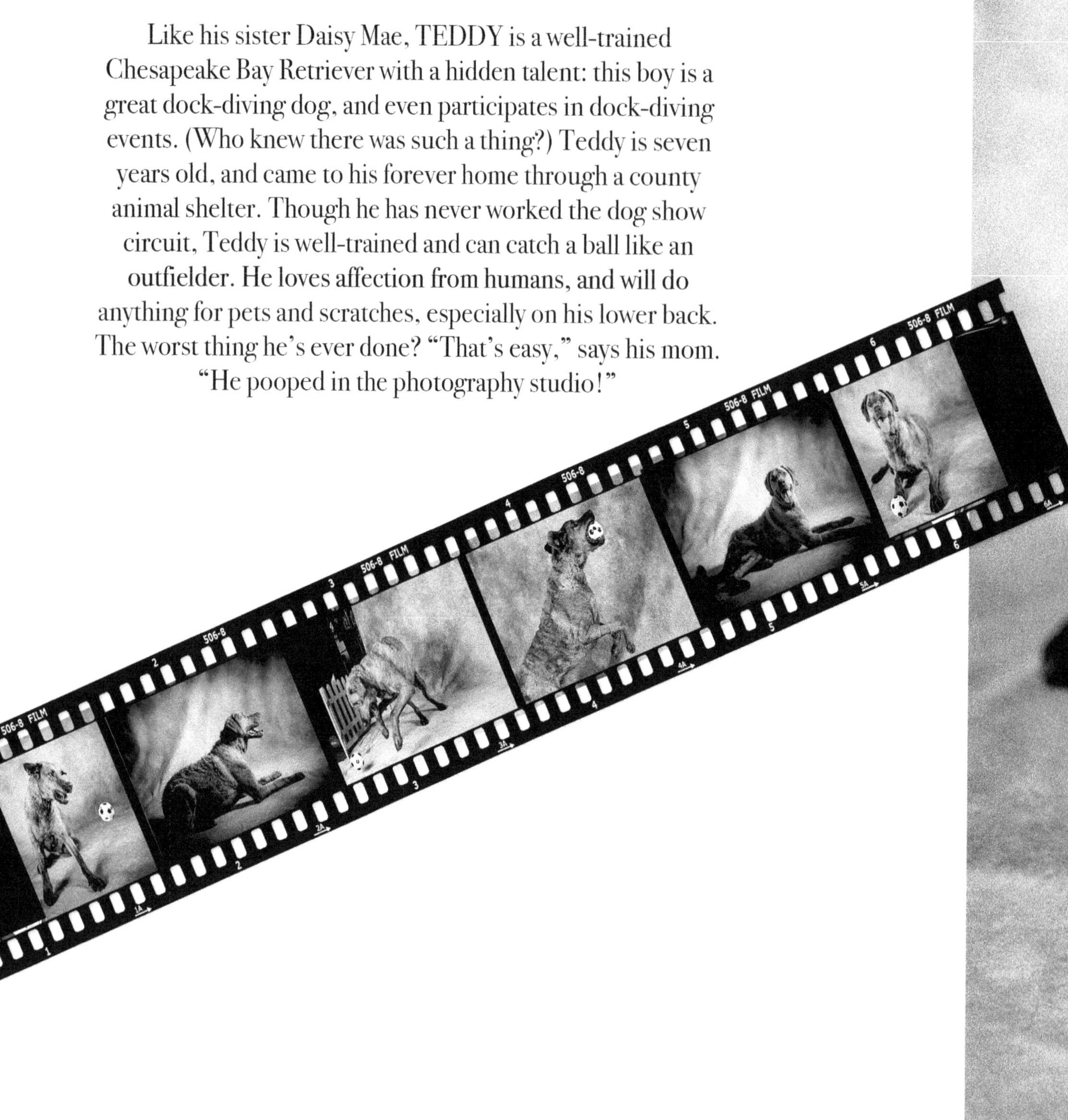

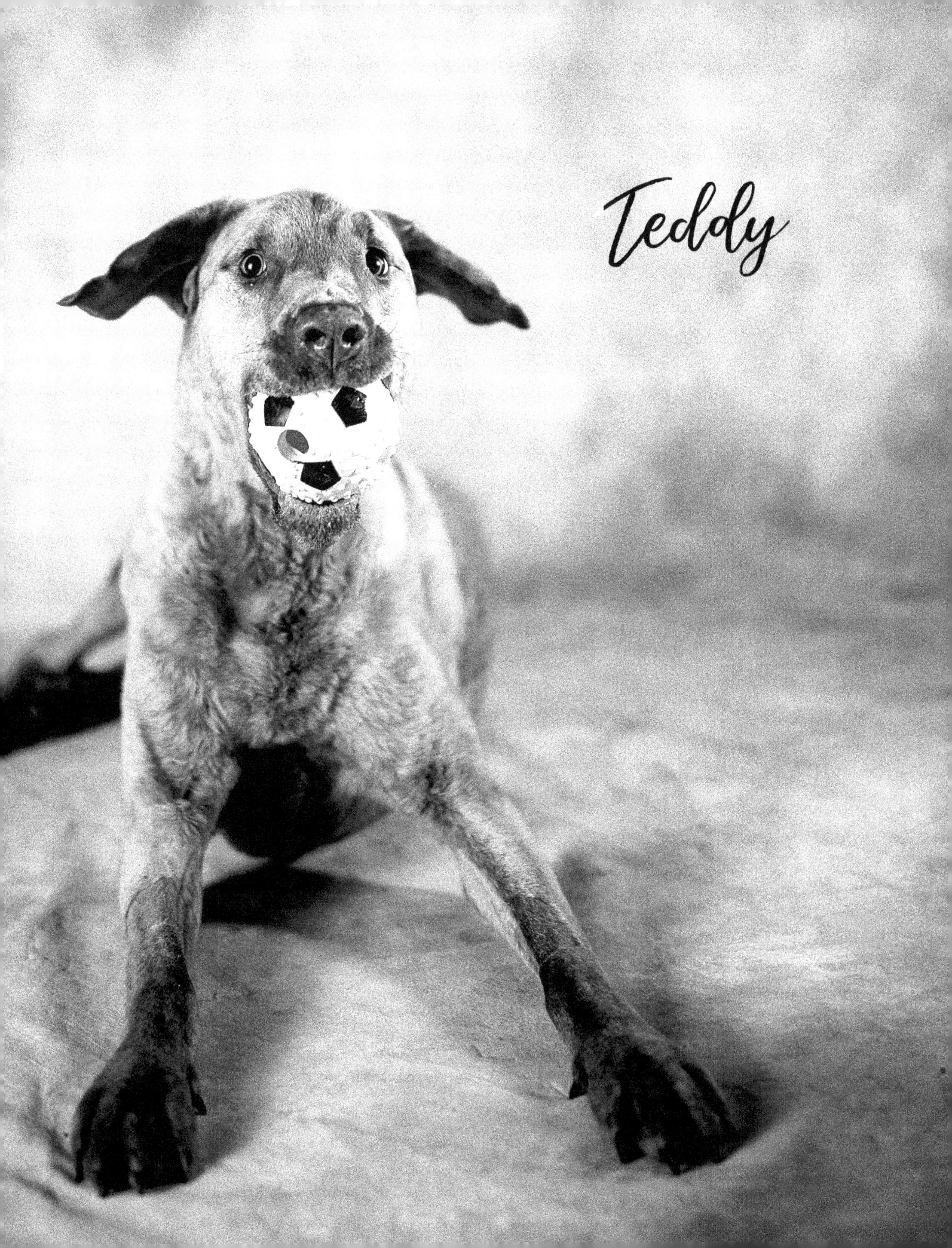

Teddy

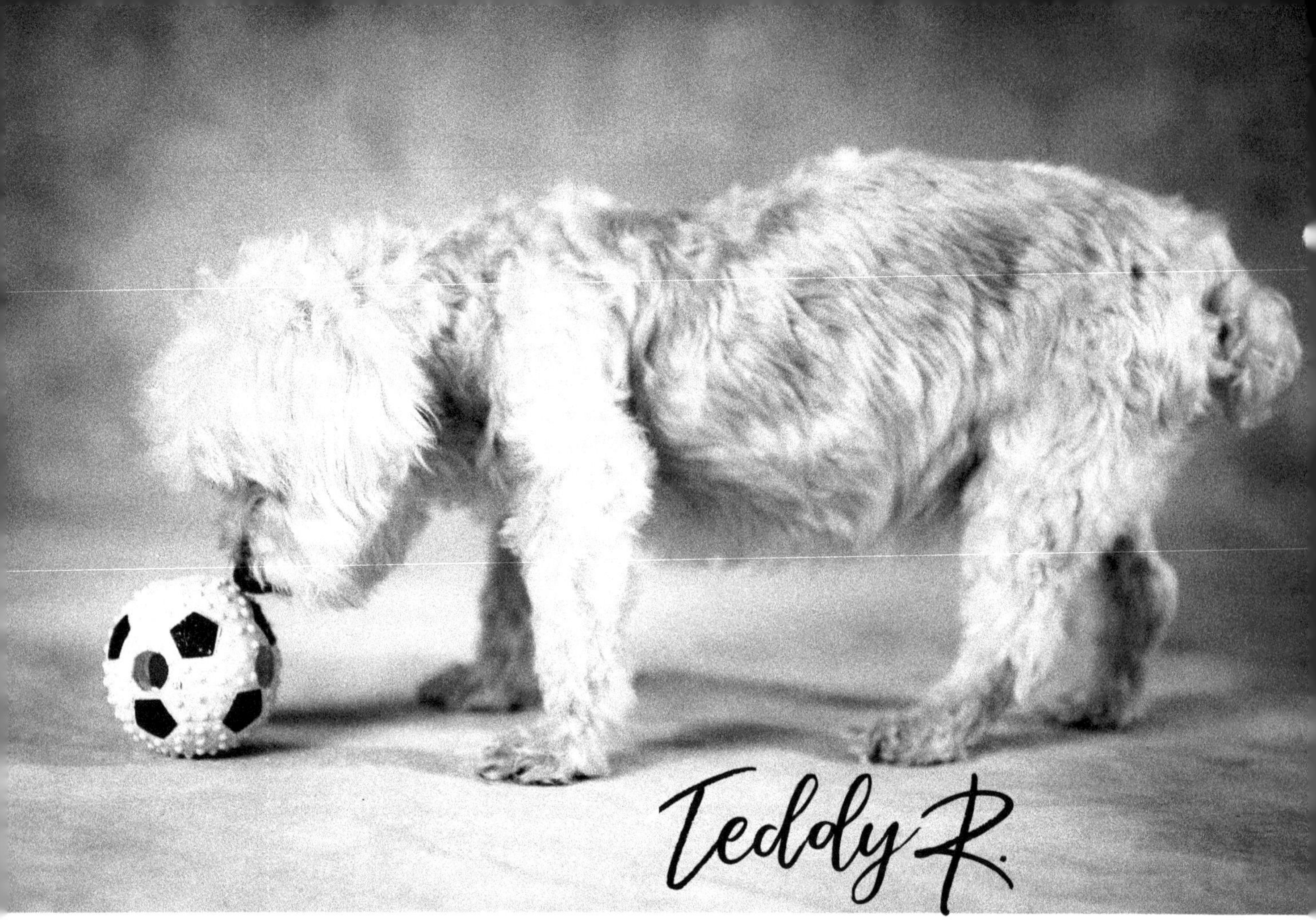

Teddy R.

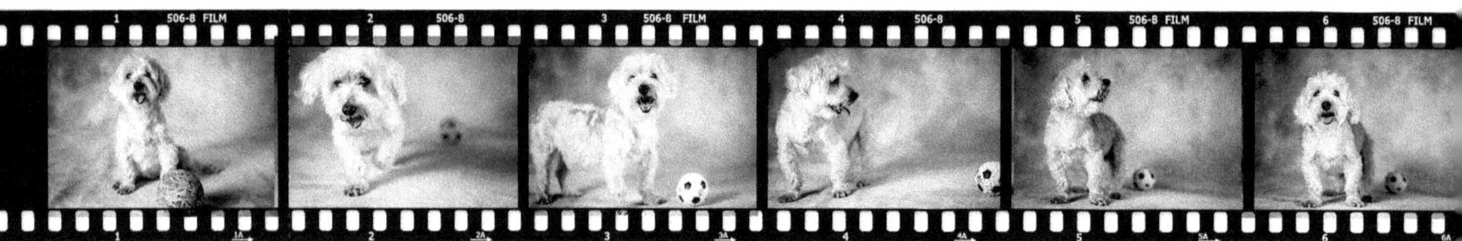

TEDDY waited two years before he found his forever home. When his owner moved and couldn't take him with her, Teddy found himself welcomed into a home where he would sit and stay. And stay. And stay. The silky terrier is now twelve years old and loves to chase lizards. He's not interested in other dogs and has no use for dog parks; he'd rather follow his human mom around all day. He has a weakness for treats, and often makes noises and moves his legs when he's dreaming. Even though he's not as spry as he used to be, Teddy is a happy boy . . . and always ready for a nice, relaxing nap.

TUCKER had been one of many, many dogs before he found his way home. The Suncoast Animal League was asked to help with a hoarding situation, and Tucker was one of the animals who needed placement. His future mama saw his picture on a website, and he looked just like the dog she'd recently lost. Her family adopted Tucker, who is now two and thriving in his new home. "Potty training was not fun," she recalls, "but we did it!" Tucker is a sweet snuggler. When he looks up with those big brown eyes, anyone fortunate enough to look back will see the grateful soul inside this much-cherished boy.

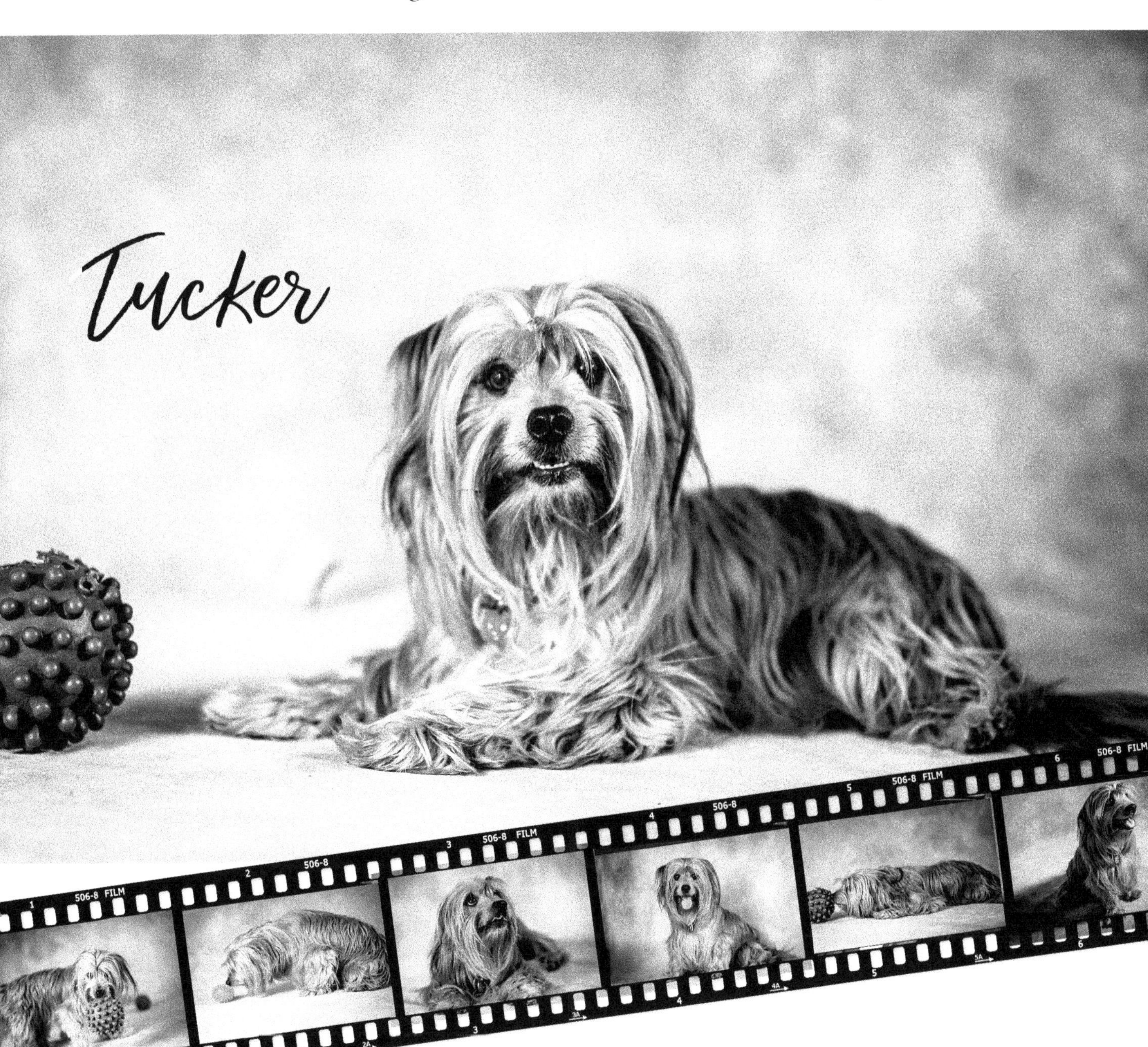

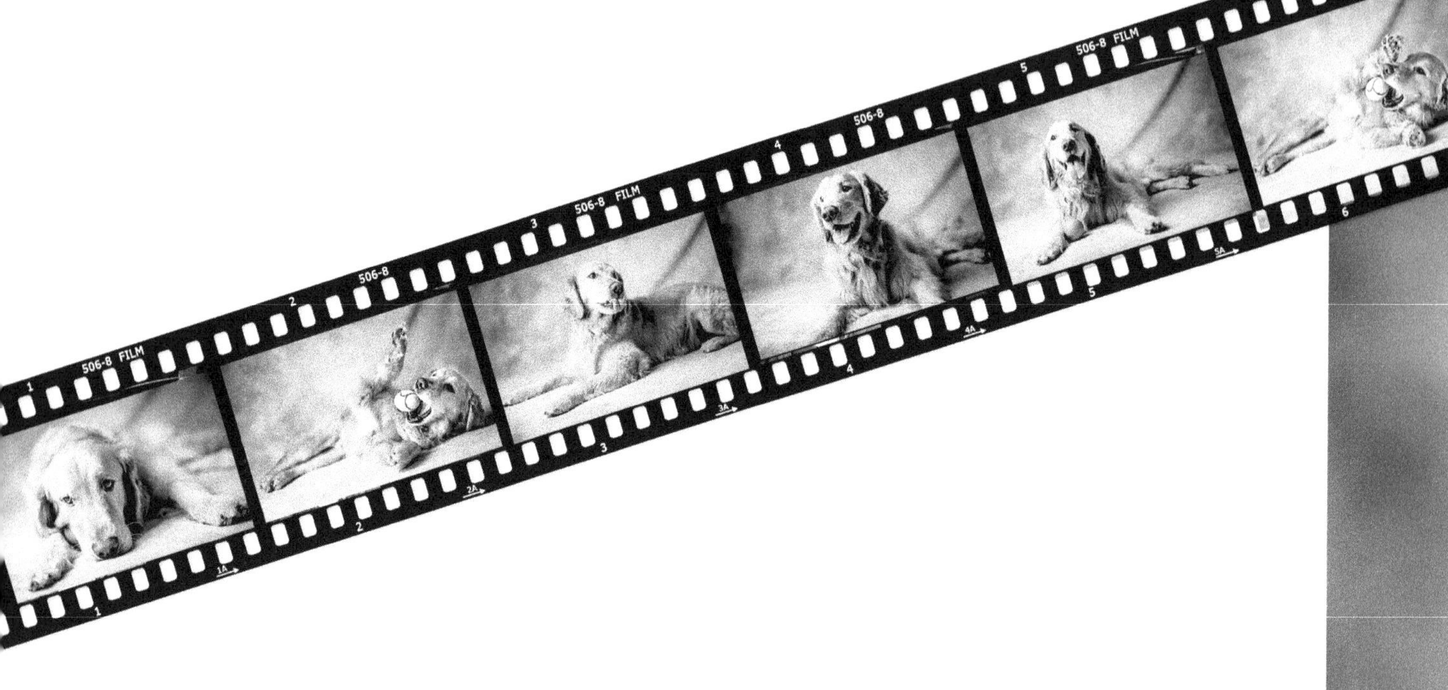

TURBO is a working dog. This five-year-old Golden Retriever works four days a week as a certified therapy dog, visiting hospice units, memory care centers, and anywhere he can find someone who needs a snuggle and a loving touch. When he was just a pup, he was adopted by a family whose vet told them he was "not a good dog--not healthy, and would be nothing but trouble." They surrendered him, but his present family found him through a Golden Rescue organization. He's been happily at home ever since.

His human mom got him involved in therapy work when Turbo fell into a depression after his canine sister passed away. Therapy gave him a new purpose in life, and he loves spending his afternoons with people who just want to pet him and love on him a while.
Every life has a purpose, and Turbo has found his.

Turbo

TWINKIE is a 5.5 year-old minature Golden Doodle whose favorite toy is a stuffed squirrel. She loves to dress up for Halloween and in years past, she has been Twink-erina (a ballerina), Twinkerella (Twinkie as Cinderella), and Wonder-Twink (Wonder Woman, naturally). She has lots of friends in her neighborhood--more, her mama says, than the rest of the family. The worst thing she's ever done is rip the heart, er, the squeaker, out of a stuffed squirrel, but that's not so bad. Most dogs believe that stuffed squeaky toys are just *asking* to be de-squeakered. Why else would they squeak?

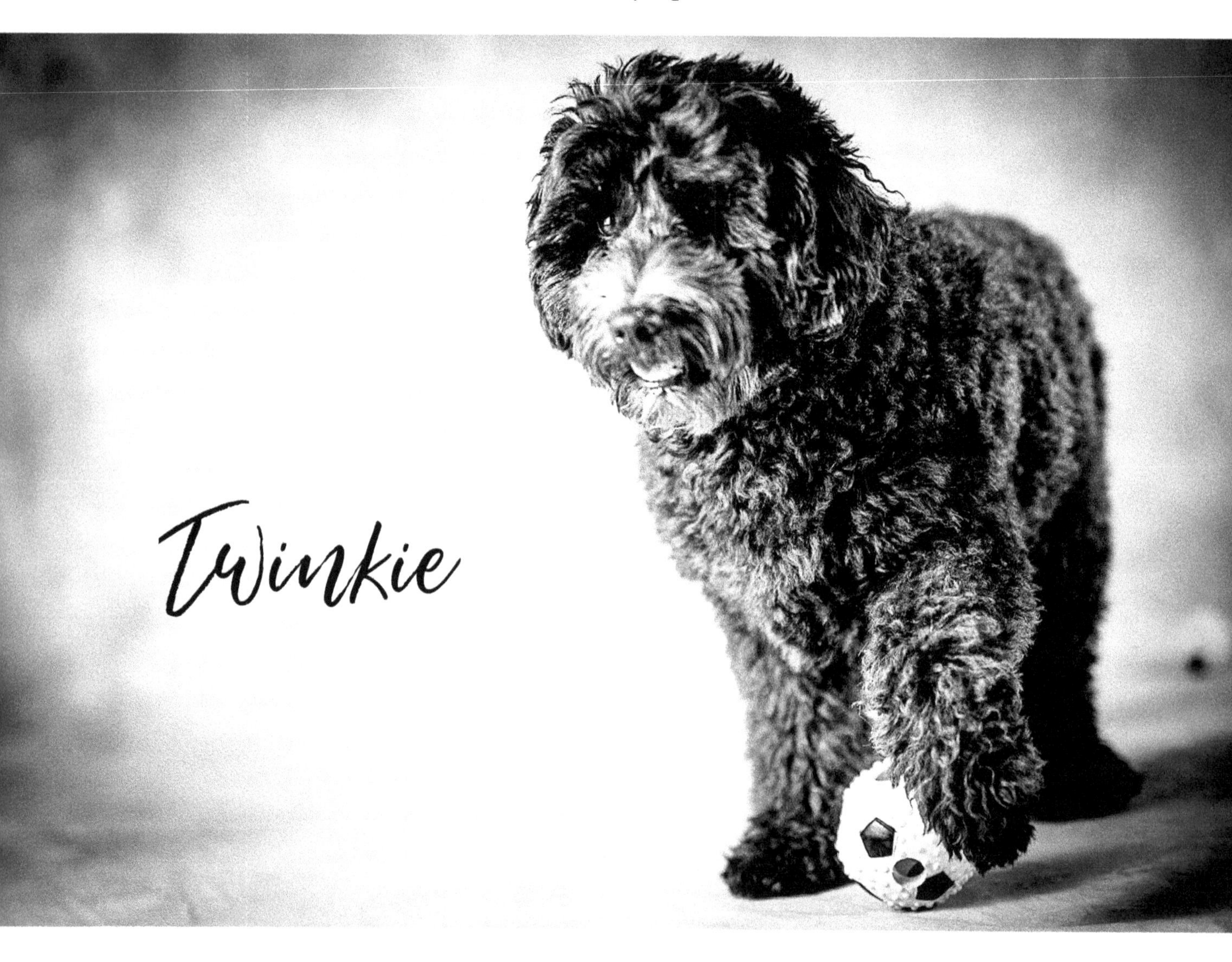

Beautiful WILLOW, a "total mutt" according to her DNA report, is nearly three years old and loves Nylabones and balls. She joined her human family as a foster, and made herself so much at home that her mom decided to adopt her. "She is the best foster sister and helper dog," says her mom. "She's wary around strangers, but loves dogs." Willow was the class clown in obedience school, probably because she has a short attention span.

But with so much life to live, who can blame her?

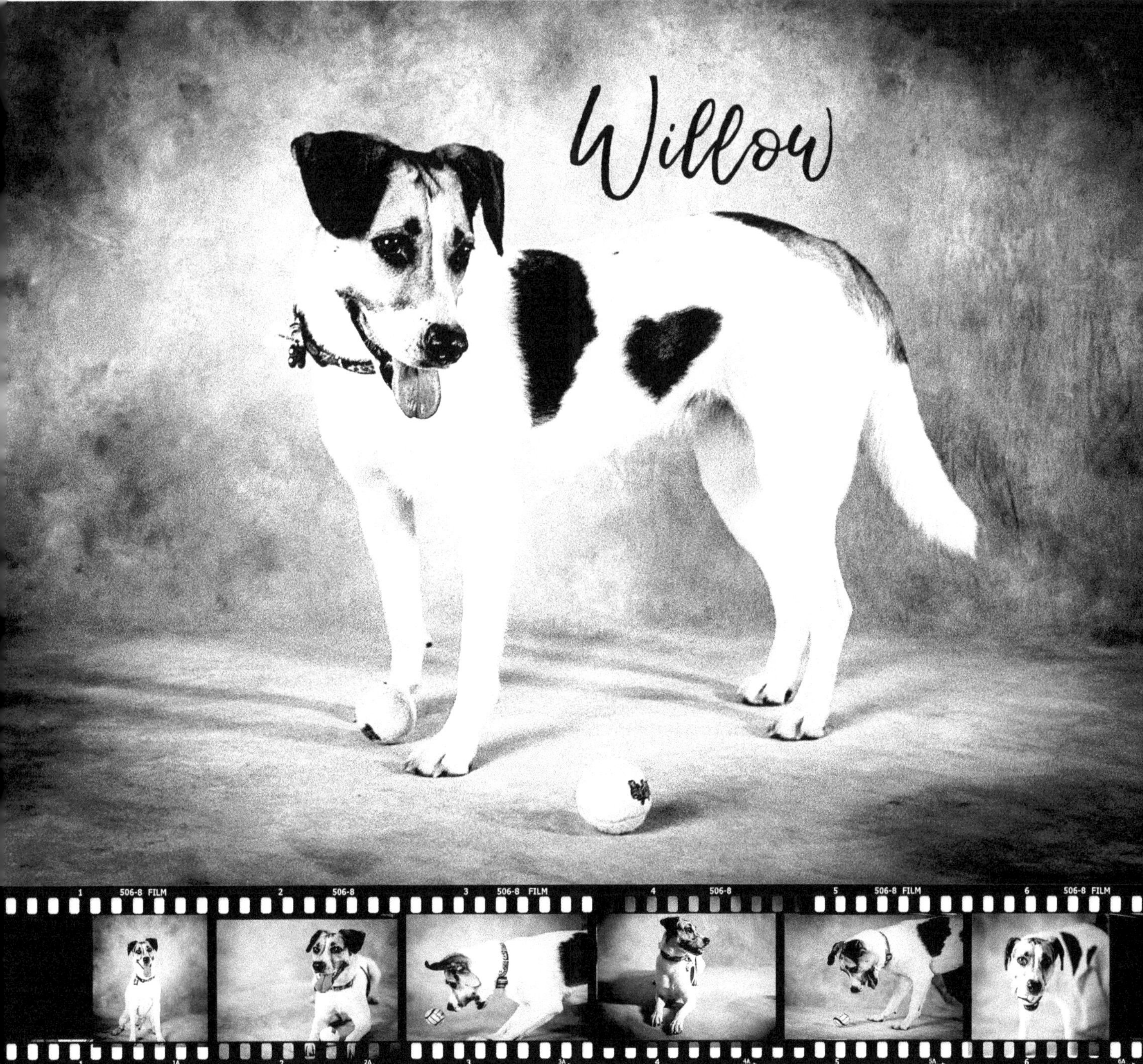

Yoshi

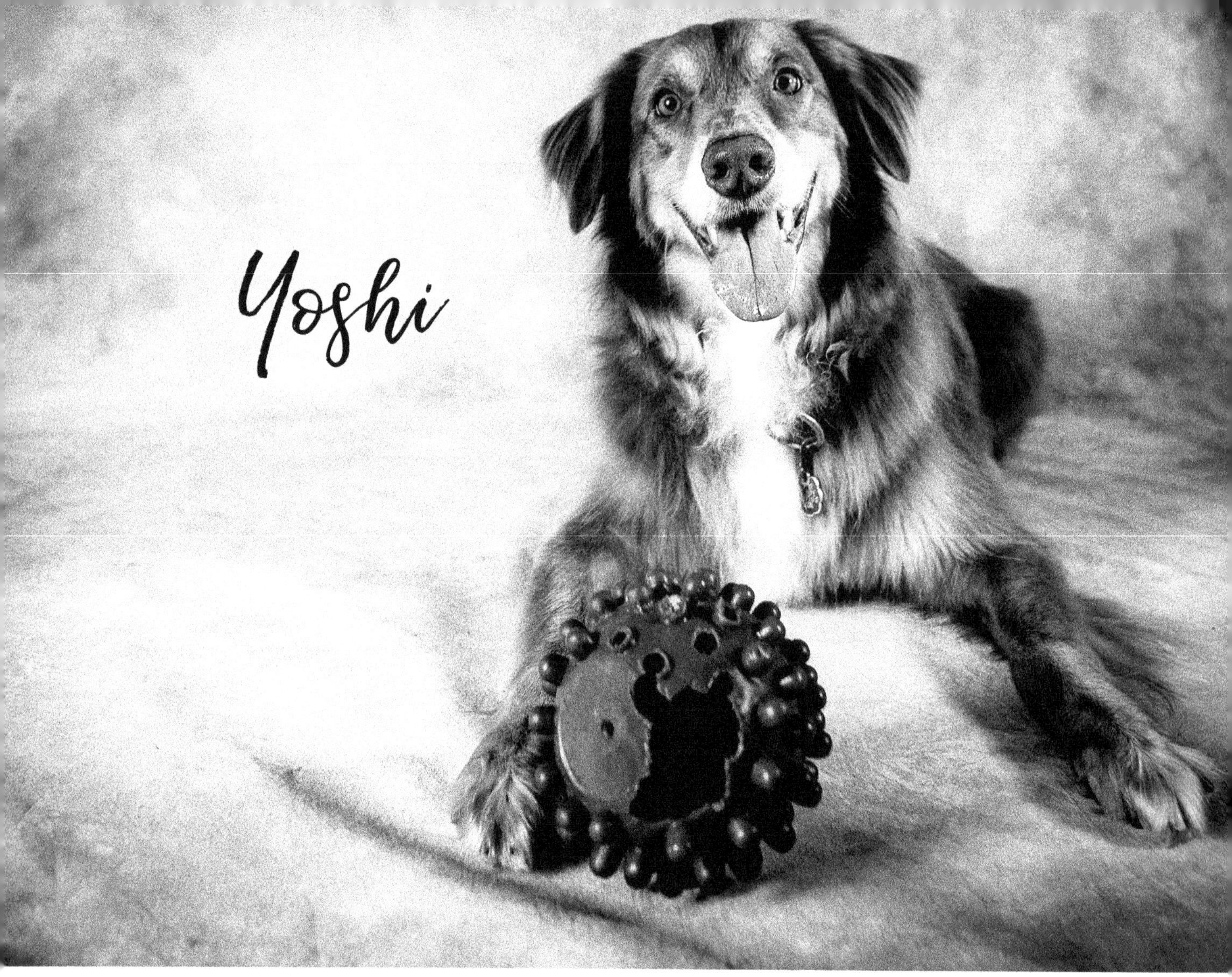

YOSHI, a four-year-old Australian Shepherd, loves his human dad and his stuffed dolphin. This enthusiastic pup has a unique quirk--he frequently jumps four feet into the air from a standing position, as if he had springs in his legs. He shares his human dad with three doggie siblings, two of which are "failed fosters." This boy is super smart. "He lives to outsmart me," says his dad, "And he often does." The worst thing he has ever done is eat the television remote--literally. His dad had to rush him to the vet for emergency surgery to take out the battery, the bits of plastic, and all the buttons, of course. Silly boy.

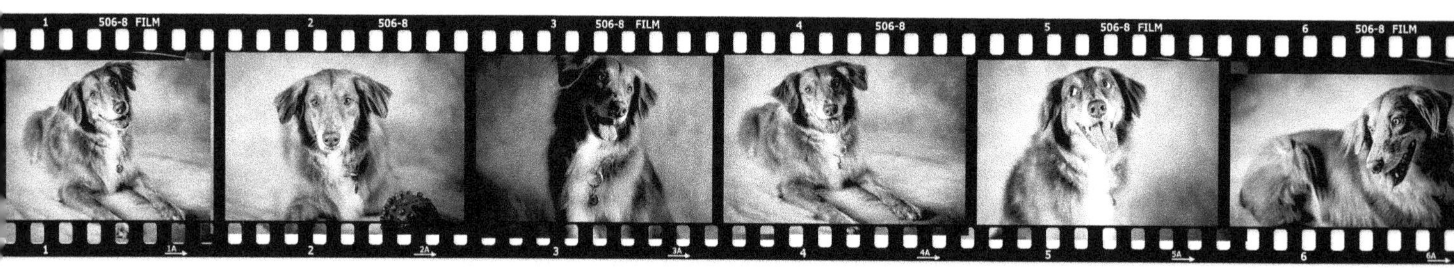

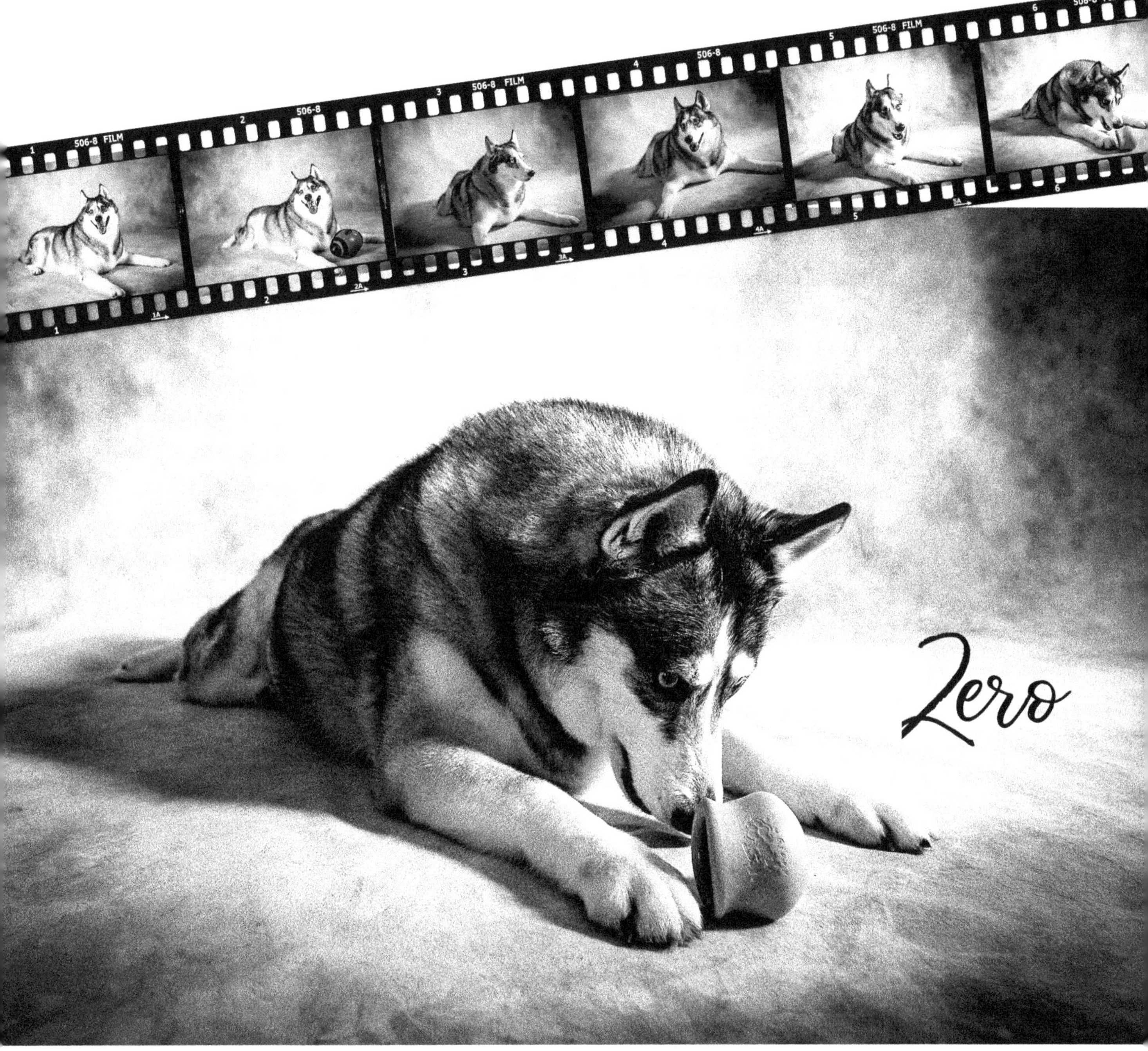

ZERO is an eight-year-old Husky whose favorite toy is “anything he can eat.” He came to his family through the efforts of the Humane Society, where he had been surrendered by a family who didn’t have time to tend to the unique needs of his breed. Now he’s turned into a hunky husky who loves nothing more than to lie around the house hoping for attention and dropped tidbits from the dining table. Zero has tons of charm--he has learned how to hug people he knows and he howls when he is really excited. Since he can be destructive if left alone for too long, his family keeps him company whenever they can.

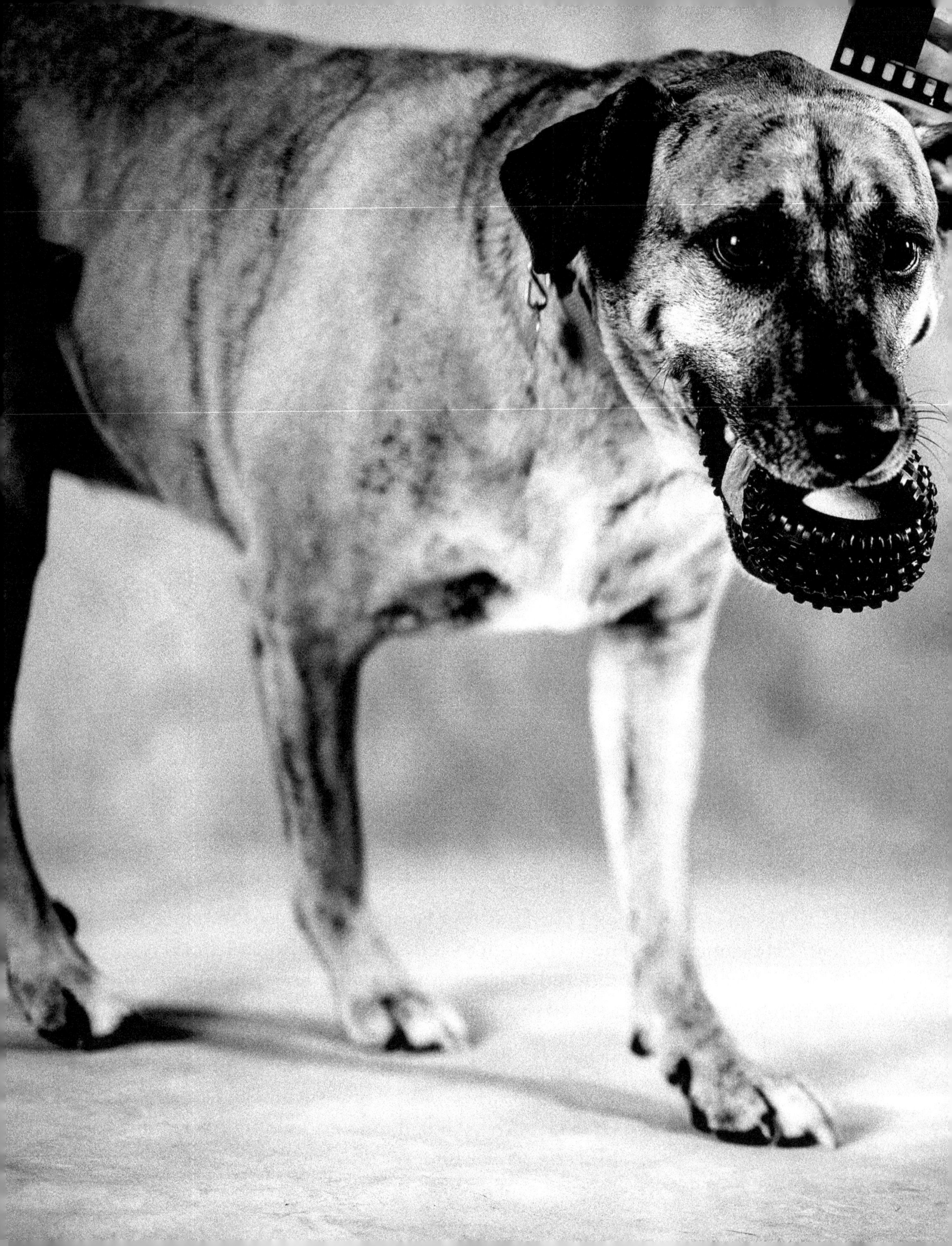

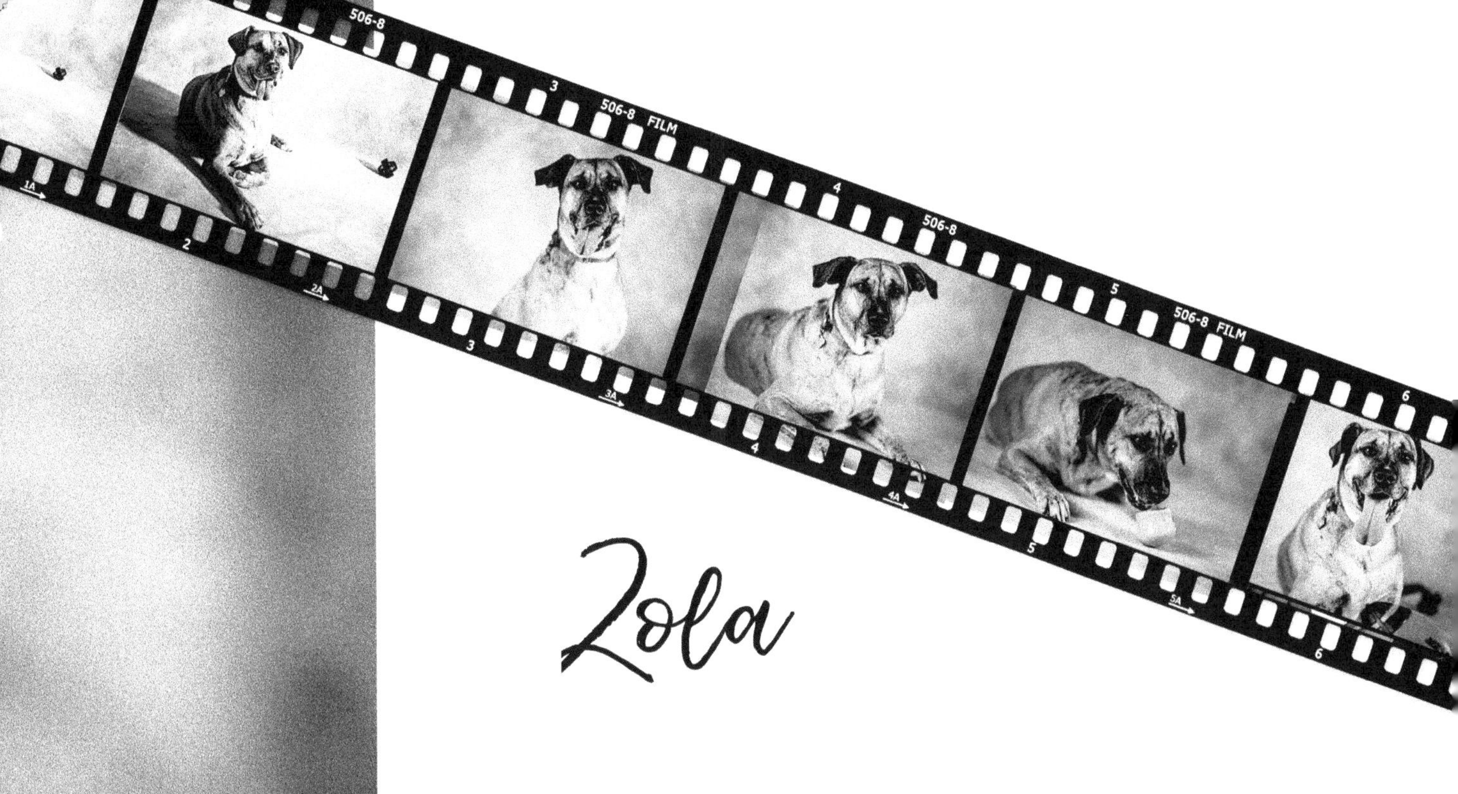

Zola

ZOLA is a six-year-old Plott Hound mix who joined her family after her human mom began volunteering at the SPCA. The two of them bonded, and Zola became part of the family. She loves any toy with a squeaker in it--but once she gets a hold of it, that toy won't last long. She also loves pizza, and makes short work of any leftover crusts. The worst thing she's ever done? She once astounded her family by jumping a six-foot privacy fence to meet the neighbor's dog . . . then she promptly jumped back.

Guess she saw that things aren't always greener on the other side of the fence.

Shelter Dog Photography

Want to make a difference for dogs *and* people? If you have a camera and a little extra time, you can learn how to take wonderful photographs to help dogs find their way from crowded shelters into loving homes.

I've written a book, *Snapping Shelter Dogs and Cats,* to give you ideas, instruction, and the confidence you'll need to approach your local shelter and begin photographing dogs . . . and cats, if you're so inclined. Your local shelter would be delighted to have more willing volunteers, and trust me--there's nothing like spending a morning with dogs to boost your spirits. Why not give it a try? Even if you can only spend a few hours a month at the shelter, the results will be worth it.

Hint: Because the book contains color photographs, the ebook version is *much* less expensive than the paperback.

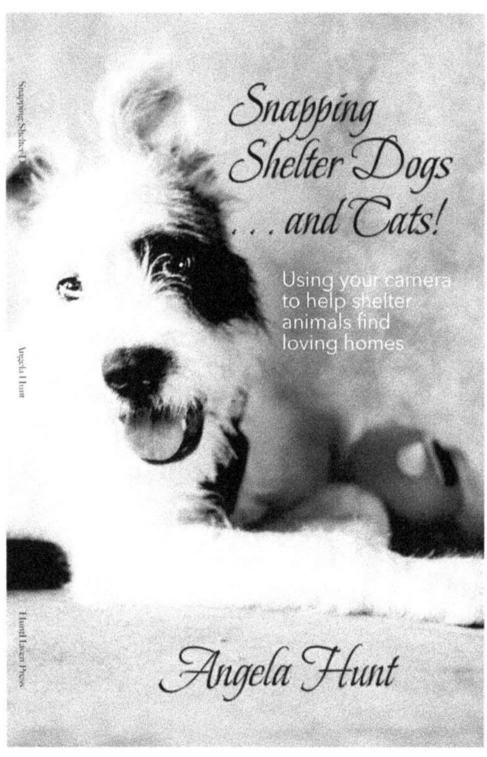

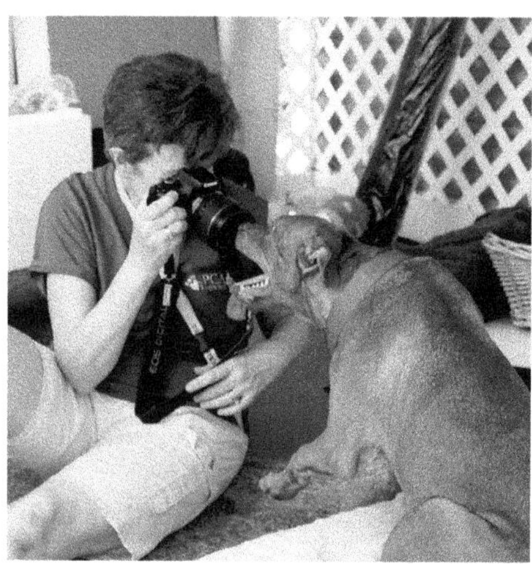

Photo: James McCook

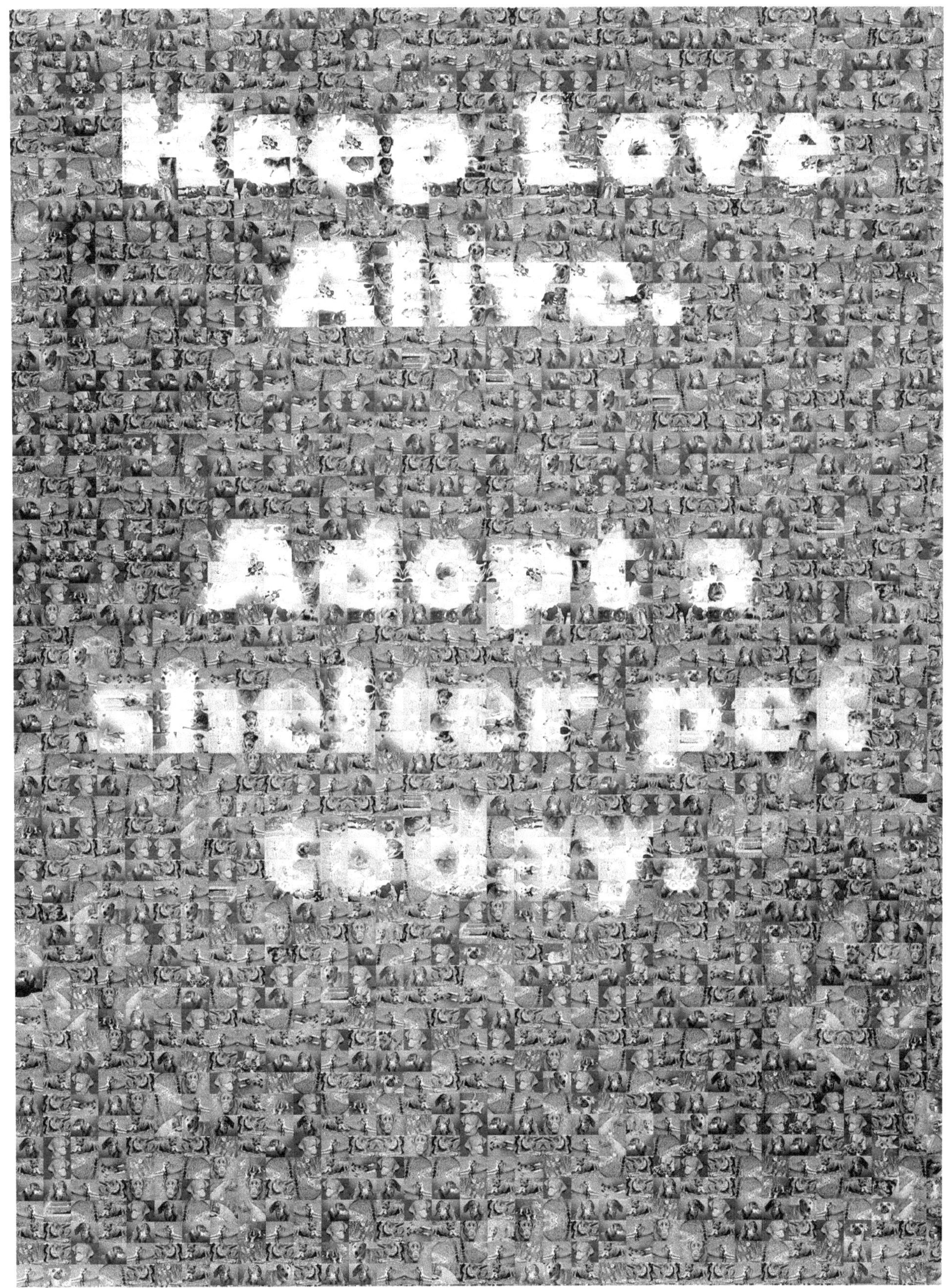

A mosaic of hundreds of shelter pet photos taken by the author.

www.ingramcontent.com/pod-product-compliance
Ingram Content Group UK Ltd.
Pitfield, Milton Keynes, MK11 3LW, UK
UKHW052232270726
14060UKWH00005B/725